MORE PRAISE FOR

BOYS

AMONG

MEN

"Expertly weaves stories and anecdotes from these players to create a fascinating retrospective on the culture, success and the continuing impact of those players in the league. . . . Abrams' book does an excellent job telling stories of these players, unearthing details that add depth to even the most-known stars. . . . Worth reading for every basketball fan as a piece of entertainment as well as for deeper insight into an era now past and the players who still shape our present and future."

—*The Sporting News*

"Abrams weaves a compelling tale about a transformational era in the NBA that also speaks to the sometimes-desperate pursuit of sporting stardom."

—*Kirkus* (starred review)

"This essential, well-researched book will appeal to readers interested in basketball's business side as well as the factors that have helped shape the modern NBA."

—*Library Journal* (starred review)

"In this excellent effort, Abrams, the gifted hoops writer late of *Grantland*, examines this controversial phenomenon from every angle."

—*Publishers Weekly*

"Will stand as the definitive dissection of an oddly brief, perpetually influential period in the history of NBA labor relations."

—Chuck Klosterman, *New York Times* bestselling author of
I Wear the Black Hat and *Sex, Drugs, and Cocoa Puffs*

"There was much I learned from this book, which covers not only the superstar 'kids' like Bryant and Garnett, but also the compelling cautionary tales."

—Jack McCallum, *New York Times* bestselling author of
Dream Team and *Seven Seconds or Less*

"*Boys Among Men* is as inside as an account can be of the paths of those players, both the famous and the forgotten. It's not merely a compelling book for any hoops fan, it's an important one."

—David Epstein, *New York Times* bestselling author of
The Sports Gene

"An indispensable book for anyone who cares about basketball."

—George Dohrmann, Pulitzer Prize–winning author of
Play Their Hearts Out

"Jonathan Abrams has transcended one of the NBA's great business and moral debates to deftly tell the inside story of the prep-to-pro phenomenon. . . . A marvelous book that will stand the test of time."

—Adrian Wojnarowski, *New York Times* bestselling author of *The Miracle of St. Anthony*

"Jonathan Abrams expertly captures this crucial era in basketball history. Yet what makes *Boys Among Men* so compelling isn't the high school players who turned out to be future hall of famers, but the stories of all the tragic would-be heroes that basketball has long forgotten."

—Dave McMenamin, NBA writer for ESPN

"A penetrating look at basketball and the time when high school players could take the great risk of moving directly into the pro game, bypassing college. Readers will devour it, as I did. One of the best sports books in a long, long time."

—Roland Lazenby, author of *Michael Jordan: The Life*

"A fascinating deep dive into the prep-to-pro generation, *Boys Among Men* is a must-read for NBA fans."

—Chris Ballard, senior writer for *Sports Illustrated*, author of *The Art of a Beautiful Game*

"Abrams is the rare reporter who unearths new details about the most famous prep-to-pro stars, like Kobe Bryant and Kevin Garnett, and tells the complex stories of those who didn't make it in the NBA. A must-read for any basketball fan."

—Zach Lowe, staff writer for ESPN's *Grantland*

"Kevin Garnett and Kobe Bryant blazed a trail in the mid-1990s, opening the NBA floodgates to every talented teen with a killer crossover and a dream. You know the success stories—Tracy McGrady, Jermaine O'Neal, LeBron James. You may know the flameouts—Leon Smith, Korleone Young, Robert Swift. You have never heard their journeys told with such rich detail and insight. Abrams's book stands as the definitive word on the prep-to-pro era, and its lasting impact on the NBA, both the good and the bad."

—Howard Beck, senior writer for *Bleacher Report*

"Prep-to-pro continues to be much debated and will be a timely issue again in the upcoming NBA collective bargaining. Jonathan Abrams gives the debate personality and life that will be entertaining and informative for basketball fans, in an inside look at the slam dunks and turnovers in the lives of those who made the leap from high school to the NBA."

—Sam Smith, author of *The Jordan Rules* and *There Is No Next*

BOYS AMONG MEN

MOSES

HOW THE PREP-TO-PRO

KEVIN

GENERATION REDEFINED

KOBE

THE NBA AND SPARKED A

TRACY

BASKETBALL REVOLUTION

LeBRON

BOYS

AMONG

MEN

JONATHAN ABRAMS

THREE RIVERS PRESS
NEW YORK

Originally published in hardcover in the United States by
Crown Archetype, an imprint of the Crown Publishing Group,
a division of Penguin Random House LLC, New York, in 2016.

Library of Congress Cataloging-in-Publication Data is available upon request.

ISBN 9780804139274
Ebook ISBN 9780804139267

Printed in the United States of America

Book design: Barbara Sturman
Cover design: Jake Nicolella
Cover photographs: (Kevin Garnett) David Sherman/Getty Images;
(Dwight Howard) Keith Allison/flickr;
(Kobe Bryant) Nathaniel S. Butler/Getty Images;
(LeBron James) AP Photo/Rich Pedroncelli

10 9 8 7 6 5 4 3 2 1

First Paperback Edition

To Tanya, my everything.

To Jayden, my motivation.

To Mom, my inspiration.

BOYS AMONG MEN

INTRODUCTION

Bucky Buckwalter carefully placed the pile of hundred-dollar bills on the orange crate that doubled as a dining room table in Mary Malone's living room. A room in the broken-down home belonged to her son Moses. A sizable hole in its wall allowed water in whenever it rained. The money for improvements and a better life had been placed before them by Buckwalter, a pro basketball executive. Buckwalter empowered Moses Malone with a choice. He offered Malone riches over poverty. Malone just had to forsake the rest of his childhood.

Moses Malone was an unassuming, gangly teenager from the South. He lived in Petersburg, Virginia, in a duplex off St. Matthews Street. The city was once a major Civil War conflict zone. In 1974, it hosted Malone, a teenager who happened to be basketball's greatest recruiting prize since Kareem Abdul-Jabbar. The sport came easily to Malone. He competed in playgrounds against adults. The kids received orange juice for winning. If they lost, they rounded up spare change to give their elders some beer money. "We'd beat them so bad, they thought they were already drunk," Malone recalled with a hearty laugh. College recruiters arrived in droves to watch Malone at Petersburg High School, where he steered his team to 50 straight victories and back-to-back state championships, leaving behind their families and checking into hotels for months. One day, a representative from Oral Roberts pledged that a higher power would cure Mary Malone's bleeding ulcer should her son bless the school with his basketball abilities.

His talent traveled by word of mouth in an era when college recruiters routinely circumvented NCAA rules of amateurism. A wink could mean a new car for a recruit and a turned head could result in the transfer of a handful of money. "It was like the Wild West," noted Howard White, then an assistant coach at the University of Maryland. Recruiters found Malone a reluctant listener. When they drove him in their cars, he feigned being asleep. When they came to his house, he pretended that he was not home. He had heard so many pitches that they had blended together by the time he finally committed to stay close to home and attend Maryland. When Maryland's coach, Lefty Driesell, learned of Malone's pending intentions, he camped outside the Malones' home. Malone awakened at about 7 a.m., wiping the sleep from his eyes. Driesell, at his bedside, came into focus. Malone signed the offer before rolling over and returning to sleep.

Then, Buckwalter, his money, and the American Basketball Association came along. The upstart league was widely viewed as inferior to the National Basketball Association's purer, more technical brand of basketball. The 11-team ABA originated in 1967 and predicated itself on showmanship, with its red-and-white ball and three-point line. The league existed in the NBA's shadow, but exploited a crack in luring talent by accepting players with remaining college eligibility. The NBA finally relented, following Spencer Haywood's antitrust lawsuit, and allowed players to leave college early and join their ranks if they could prove a financial hardship. But no high school player had ascended straight into basketball's major leagues. (The Detroit Pistons had drafted Reggie Harding out of high school in 1962, but he first played in basketball's minor leagues before joining the NBA.) By chance, Buckwalter, the director of player personnel for the ABA's Utah Stars, had stumbled upon one of Malone's high school All-Star

Games. He marveled at Malone's blend of height and quickness. A hard wind would have blown Malone over. He stood 6 feet 11 inches tall and weighed just over 200 pounds. But his feet danced like those of a boxer. They never stopped moving on the basketball court. The colleges wanted the best basketball players. Buckwalter did, too. The Stars drafted Malone in the third round of the ABA's 1974 draft. Most viewed the selection as little more than a publicity stunt, although it granted the Stars the ability to negotiate a contract with Malone.

Buckwalter had heard rumblings about the envelopes stuffed with money that one of Malone's uncles requested just to let a recruiter meet with the teenager. Buckwalter had to sneak under a fence and narrowly avoided the jaws of a dog simply to knock at their front door. Mary Malone answered the door. Buckwalter glanced at the scarce furnishings. Mary Malone had four pictures on her mantel: one each of Jesus Christ, Martin Luther King Jr., John and Jackie Kennedy, and her son, Moses.

Buckwalter knew that Moses Malone had heard every possible spiel. He discussed being a pioneer with Malone. Malone stared and mumbled. Buckwalter offered to build the family a new house.

"This is yours," Buckwalter said after he put the money on the crate. "This is for you and your friends. This isn't like Maryland, where you never really see anything."

Malone nodded and mumbled some more. He left the room and phoned Lefty Driesell. "Coach Buckwalter is over here and he's got $25,000 in cash lying on my table," Malone told Driesell. "He wants me to sign this thing. Should I sign it?"

Driesell did not miss a beat. "Tell them to leave," he said. "And if they don't, call the police. Now, if he puts a million dollars on your table, then call me back."

Driesell's enthusiasm could drown out the voices of the hundreds of other coaches who lusted after Malone. Driesell was a marvelous, relentless recruiter. He had told Malone that they could start counting their national championships together. He planned to pair Malone with John Lucas, a talented guard, and purchase him an insurance package should an injury derail his future professional career. Driesell sold the university to Malone. More importantly, he sold himself to Mary Malone. She supported herself and Moses, first as a practical nurse and then as a meatpacker. Moses's father had left the family before his son turned two. Driesell told Mary Malone that he was a God-fearing man and Maryland was a Christian-based program.

He was not going to lose Moses Malone without a fight. Driesell had successfully and skillfully fended off the other college recruiters. He now planned on struggling for Malone all over again. He preached the sanctity of college. He told the Malones that he had their best interests at heart and recommended that the Malones talk to an agent acquaintance, Donald Dell, and his partner, Lee Fentress, before making any decision.

The Malones agreed to the meeting. Dell found Malone to be aloof—as all the college coaches had. He wanted his attention.

"Moses, have you ever heard of slavery?" Dell asked.

Malone's head snapped up. "Well, this contract you've been offered is slavery." The contract, Dell said, ran for 16 years. Utah only guaranteed the first four years, with a team option for the next dozen years. "I hated the contract they offered him," Dell recalled. "I thought it was chickenshit that they arrived at their house and put all that money on the dining room table of a poor person's home. The whole thing smelled." Dell wearily agreed to represent Malone in the negotiations. "I was very, very worried that he wouldn't make the team or he would turn into something less than he wanted to be," Dell said. "A young eighteen-year-old with no education. That's what I was really worried about and I really didn't sleep for a couple of weeks thinking about it."

But Malone's decision had been made long ago. At 14, he had scribbled in the back of his Bible that he wanted to be a professional athlete. To reject this opportunity meant turning his back on the gift. "I said if I make this decision, this decision is going to be on me," Malone said. He had remained mostly quiet throughout the process. His muteness did not reflect the lack of interest it often projected.

"What I do is listen and pay attention," Malone said. "I listen to words and I can tell if they're trustworthy or if they're honest."

The Maryland players offered Malone their combined per diem for food and laundry, about $15 a month from each player, in an effort to make him stay in college. His college career lasted all of five days. John Lucas, his roommate, tried stirring Malone one morning. "C'mon, we've got to go," Lucas said.

"Big Mo going pro," Malone replied. "Big Mo can't take these damn college hours." He signed a seven-year contract with Utah that would pay him up to $3 million.

• • •

M oses Malone's leap from high school did not immediately change professional basketball's landscape. In a hierarchy of natural progression, players starred in high school and made their names in college before graduating to the pros. Darryl Dawkins and Bill Willoughby jumped to the NBA from high school a year after Malone's decision. Malone joined the NBA in 1976, when the league absorbed much of the ABA, and carved out a Hall of Fame career. But Dawkins and Willoughby provided cautionary tales for different reasons as to why teenagers, both physically and mentally, were not prepared for the NBA's rigors.

That thought persisted until a lanky teenager named Kevin Garnett reopened the dormant door in 1995. The game had been transformed by the time of Garnett's arrival. Players commanded millions in salary, a large jump from $130,000—the average salary of an NBA player in 1976. Malone's decision ultimately birthed the route into the NBA for one of the game's greatest group of players, from Garnett to Kobe Bryant, Tracy McGrady, LeBron James, and Dwight Howard. They grew into stardom, while quickly advancing from their proms to playing against grown men whose paychecks accounted for how they fed their families. "When I see guys like Kobe, LeBron James, Kevin Garnett still doing what they're doing, it just makes all the high school players that came before very proud," Malone said. "We're doing what we're doing because we were the best in high school and we ain't got to go to college for four years to be the best." Malone was proud of his place in history, before his death from heart disease in September 2015, just a few weeks after Darryl Dawkins died from a heart attack. They did not first toil in minor leagues, as in professional baseball and hockey. They did not have to wait three years after high school before becoming professionals, like NFL players. Most became successful and, lacking stardom, made more money than they would have otherwise dreamed of. A few failed and faded with their chance at fame and fortune eternally lost.

They all started at the same place. At an early age, they showed remarkable physical gifts and someone pegged each of them as a phenom. The days of a talent undiscovered until college are long gone. High school games are televised across the country. Elementary-school children are ranked nationally. "It's the same reason we want to see young, gifted actors, musicians, or pianists," said Jeremy Treatman. Treatman served as one of Kobe Bryant's high school assistant coaches and later scheduled and broadcast marquee high school games. "They're phenoms," he continued. "They're prodigies. LeBron James was a prodigy. Dwight Howard's a prodigy. Kobe Bryant's a prodigy. When someone can do things that no one else can, you're just blown away by it. Even when you're seeing a seven-year-old girl sing the national anthem perfectly and you're blown away for days. It's that kind of thing." But the attention often came with a price: an abbreviated childhood and mostly unrealistic expectations. "The hustle and bustle, prostitution, drugs, gang banging, and all that [in his neighborhood] to the AAU [Amateur Athletic Union] circuit was no different," said Tyson Chandler, taken second overall in the 2001 draft out of high school. "It was the same hustle. It was just legal. It was definitely the same characters I would see on my street corner, just disguised different. My life was accelerated because I had to learn how to protect myself and use people who thought they were using me and do all of that to get to where I wanted to get to.

I was very aware of what was going on at such a young age. That innocence is kind of thrown out the window."

Malone's decision to fulfill his own prophecy mutated over the years. A decision faced by a modern NBA prospect who considered the jump from high school became saturated with too many parties all with a stake in his future: the coaches, the families, the shoe companies, the NBA, the handlers, the agents. Former NBA commissioner David Stern began presiding over NBA drafts that may as well have been high school graduations. The procession stopped in 2006 with a rule mandating draft-eligible players be at least one year removed from high school. "It's a failing of so many institutions, for which I think we are drawn into it," Stern said. "I don't mean to take any attention, cut away any responsibility, because we're part of the system, but we're not the lead part of the system."

They are the end goal, the league kids dreamed of and, for a while, played in. The ban on high school players is continually discussed. Some want it eliminated. Others want to extend the league's age minimum to at least 20 years. "It's just not right," said Jermaine O'Neal. He jumped to the NBA from high school in 1996. "You can go to the military and fight a war at eighteen years old and give your life at eighteen years old. Those people are going to war to try to better their lives. It's life or death in the military. You're allowed to carry a gun and give your life. That's the ultimate sacrifice. So my question is, Why aren't you allowed to do something as simple as play basketball?"

1.

This kid is about to hyperventilate, John Hammond worried to himself. Hammond, a Detroit Pistons assistant coach, had flown to Chicago in 1995 for the NBA's annual predraft camp. The league's movers and shakers attended to mix and mingle. Hammond had walked into the Hyatt Regency's lobby a couple of days earlier and run into the agent Eric Fleisher. Fleisher asked Hammond if he would conduct a workout in front of NBA executives for one of his prospects, a youth named Kevin Garnett. Hammond quickly agreed. He had heard of him. Everyone had. Garnett vied to become the first high school player to enter the NBA directly since Darryl Dawkins and Bill Willoughby had done it two decades earlier. Garnett attracted NBA royalty the day of his workout at the University of Illinois–Chicago. Elgin Baylor, Pat Riley, Kevin McHale, Donnie Walsh, Doug Collins, and other basketball dignitaries packed themselves into a bleacher beneath one of the baskets for a firsthand peek at Garnett.

The NBA had seen robust growth in recent years, gaining greatly in popularity and profitability. When Magic Johnson and Larry Bird entered the league in 1979, it "was seen as far too black, and the majority of its players, it was somehow believed, were on drugs and willing to play hard only in the last two minutes of the game," wrote the journalist David Halberstam. Interest in the college rivalry shared by Johnson and Bird carried into their professional careers. Still, CBS continued airing some NBA championship games in the early 1980s on tape delay. The network played the games near midnight, when people who did watch television that late routinely tuned in to NBC's Johnny Carson. Nearly the whole country watched *The Dukes of Hazzard* and *Dallas* in 1980, instead of the sixth game of the NBA Finals between the Los Angeles Lakers and the Philadelphia 76ers. A fresh-eyed Johnson played all five positions in the absence of an injured Kareem Abdul-Jabbar and put on a masterful, transformative performance. But few had watched it. An ambitious David Stern sought to change the league's image as its commissioner four years later. Stern cracked down on the league's drug problem and promoted the All-Star Game as its signature event. His ascension as commissioner coincided with Michael Jordan's NBA arrival. Jordan became the vehicle Stern used to vault the game's popularity into the corporate stratosphere. Jordan played gracefully on the court and, at times, appeared to defy gravity. He evolved into a worldwide icon, more recognizable than most actors and politicians. Companies enjoyed partnerships with Jordan and, in turn, with the NBA, and lucrative television deals resulted in surging salaries.

By the summer of 1995, the average NBA salary had ballooned to nearly $2 million. That provided a monetary incentive for collegiate players to declare for the NBA before their amateur eligibility expired. Among the first 15 picks of the 1990 draft, 13 had been college seniors. By 1994, only one college senior was drafted in the first seven selections. The NBA had become a high-stakes, cutthroat business. Executives drafted players based on potential as much as on proven talent. A younger prospect meant a higher ceiling. A higher ceiling meant a prospective star in a sport where one dominant player can carry a franchise. The high school–to–pro route was thought to be closed, but no rule prevented a player from trying. Shawn Kemp had become a star by jumping to the NBA in 1989 after leaving the University of Kentucky and Trinity Valley Community College without ever having played a game at either school.

The storyline of a talented prodigy proved too tantalizing for NBA executives not to evaluate Garnett's workout. Garnett had been compared to everyone from Bill Walton to Alonzo Mourning to Reggie Miller. Hammond had spent his life around basketball as a player and coach. Players, in his experience, usually masked their nervousness with an overabundance of confidence as they got older, wearing it like a cheap cologne. Garnett did not disguise anything. He couldn't. He was what he was, a kid who would have his entire future determined over the course of the next precious moments. The workout had not even started. The boy could not catch his breath. His heart thumped. His chest heaved up and down, up and down. Hammond walked Garnett away from the executives to the court's far side. "Stand here and get your breath," Hammond advised. He positioned Garnett at the free-throw line. Garnett leisurely shot a couple, trying to regain his composure. He had once dreamed of playing college basketball. So many people told him he could jump straight to the NBA that he had changed his mind. Garnett glanced at the executives. Some looked bored, as if they had come out of deference to Fleisher, who had player clients scattered throughout the league. Maybe they were right. Maybe he and Bill Willoughby were wrong. Willoughby had encouraged Garnett to opt for the NBA in a telephone call arranged by Fleisher. Garnett was a historian of the game and listened intently. Many, after all, considered Willoughby the primary reason no high schooler had attempted the sizable jump in years.

• • •

College coaches recruited Bill Willoughby in 1975 with the same fervor used on Moses Malone and Darryl Dawkins. Willoughby stood 6 feet 8 inches tall and played forward. Yet he snaked in and out of the lane like a guard. Lefty Driesell's sermons to him landed on deaf ears. Willoughby nearly ended up at North Carolina. But Kentucky's Joe B. Hall became the coach who ultimately got Willoughby's signature on a letter of intent. "Big arena, beautiful women, eating Kentucky Fried Chicken, watching horse races" is how Willoughby described Lexington. He returned to finish his senior year at Englewood's Dwight Morrow High School in New Jersey, intent on becoming a Wildcat.

One recruiting trip still nagged at Willoughby. He had visited Maryland during the summer when Malone still thought he would attend the university. Willoughby spied Malone working at a construction job. The image of Malone, nearly seven feet tall, wearing dirt-caked clothes and a hard hat, remained with Willoughby. Driesell had secured Malone the gig so he could have a bit of spending money. "He had to be at this guy's house at 6:30 every morning," Driesell recalled. "These college kids with jobs, you tell them to get there at 6:30, they don't show up. He said that Moses was sitting on his front porch at 6:00 a.m. every morning waiting for him, never missed a day, was never late." Malone had no use for that hat now, Willoughby thought. He had become a pro and made hundreds of thousands. "*This guy went to the ABA*," Willoughby said of his thinking at the time. "*He's playing against George Gervin and Julius Erving. I could be next.*" Willoughby instructed Bob White, his high school coach, to return interest should any pro scouts inquire about him.

One NBA executive had paid close attention to Malone's assimilation before training his eye on Willoughby. Pat Williams had inherited the hapless Philadelphia 76ers, a once-proud franchise fallen on troubled times. The team slipped and staggered to a record 73 losses in 1972–1973. Williams, Philadelphia's general manager, tried everything to revive interest in the franchise. Long ago, he had played minor league baseball, where players would be routinely drafted into the sport from high school. He assumed basketball players could not take the same route.

That is, until he saw Malone on the Stars. Malone more than held his own, Williams mused. No college prospect enticed him in the approaching draft. Williams wondered if another Malone was out there somewhere. If so, he could outsmart the rest of the league and jump-start the franchise. Williams homed in on Bill Cartwright and Darryl Dawkins. Cartwright stood taller, but was also much thinner. Word trickled back that his mother insisted he attend college. Dawkins, an Orlando native, was about 6 feet 10 inches tall with a chiseled frame. "Man-child" was the oft-used description. Williams selected Dawkins fifth overall in 1975, making Dawkins the first player drafted directly from high school who would immediately play in the NBA. Williams pointed Dawkins toward Herb Rudoy, an agent who did not share the same moral concerns as Moses Malone's agent. "I am a believer in capitalism, that if a young person has a talent that's good enough, he ought to go to the pros," Rudoy said.

Williams figured he had one-upped the league and could draft all the top high school talent, develop them, and field a super team in a few years. He told Willoughby that he would pluck him as well with Philadelphia's next pick. A reporter called a surprised Willoughby and alerted him that the Atlanta Hawks, instead, had chosen him 19th overall. In some ways, the Hawks had outsmarted themselves. Atlanta took David Thompson and Marvin Webster in the first round. Thompson and Webster chose the ABA and Willoughby now merited more money. The ABA's Denver Nuggets had also selected Willoughby.

He had choices, and college looked less likely among them. Willoughby's mother worked at a factory. His father was a mechanic. They left the decision to him, Willoughby said. He went to the NBA, signing for $1.1 million over five years. "I had clothes," Willoughby said. "It didn't strike me until I turned 18 that I didn't have no money in my pocket. You want to go to the movies, you have to ask your mother or father. I never had a job. I wasn't allowed to cook. I wasn't nothing."

The move stunned Joe B. Hall. The Kentucky coach had also recruited Malone and Dawkins, losing all three to the professional leagues. Hall blamed some of the people around Willoughby for trying to capitalize off him and pointed a finger toward his high school coach. "[Bob White] wanted to go with him [to Kentucky]," Hall said. "I had no place for his coach. I was real surprised about Willoughby because we had talked it over with his parents and they were happy that he was not going to turn pro. They didn't feel he was ready. Not basketball-wise, but just socially mature to handle it." Willoughby lacked life experience. All he had done in his first 17 years of life was play ball, first in New Jersey and then on the famed courts in New York. His parents offered to move to Atlanta with him. Willoughby decided he wanted to learn and live on his own. He took his driver's test after purchasing his first car, a Lincoln Town Car. He only used it to drive to the arena, home, the airport, or a diner. "I just felt by myself," he said. "I was a loner." He still thought about his future. Willoughby received a $500 monthly allowance from his agent and wanted to preserve the bulk of his earnings.

He planned on dominating the NBA as he had in high school. "They thought I was going to be the next Dr. J," he whimsically reminisced. His adolescent body did not allow it. Willoughby's pushes against high school kids became gentle nudges to his grown opposition in the NBA. He suffered in the face of the game's physicality and withered when he encountered any coaching criticism. He had always been the star and critiques were foreign and unwelcome.

In an early game, Willoughby drove toward the basket and dribbled through his legs. The ball bounced helplessly off him, out of bounds. "This isn't the playground," said Cotton Fitzsimmons, Atlanta's coach, as he yanked him from the game. Fitzsimmons's departure the following year did not improve Willoughby's outlook or up his playing time. The Hawks hired Hubie Brown away from the ABA. Brown was a disciplinarian and a tactician, known to time his practices to the second. He had little use for a player unprepared to treat the profession like a job—even if that player was only a year out of high school. The coach, Willoughby said, relentlessly cursed at his team and played favorites. But Hal Wissel, Brown's assistant coach, recalled those days much differently. Wissel said Willoughby had "potential with no fundamental skills." Brown once asked Wissel to teach Willoughby a few post moves before practice. Someone from the front office interrupted practice a couple of days later, telling Brown he had an urgent phone call. It turned out to be Willoughby's agents complaining about his having to arrive early, Wissel said. Brown requested two things from every player: be on time and do your job. "Bill Willoughby didn't do number two," Wissel said. "He didn't do his job. These are pros. These are men. And he wasn't ready for that."

In Philadelphia, Darryl Dawkins also came into the league unprepared. Without school, he suddenly had money in his pocket and hours of the day to fill. "The hardest part is what are you doing during idle time?" he said. "I started writing poetry. I stated cooking and tweaking recipes. I've always had a fetish for cars and I did like women. So I occupied my time that way, besides playing basketball." Dawkins offered colorful quotes, wore even more colorful clothing, and shattered backboards with his thunderous dunks. He named his finishes: the Rim Wrecker, the Go-Rilla, the Look Out Below. He claimed he came from the planet Lovetron. Dawkins volunteered whenever the team needed someone at a community event. He was also the first to attend parties. He wore a lime-green suit to his 19th birthday celebration. "You could see him coming from five miles away," said his teammate World B. Free. Dawkins's mind seemed forever split between the game and what to do after the game. "Present," he once called before realizing Coach Gene Shue was not taking roll call, but subbing him into a game. Dawkins was good. Many expected him to be great. But he considered the game to be a game, while his older teammates regarded it as their livelihood. Entering the NBA early prolonged his adolescence, instead of hastening his maturity. "He was immature when he came in," said teammate Steve Mix. "The physical part was there. The mental part wasn't."

Dawkins at least enjoyed the game. Willoughby had an undistinguished career, meandering through six teams in eight years. He had trouble accepting that he would never become the star he was once projected to be. His career highlight arrived in 1981 as a Houston Rocket when he did the impossible and blocked Kareem Abdul-Jabbar's skyhook in a playoff game. Del Harris, his coach in Houston, remembered Willoughby as softhearted and likable, but, also as an introvert who masked his feelings. Harris once requested that Willoughby run sprints when he sustained a hand injury. "He insisted to my assistant, Carroll Dawson, that I was punishing him for being hurt," Harris recalled. "He could not accept that I was trying to keep him in shape while he was out."

Life had come full circle. Bill Willoughby had started as a phenom in New Jersey. He tried to hang on to the tatters of his NBA career by appearing with the New Jersey Nets in their 1985 summer camp at Princeton's Jadwin Gym. The roster featured rookies and free agents, players with little chance of making a regular-season roster. Willoughby glanced across the court during a summer game against the Knicks and noticed some unwelcome faces. Willoughby said that he had been battling concussions and that some of the Knicks players sought to inflict further injury on him during the game.

Willoughby played four minutes and ran into a hard screen. He remembers hearing Knicks players saying, "Get this motherfucker." Bob MacKinnon, the Nets general manager and acting coach, tried reinserting Willoughby into the game's second quarter. "I don't want to," Willoughby said. "Then go home," MacKinnon instructed.

"And he did," MacKinnon said to the *Record*, a newspaper in New Jersey. "I have no explanation for it."

Willoughby asked the team's athletic trainer to open the locker room so he could collect his belongings. "You're not going to make the pros going down Route 80," the trainer told Willoughby. "They can take my money," Willoughby responded. "But they're trying to hurt me."

Willoughby had a couple of other tryouts. He later waited day after day, week after week, year after year for a phone call that never came, one from an NBA executive offering a last chance. Willoughby's basketball career ended when he was 28 years old. Retirement did not treat Willoughby any more gently. His agents—whom he had awarded power of attorney—had embezzled most of his savings. Willoughby won a judgment for $1.1 million, but could not collect the majority of the sum when one of the agents declared bankruptcy. Willoughby lost his home, moved in with his parents, and battled depression. He came to symbolize everything that could go wrong when a franchise hitched its hopes to a high school player. Willoughby was a man among boys in high school. He was a boy among men in the NBA. The Hawks saw Willoughby's potential and predicted his future. They did not factor in his physical immaturity and emotional instability as significant hurdles. Years later, Willoughby took steps to straighten out his life. He enrolled in Fairleigh Dickinson University's regular day program on the persistent advice of a close friend and with assistance from the NBA's Retired Players Association. He kept cramming his frame into his 1984 Mercedes-Benz, day after day, to attend class.

Willoughby graduated from Fairleigh Dickinson in 2001 at the age of 44. He cried upon realizing that Continental Airlines Arena was hosting the commencement—the same building where Willoughby had played his final NBA game in 1984. False hope and faded dreams had followed that appearance until now.

The school asked Willoughby to address the graduates.

"I chose basketball over education," he said. "I chose a big contract over education. I soon found out that life is about so much more than money and that success on the court lasts a very short time."

Willoughby had just started to emerge from his troubles in 1995 when he offered Garnett much different advice.

"Yeah, I'm broke," Willoughby said. "I'm scared because the guy is saying he's bankrupt and I could win and still not get anything. Know what's happening. You got your agent. You got your business manager. You got your mother, your father, sister, brother, girlfriend. What's really yours? Even if you buy them a house, now they want a car, now they want jewelry. Now they want clothes." Garnett told Willoughby how much money he expected to make should he declare for the NBA. "And you thought twice?" Willoughby asked. "What are you going to do in school? Take wood shop? Ceramics? Theater? You're still thinking? I'm in school now. You can go to school in the off-season and take classes. Then, you can finish when you retire."

2

Today, he is known as the Kevin Garnett who scowls, growls, and talks trash, not as the bundle of raw nerves that showed up in 1995 before the executives. But Garnett's nervousness had bubbled over before. His formative basketball education took place at Springfield Park in Mauldin, a city outside of Greenville in South Carolina. The park housed a playground, benches, and baseball fields. Garnett only cared for the blacktop basketball court and its chained nets that rang like a cash register whenever a ball snapped through them. One measured his manhood in points and his self-worth in aggressiveness at the park. No one was more man than Baron Franks. They called him Bear for good reason. Franks stood 6 feet 4 inches tall and weighed nearly 300 pounds. Garnett was about 13 or 14 years old, with no discernable skills, when he mustered enough courage to play at Springfield. Franks was about four years older and light-years ahead in the art of trash talk. He saw Garnett and sized down another victim. "I've got your mind in my pocket," he told Garnett after he scored. "I own you," Franks said, scoring again. He talked about Garnett's mother, Shirley Irby, and his sisters. "Get off my court," Franks yelled to Garnett after each inevitable loss. Garnett did not verbally retaliate. He maintained a straight face and returned daily. He leapfrogged Franks in height within a year. Garnett still wondered why Franks seemed to have it in for him. The trash talk never stopped. Word of Garnett's frustration over Frank's verbal assaults filtered back to the source. Franks addressed it by wrapping his arm around Garnett. "Basketball, it's my love," Franks explained. "When I play, nothing else matters. I take it seriously, whether it's a pickup game or not. It's that big."

Franks found that Garnett appreciated the game in the same way. Garnett bickered often with his stepfather, Ernest Irby. Irby did not see any need to put up a hoop in the family's backyard when Garnett requested one. Garnett's biological father sent checks, but was mostly absent from his life. The park became Garnett's soothing confidant, where nothing existed except the ball, himself, and the basket. Garnett stayed at the park so late that police chased him home. He sometimes arrived so early, dribbling a ball over rocks and gravel from his home on Basswood Drive, that he beat the day's sunrise. The game meant so much to him, something his teammates at Mauldin High soon realized. Garnett made varsity as a freshman, despite Coach Duke Fisher's preference for underclassman to first pay their dues at a lower level. Fisher had played on the freshman team at the University of North Carolina and seared discipline and defense into his team's DNA. Garnett accepted and excelled at both, gradually becoming more aggressive on offense. The team lost one Friday night during Garnett's freshman season. Sal Graham, a sophomore guard, walked into the locker room and discussed weekend plans with the rest of the team. "Hey, man, you coming to the party with us tonight?" Graham asked Garnett. But Garnett was despondent. He covered his face with a towel. "We lost the game because of me," Garnett said in tears. "He took it so personal that no matter what the score was, he felt, as a fourteen-year-old freshman, that he should have won the game for us," Graham recalled.

Garnett loved the aspect of playing on a team, the strength of a group with a common goal. He preferred blending in among his teammates and classmates away from the court. But the same size that helped him excel on the court prevented him from fading into the background off it. Garnett would pull a teammate into the frame when a fan wanted a picture of just him. If Garnett signed a program for a spectator, he passed it along to a teammate and had him autograph it as well. "He was so much taller than everybody else," recalled Betty Mitchell, a guidance staff officer at the school. "You could spot him at the end of the hall. He wanted to be a regular teenager, like everybody else at the school. The adults here in the building probably put a little bit more on him than he was ready for at the time." Garnett's history teacher, Janie Willoughby (no relation to Bill Willoughby), became a second mother to him. Garnett couldn't sit at a regular desk without doing contortions, so Willoughby brought in an old living room chair from her home. He was a reluctant student. She knew how to push, prod, and edge him along. He once delivered an oral report on the Boston Tea Party, pausing every few moments to ask Willoughby if he had done enough to warrant a passing grade. "No, not yet," Willoughby patiently replied several times before finally accepting his plea to finish. Another time, Garnett helped a student as she nervously stumbled through her oral report. Garnett asked a question each time she paused to get her back on track. Willoughby beamed, thinking that Garnett did not want the spotlight on himself, but would help others on their way.

Garnett earned an invite to the Nike All-American Basketball Festival in 1993. The nation's top 125 high school players gathered to be judged by about 500 college coaches over a five-day period in Indianapolis. He teamed with players whose high schools treated them like royalty, a far cry from how he felt at Mauldin. The boys broke into teams for scrimmages. William Nelson, the coach at Chicago's Farragut Career Academy, noticed all the camp's top players walking toward other instructors. A sinewy Garnett came up to him. *I got the skinniest big man?* Nelson thought. *That's not fair.*

"How you all give me the little guy?" Nelson asked the tournament's planner.

Garnett was within earshot. "Come on man, quit tripping," he said.

"Quit tripping?" Nelson retorted. "You skinny, man."

Nelson prepared for a long day of watching Garnett being shoved and bullied on the court. He figured his team could only win by pushing the tempo and instructed them to run every possession. They did, winning 13 of 16 games behind the play of two juniors, Garnett and Antawn Jamison. Garnett experienced liberation during the games. In South Carolina, Fisher rebuked Garnett whenever he screamed after dunking. Fisher was a purist and considered the outburst a form of showboating. "Scream louder if that's what works for you," Nelson advised. Garnett looked at Ronnie Fields, Nelson's star guard, whom he had befriended at the camp. "Is that your coach?" he asked Fields. "Our coach is nowhere near that. It's like night and day. I didn't know they had coaches like that."

He had grown more that summer, to the point that the Mauldin coaching staff needed a moment to recognize Garnett upon his return to South Carolina for his junior year. Every year the Mauldin Mavericks looked forward to the annual Beach Ball Classic in Myrtle Beach. The Christmas tournament brought together some of the country's most talented high school players on the East Coast. Mauldin had hopes of a high tournament placing in January 1994. Garnett was eager to become better known nationally, like one of the team's early opponents, LaMarr Greer. Greer played for New Jersey's Middle Township High School and few around the country could fill up a basket like the Florida State recruit. In the game, Greer dunked on Garnett early on, letting Garnett know about it. "You're mine," he said. Garnett's mind returned to Bear, the playground, and the taunts. But he was older, better, and stronger now. Garnett retaliated with his own dunk and chirped right back at Greer. "It turned into a one-on-one show between those two guys, everybody else get out of the way," said Murray Long, Garnett's teammate. "It was just a tremendous display of who he was getting ready to become." Garnett and Greer went back and forth. Whenever Greer made a shot, Garnett answered. Mauldin lost, 69–62. Garnett had 35 points, only missing 2 of his 17 shots, with 7 blocks. Greer countered with 37 points and 11 rebounds. Garnett finished with 40 points, 26 rebounds, and 8 blocked shots in another tournament game that went into five overtimes, prevailing over Los Angeles Loyola. In just three games, Garnett totaled 101 points, 56 rebounds, and 21 blocked shots. "We had seen flashes of greatness before, but that stands out in my mind as when I really was able to step back and think, *Wow, this guy is the real deal*," Long said.

Garnett averaged 27 points and 17 rebounds his junior year. But Mauldin fell in the upper-state championship game in March 1994. The team was lucky to advance that far. Garnett had nearly transferred before the season to Oak Hill Academy, a powerhouse secondary school in Virginia. He had forwarded his transcripts and application to Steve Smith, the school's coach. Garnett's mother nixed the plan. But Garnett had already noticed the hypocrisy in others benefiting from his work and talent. It weighed on him. His Mauldin team sold out every game. Yet, the team performed in tattered jerseys. The players Garnett formed friendships with over the summer had received shoes and jerseys from sneaker companies. "He didn't feel appreciated," Graham said. "I can see how he felt that way. Our uniforms looked bad. They were a wreck." Fisher's combative coaching style also grated on the team, Graham said.

Two months after the lost state championship, members of the team milled around on the final day of school. Some described the ensuing incident as a fight. Others characterized it as innocent horseplay. Someone had written racial epithets on the basketball players' lockers earlier in the school year. They circled around the suspected student perpetrator this day and, according to different accounts, either playfully or forcefully punched him. The student reported a foot injury to authorities and Garnett as one of the participants, even though Garnett had only watched. His size again made it impossible for him to fade into the background.

Garnett rushed into Willoughby's classroom. She immediately recognized the distress in his voice. She stopped teaching her class and escorted him into the hallway. "I was just there," he told Willoughby. "I did not throw a lick. I just looked." A school administrator and a police officer arrived in the classroom, looking for Garnett. "If you are going to take him, do not cuff him, because he will not run," Willoughby pleaded. "He has nothing to run from." Police charged Garnett, Graham, and three others with second-degree lynching, defined in South Carolina as an act of violence by two or more people against another, regardless of race. He was taken to jail and released on $10,000 bond. "When you are looking at this kid, there wasn't one scratch or scar and they're looking at us like we robbed a bank," Graham said. "Kevin was in the circle and didn't even touch him." Graham said that he jokingly hit the accuser's shoulder twice. The only injury the student suffered occurred when he kicked a locker out of the frustration of having his pride damaged, Graham said. "I thought it was a relatively low-level encounter, but then the boy got real upset and kicked the locker and ended up with a broken foot," Stan Hopkins, the school's athletic director, remembered.

The students avoided a jail sentence through a pretrial intervention program for first-time offenders. "[Kevin] just wanted to be a regular kid," said Joe Broadus, Mauldin's principal at the time. "Unfortunately, sometimes he paid attention to social acceptance more than he should have, but, in this situation, I'm not sure how he could have handled it better." But lines had been drawn. Garnett thought he had the support of the school and community. He now believed he had neither. People treated him differently, even though he had done nothing wrong. "I think it was the biggest mistake that we as a school and as a community made," said Mitchell, the school's guidance counselor. "I still have a sour taste in my mouth about the whole thing that went down. I just don't think it was right."

The incident and the mounting spotlight on him contributed to Garnett calling Nelson, asking to attend Farragut. "You ain't live in Illinois," Nelson said. "You ain't live in Chicago. That's the craziest thing in the world. Why you gonna come to Farragut when you live somewhere else?" Garnett insisted that he was serious. His mother now agreed to a relocation. She had tired of the skepticism toward her son and the media that constantly hounded the family. They moved into an apartment one floor above Nelson's on Chicago's West Side. "Kevin was with me for most of the time," Nelson said. "His mother and his sister was always together. Guys with the guys, girls with the girls." Not all the time. Shirley Irby worked long hours in a government office near a gang-infested area. Garnett often hurried home to watch his sister, Ashley, before playing pickup games for spare money. The *Greenville News* reported that Nike had paid for the move and helped secure an apartment in Chicago for Garnett and his family. Nelson dismissed those allegations. "I wasn't even on that level," Nelson said. "Getting players from out of town? I wasn't even getting players from across the other side of town, so it was a joke to me." Nelson's team was already one of the state's best. Garnett improved them and immediately became a leader. Nelson sometimes arrived late to practice after teaching his final math class of the day. Garnett would already have the team sweating through drills. "I could sit back and just admire what he was doing," Nelson said. "He actually had those guys working hard. Man, I miss those days." If Garnett took undergraduate courses in the art of trash-talking from Franks, he received his master's from Ron Eskridge. Eskridge, an assistant coach, grew up playing in Philadelphia. He knew that you could simply talk opponents out of their game and relayed that to Garnett. "Personal, but nonpersonal," Eskridge said of the art of talking trash. A competitor reacts to trash talk by playing harder, Eskridge said. A weak player wilts away. "Nervous man—that's what he used to say when someone came onto the court," Eskridge said. "That was Kevin's favorite."

NBA scouts caught wind of the talented high school basketball player—possibly the best in the country—who might not qualify for college academically. Shawn Kemp's declaration for the NBA in 1989 had caught most executives off guard and many feared being blindsided again. Kemp left the University of Kentucky without playing a game amid allegations that he had pawned two gold chains stolen from a teammate. NBA scouts had little to go on as the draft neared— just grainy video footage of Kemp playing against subpar competition. He worked out for several teams prior to the draft. In Seattle, Bob

Whitsitt, the general manager of the SuperSonics, thought of an original way to gauge Kemp's basketball acumen. "Would you mind playing a game?" Whitsitt asked Kemp at Seattle University, motioning to a game on another court that featured some of the area's better amateur players. "Just play. We're not going to drill you and do all the footwork and all the stuff everybody does. We're just going to have you play basketball." Kemp smiled, nodded, and obliged. He played for more than an hour. "I was watching him handle the ball full court, do bounce passes from twenty-five feet," Whitsitt said. "He was the best player, knocking down three-point shots, like he was Reggie Miller." Whitsitt reported back to his coaching staff: "I've got this guy that, if it really comes together and that's a big if, he's a combination of Dominique Wilkins and Charles Barkley. He's got the physicality of Charles and he can just explode and jump like Dominique." Kemp lasted until the 17th pick in the first round of the 1989 NBA draft, going to Whitsitt and the SuperSonics. There he blossomed into an NBA star. "I remember some of my peers subtly letting everybody know how stupid I was and how smart they were for not taking this high school kid," Whitsitt said.

Times changed. Most teams had cobbled together detailed reports on Garnett by the end of his senior season in 1995. Lee Rose routinely brought his wife, Eleanor, on scouting trips. "Now, if you can't tell me who I'm looking at, then I'm not seeing a good player," said Rose, the vice president of player personnel for the Milwaukee Bucks. His wife immediately pointed to Garnett. *Shows you how important scouting is,* Rose thought. Ronnie Fields and Garnett developed into a devastating combination. They led Farragut to a 28–2 record and the city championship.

Most players Garnett's height of around seven feet pushed and pummeled inside. Garnett could do that. He could also play outside among the guards. "Run a three-point play for Kevin," Nelson would instruct. "The other coach would look at me like, *Who in the hell lets this seven-footer shoot a goddamn three?*" Nelson said. "Hell, one who knows he's going to make it." But Garnett missed a three-pointer with three seconds left that would have tied a Class AA state quarterfinal game against Thornton High School. Instead, Farragut was stunned, 46–43. Garnett sank just 6 of his 17 shots to go along with 16 rebounds and 6 blocks. "We didn't pass him the ball," a frustrated Nelson lamented to reporters after the game. "We had some guys who definitely didn't play our style of ball—they wouldn't pass it to him."

For years, Garnett had received grocery sacks of recruiting mail. In South Carolina, Willoughby had devoted a desk drawer in her classroom to them. Garnett sometimes came into her class, stretched out, and sifted through them. Michigan, South Carolina, and North Carolina were his favorites. He struggled to achieve qualifying ACT and SAT scores for college. He contemplated attending junior college for a year before advancing to a university. But he could not ignore the NBA scouts watching his every move. He would audition in front of them before taking the qualifying tests one more time.

· · ·

E ric Fleisher crafted the workout for Garnett in front of the executives after Garnett retained him as his agent. Fleisher's job was to point up Garnett's strengths and mask his weaknesses. Fleisher noted Garnett's shakiness in front of the NBA executives and wondered if he would bottom out, as he had at an earlier private audition that only Fleisher had watched. Fleisher was the son of Larry Fleisher, the onetime president of the NBA players union. Larry Fleisher helped found the union and presided over it during the mid-1960s, when pensions and minimum salaries would rise. He worked as a general counsel for the association when Moses Malone, Darryl Dawkins, and Bill Willoughby matriculated into the NBA. His son proved pivotal to the next generation of high school players who entered professional basketball. Agents had continually approached Garnett during his senior year of high school. Garnett planned on vetting them under his terms at his own time. He requested a meeting with Eric Fleisher a few weeks before the Chicago workout. He knocked on Fleisher's hotel room door at about 2 a.m., tardy by a mere seven hours. The knock stirred Fleisher. He thought Garnett had stood him up. Garnett, accompanied by five friends, wanted to talk from a position of power. He had deliberately arrived late. "I'm not signing anything," he told Fleisher. "I'm not committing to anything. I don't owe you anything."

Fleisher yawned. "Fine by me," he said.

Fleisher had performed his due diligence. He peppered Garnett with questions for nearly an hour. "Why do you want to do this? What are you thinking?" Garnett did not reveal his hand. Still, Fleisher predicted that Garnett planned to declare for the draft. "I think he understood the economics for a young man," Fleisher said. "He understood that if he went to college, they were going to sell his jersey. They were going to sell tickets. They were going to get tremendous benefits and he wasn't." Fleisher finished the meeting and gave Garnett his card. "If you ever want to talk again, just call me," he said. Garnett phoned about three weeks later. "Are you going to be in Chicago again?" Garnett asked. Fleisher had never seen him play and put him through an NBA workout at the Lakeshore Athletic Club. He had heard the stellar reports of Garnett's athleticism, but wanted to see it firsthand before he attached his established reputation to Garnett's nonexistent one. Garnett missed shot after shot at the workout. The misses made him irritated and flustered. He missed more. He became more irritated and more flustered. "He was terrible," Fleisher remembered. "I mean honestly, truly, really bad. His footwork was horrible. He couldn't make a shot." Garnett approached Fleisher afterward. "But really, I can play," he insisted. A pickup game among college players had broken out on an adjacent court. "Just watch me play," Garnett said.

"We waited and he got into the next game and within two minutes of watching him play, you could see it," Fleisher said.

Fleisher now prayed that Garnett would show that talent in front of the executives.

Flip Saunders and Kevin McHale conversed among the throng. They had played together at the University of Minnesota in the 1970s. McHale was the son of a mine worker who figured he would embark on a coaching career after graduating. The Boston Celtics drafted him with the third overall pick in the 1980 draft, the beginning of a prosperous professional career and teaming with Larry Bird. It was Saunders, instead, who immediately coached after college. He started at Minnesota's Golden Valley Lutheran College and later coached in the Continental Basketball Association. The two had joined forces again, tapped to jump-start the Minnesota Timberwolves. It was a fledgling franchise that had languished in the NBA's basement during its first six seasons. McHale, the new vice president of basketball operations, and Saunders, the new general manager, eyed the draft as a new beginning. The 1995 draft contained four college prospects viewed as franchise players: North Carolina's Jerry Stackhouse and Rasheed Wallace, Maryland's Joe Smith, and Alabama's Antonio McDyess. The Timberwolves were slotted to draft fifth. "Yeah, we are going to take the high school kid," McHale bluffed to his brethren at the workout, hoping that one of the teams choosing before him would gamble on Garnett, allowing him access to one of the coveted college players.

John Hammond had worked out hundreds of players before and picked up on their patterns quickly. He felt that Garnett had finally calmed down enough to begin the workout. He returned Garnett to the near side of the gym. Garnett performed shooting drills. The uninterested glances he had caught from some of the executives had left him enraged. Saunders elbowed McHale five minutes into the workout. Each knew the other's thought. They now hoped that Garnett would last until the fifth pick. He stood an angular 6 feet 11 inches tall. He moved like a player half a foot shorter. The gym was so hot that it felt as if all the city's heat and humidity had converged on the court. Perspiration soaked through Garnett's clothes. The executives even sweated. Garnett kept going. *This kid runs like the wind,* thought John Nash, Washington's general manager. Nash's Bullets possessed the fourth pick in the draft. Garnett had arrived late to the workout, already a strike against him in Nash's mind. He was now intrigued. Most college players were out of game shape by the June draft. Their seasons had come to a close a couple of months earlier. Garnett ended the workout with the same enthusiasm that he had begun with.

"Jump and touch the box," an executive requested, meaning the square that hovers above the rim. Garnett tapped it with ease. Another asked that he touch the square's top. He did it with each hand and screamed with each ascent.

Hammond took Garnett to the right side of midcourt as the workout ended. "Hey, Kevin, why don't you do this?" Hammond said. "Put the ball on the floor and be as creative as you can and then finish by giving a great dunk at the end of it." Garnett did. Hammond smiled. Jaws dropped. They performed the same move on the other side of the court. Garnett dribbled the ball between his legs, around his back, and crossed over before finishing with a yell and a crashing dunk. McHale made a point of introducing himself to Garnett before leaving, offering some shooting tips. "Make sure you square your shoulders," McHale said. "Don't fade away on your shot." McHale just wanted to be kind and thank Garnett for the show. McHale now thought he had no chance of landing Garnett.

Garnett waited for the gym to empty. He laid down on the court, sleeping for the next couple of hours. He had literally left everything he had on it. Garnett was now expected to be taken within the first few picks. John Nash returned to Washington and huddled with Abe Pollin, the team's owner, and Coach Jim Lynam. The franchise desperately needed a shooting guard or a small forward. Nash discussed Rasheed Wallace and Jerry Stackhouse with the pair. He mentioned Garnett and described the impressive performance. "John, I would appreciate it if we didn't draft a high school player," Pollin said. Nash respected Pollin and was unsure himself if he wanted to assume the risk in drafting a high school player. He dropped Garnett from consideration.

Even with Garnett's name on the tips of every NBA executive's tongue, Shirley Irby wanted Garnett to attend college. For an urban kid, college was a dream, not a realistic destination. But now, schools wanted to *pay* for her son's education if he qualified. It seemed like too good a deal to pass on. Nelson explained another offer too good to pass up. "If he went to college and got every degree in school, he wouldn't be making the kind of money he could make right now," Nelson told her. "I wouldn't advise him to go to college at this point. Hell, he can buy the damn college if he wants to." Garnett scheduled a press conference at the Home Run Inn, a pizza restaurant on Chicago's Southwest Side. "Um, I declare myself eligible for the NBA draft," Garnett began in front of an assembly of family, media, coaches, and teammates. "Recently I received my ACT scores, which was not high enough to play Division I ball . . ." He said he would like to keep his options open, should he qualify academically. An NCAA spokesperson told the *Chicago Tribune* that Garnett would lose his college eligibility if he declared for the NBA. But he could petition for reinstatement as a Proposition 48 student-athlete if he paid his first year of college expenses and did not play basketball. The NCAA had enacted the regulation in 1986 in an effort to raise eligibility requirements and respond to criticism of undereducated athletes who rarely graduated. A freshman now needed a 2.0 grade point average and at least a combined score of 700 on the Scholastic Assessment Tests to qualify for eligibility. Blacks became disproportionately ineligible because of the regulation. Garnett seemed like another casualty among hundreds until he decided to bypass the amateur route into professional basketball.

At the press conference, he looked uneasy. The confidence he showed on the court eluded him.

"Why not go to junior college?" a reporter asked.

"Why go?" Garnett responded.

He was 18 years old and he looked like it. Another journalist asked if he would like to be the role model for others to enter the NBA out of high school. "Oh, man," he answered. "I don't want that on me. All I'd do is wish them good luck."

The question remained: Which team would pull the trigger on a high school player? Fleisher declined private workout requests from NBA teams—afraid that a knee injury Garnett had suffered at the time would scare teams away. Instead, he allowed franchises to interview

Garnett. Some still questioned Garnett's maturity after his transfer from South Carolina to Illinois. Doug Collins, the Pistons coach, had one of the first sit-downs with Garnett. "In a nice way, he really peeled back some of the layers," Fleisher said. "I walked away from that day with a real sense that Kevin was going to go very high." Fleisher offered an interview with Garnett to Isiah Thomas. Thomas declined. He was formerly the dynamic point guard who played under Bob Knight at Indiana before piloting the "Bad Boy" Detroit Pistons. In 1994, he became a part owner and executive of the expansion Toronto Raptors. He knew Garnett inside and out. Thomas first saw Garnett play at a camp in South Carolina and monitored him closely once Garnett emerged in the Windy City. Anthony Longstreet, a childhood friend and assistant coach at Farragut, provided him with updates. Thomas envisioned Garnett evolving the game, a big man who could play outside among the guards. Thomas promised that Garnett would not slip beyond Toronto's seventh pick.

McHale phoned Thomas before the draft. The two shared a longstanding friendship. McHale had heard the rumors of Garnett being immature and asked for Thomas's input.

"Whatever you're hearing, don't believe," Thomas told McHale. "If you don't take him, I'm definitely taking him. What you're seeing in him is all true. What you're hearing about him, none of that is true.

"Kevin, you and I have known each other since high school. He would be the perfect guy for you and he's the perfect guy for me. I wouldn't tell anybody else that, but out of respect for our friendship, I would [tell] you."

The honesty seemed misplaced in a competitive business. Truthfully, Thomas had minimal concerns about Garnett's ability. He worried more about his own organization's impact on the teenager. The Raptors had inherited the players that other teams offered to give away through the expansion draft. Thomas did not want any jaded players rubbing off on an impressionable teenager. Had he drafted him, Thomas would have insisted that Garnett remain home during some road games and enroll at a university to ease into adulthood in a spotlight. "Garnett, coming out of high school to a foreign country in Canada, I didn't know," Thomas said. "I was going to have to put a totally different type of program around him to make sure he had success and make sure he was comfortable because he was such a young player. The mentoring and tutoring that was going to be required was going to be different. I had put together a plan for Garnett."

Meanwhile, McHale told Glen Taylor, the owner of the Timberwolves, that Garnett would develop into a good player, likely a star. "I just don't know when," McHale said. Taylor left the decision to McHale and Saunders. Celtics legendary coach Red Auerbach once advised McHale that everyone fumbled draft picks. If he did not, he would become the first executive in NBA history not to do so. "Hey, if we pick guys who don't work, we'll just tell them we don't know any better and it's our first draft," McHale joked to Saunders. The pair decided that if Garnett was available with their fifth pick, they would take him. They had once declared that they coveted him when they did not. They now told others that they wanted a college player who could contribute immediately in hopes that Garnett would fall to them in the draft.

Toronto hosted the NBA's draft in 1995. Garnett, as one of the top projected selections, attended at the NBA's request. Nelson called him moments before the draft. "You passed," Nelson said. *Passed what?* Garnett wondered. Nelson had not bothered opening the results of Garnett's last and latest SAT once Garnett had declared for the draft. Nelson had unsealed it on a whim. Garnett had earned a qualifying score, but it was too late for college now. His professional career beckoned. The college players went as expected. Golden State drafted Joe Smith first overall. Antonio McDyess went second to the Clippers (which traded him to Denver) and Philadelphia selected Jerry Stackhouse. Nash eagerly took Rasheed Wallace, a versatile forward. McHale alerted Clayton Wilson, Minnesota's equipment manager, that the organization would take Garnett. Garnett rose to greet David Stern, passing several older, more established college players on his walk to the podium. He said a prayer of thanks as he walked, he later told *Sports Illustrated*, and finished it as he took Stern's outstretched hand.

Wilson had packed the shorts of Terry Porter, a guard, and figured he would have some fun with the teenager. He requested that Garnett take a picture in full Timberwolves garb. Wilson held up Porter's shorts that would have resembled Speedos had Garnett worn them. "The bad news is, I thought we were drafting a guard," Wilson said. "The good news is, next year, we can get you some longer ones."

"Word?" Garnett said in amazement. He was not offended, as Wilson had predicted. Garnett admired the shorts. Wilson laughed, pulling out a Timberwolves jersey. "This is the first jersey I've ever had like this," Garnett said, running his hands over his name. "Look at it, it's stitched in."

A tear formed. His life had changed so much the past couple of years from the rural, choking spotlight in South Carolina to the urban, gang-packed Chicago streets to becoming a NBA draft pick in Toronto on his way to being a professional in Minnesota. Basketball remained the common thread.

Saunders, in the years to follow, would recognize Garnett's display of nervousness in that first workout from a different perspective. "His shaking is not that he's scared," Saunders said. "It's his adrenaline pumping. He always drank two Gatorades, one in each hand, and they would be almost coming up over the edge he would shake so much. It's not nerves. It's an unbelievable adrenaline rush."

3.

Kevin Garnett slouched on a bench. Ice and tape left his body mummified. Everything hurt. Everything. "The league ain't no joke, man," he mumbled to himself again and again. "The league ain't no joke." Garnett had just begun his first NBA training camp with the Timberwolves at St. Cloud State University deep into the fall of 1995. Minnesota opened with grueling twice-a-day practices. The veterans could coast. Rookies and others with playing time to earn and reputations to make went full tilt each session. League turmoil had nearly delayed Garnett's debut. The NBA's first lockout threatened the 1995–1996 season. An agreement between the league and the players union in September ended the three-month standoff. The arrangement closed loopholes that creative teams used to circumvent the league's salary cap in adding players. The deal birthed a sliding salary scale that specified how much rookies earned, based on their draft position. The increasingly enormous contracts that rookies signed before having ever played an NBA game—Glenn Robinson had signed with Milwaukee a year earlier for $68.2 million for ten seasons—ended. Garnett inked a comparatively paltry contract, three years for $5.6 million. But Garnett could enter unrestricted free agency after three years, a provision that proved to be a windfall for many players—himself included—in the future.

That would come later, much later.

But first Garnett had to survive training camp. Clayton Wilson figured he would play another joke on the aching teenager. Garnett had just gone through two practices and was more ice than man when Wilson approached him. "Young fella, it's your cardiovascular night," Wilson said. "You've either got to do an hour on the treadmill or walk back to the hotel." Garnett glared incredulously at Wilson. "I can barely walk," Garnett answered. "The league ain't no joke, man."

The entire NBA wanted to know if Garnett could adapt to the league's physical play, frequent travel, and lifestyle. The curious included Minnesota's staff. Jerry Sichting had played with Kevin McHale in Boston before becoming Minnesota's director of scouting. Garnett had stated that he wanted to be the Deion Sanders of basketball, a flashy prima donna, in an article Sichting had read. Sichting anticipated the worse when Garnett arrived. "When he got here, he was the most humble, shy person," Sichting remembered. "Clayton Wilson gave him a bag of 'Wolves gear and he was like a kid in a candy shop. He was totally different than the persona he was trying to project." Garnett missed his first workout with the Timberwolves because of a sprained ankle, sustained while shooting a Nike commercial. He debuted a couple days later with a number of free agents, journeymen, and others looking to break into the NBA. The game's pace hit Garnett like a wall. He could not take in oxygen fast enough. His chest heaved in and out. He finally settled into a rhythm. Then his nerves kicked in. His shot continually fell short. He muttered curses to himself up and down the floor. Bill Blair, Minnesota's coach, saw in him a prodigy who possessed the total package, years away from knowing how to use it. "He had some toughness," Blair said. "He would get mad quick. He had that thing that the special ones do about being such a good competitor."

Garnett needed it when the rest of the team convened at St. Cloud

State. Minnesota had never finished above 29 wins in its short history and wanted to turn the bleak past into a better future. The team's veteran players quickly introduced Garnett to the NBA one hard pick and tough foul at a time. Garnett only weighed about 215 pounds and each one of them felt sore after those first few practices. Eric Fleisher knew the transition would likely be jarring and he would have to be at Garnett's disposal more than he would be for other clients. He urged Garnett to call whenever he wanted. Garnett phoned after his second practice. Fleisher heard muffled crying. Garnett had gone up for a layup earlier in the day when Sam Mitchell, a six-year veteran, roughly rerouted him back to earth.

"Kevin, what do you expect?" Fleisher asked. "You're trying to take their job. This is a business now. You've got to understand that."

"I didn't think it was going to be this way," Garnett said.

"Guess what?" Fleisher promised. "It's going to get worse."

Kevin McHale devised a weight-lifting program with Sol Brandys, the team's strength and conditioning coach. They hoped Garnett would add about 25 pounds to his boyish frame by the end of his rookie season. Skinny players carry less muscle mass, leaving them more prone to injury. But Garnett despised lifting weights and figured he would take the bumps and bruises as they came. McHale trained a close eye on Garnett during those nascent days. He approached Garnett between practices one day. Garnett rested his back against the bleachers. His body would have collapsed without the support. "This is really hard," Garnett told McHale. "How did you do this for so long?" McHale wanted to walk the fine line between coddling and nurturing Garnett. "You're supposed to be tired," McHale said. "Training camp is tiring. The first one is always the toughest." McHale left Garnett alone to prepare for the day's next session. He figured Garnett would deliver a lackluster performance. "Then practice started and you would've never known he was exhausted or tired because he had a motor to play that was so impressive," McHale said. "I remember thinking at that moment that he was going to be OK." Garnett's exuberance rejuvenated the rest of the team. Mitchell had only wanted to test him out with the hard foul. He became a mentor to Garnett and their lockers were next to each other's. "We all knew about Kevin Garnett," said Mitchell, who later became an NBA coach. "We had read about him. The thing that we didn't know was how intense, how dedicated, how motivated he was to become a great player. The very first practice we had, we kind of turned to each other and said, *We're going to look back at this day and realize we played with a truly great player.*"

Bill Blair summoned Kevin Garnett midway through the first quarter of Minnesota's season opener in Sacramento on November 3, 1995. Garnett jumped up and walked slowly. He chewed bubble gum, wore a rubber band around his right wrist, and walked onto the ARCO Arena court, becoming the first person to play in an NBA game out of high school in two decades.

He needed less than two minutes to score a basket, banking in his first attempt off a feed from teammate Tom Gugliotta. He had grown up admiring Walt Williams, the Sacramento forward. Garnett was now guarded by Williams. Williams scored 20 points in the game, some off Garnett. Garnett mostly held his own. He took only four shots in his 16 minutes, sinking all of them in Minnesota's loss. "For a guy who's as young as he is, you'd think he'd be out of control or nervous, and he wasn't," Williams told reporters after the game.

Garnett simply wanted to play basketball, maintaining the mentality of the kid shooting every hour of the day at Springfield Park. He became the ideal player to reopen the avenue for high school players to join the NBA. His interests did not include partying or burning through money—not with all the basketball to be soaked up. "He just kind of seemed born to play," Sichting said. Garnett's checks piled up in his locker. He simply told Clayton Wilson that he was saving them up. "Money didn't really matter to him," Wilson said. "If the going rate was $30,000 for an NBA player, he'd still play." Like Isiah Thomas, McHale and Flip Saunders scripted a transition program for Garnett. They planned to place him with a host family, maybe one near the University of Minnesota, so that Garnett could be near some of his peers. "I think you can imagine Kevin's reaction to that," Fleisher said.

Garnett moved into a three-bedroom luxury condominium in Minnetonka, a Minneapolis suburb. He lived with Jamie Peters, a longtime friend from Mauldin. "We had spent a lot of time preparing for all these contingencies that ended up being a waste of time," McHale said. "We didn't have to do any of them."

The newness led to a series of light moments that reflected a teenager's adjustment.

Fleisher once called the organization. Garnett, he said, could not attend practice with the ongoing snowstorm and all. "Snowstorm?" Wilson asked Eric Fleisher. "It's a light drizzle outside."

"Really?" Fleisher said. "He made it sound like a blizzard."

Garnett tried entering one game, forgetting to change from his warm-up shirt into a jersey. He looked for it under the team's bench as the game halted. "Kevin, it wouldn't be under there," Blair said. "Try the locker room." Occasionally, Garnett would forget to pack for a road trip. The team left after home games and a friend had to scramble to gather Garnett's possessions. "They would meet him at the airport with literally just a garbage bag of clothes," Wilson said. Garnett racked up long-distance phone bills on the road by constantly talking to his friends. The organization finally bought him a phone card.

Clayton Wilson had also never seen someone so superstitious. Garnett barely paid attention to his paychecks. Yet, he always wore a lucky $2 bill in his game shoes. During Garnett's rookie season, Wilson came into the locker room at halftime to find him irate. "Who's in my locker?" Garnett asked. "You tell these motherfuckers to stay out of my locker. Someone stole my $2 bill."

"K.G., look in your locker," Wilson said. "You have hundreds and hundreds and maybe thousands of dollars in there. No one is going to take a $2 bill and leave the rest." Sam Mitchell listened to the conversation from his adjacent locker. "You mean this?" he asked, pulling out the wrinkled bill. "Man, I found this in the hallway. I didn't know it was yours." Garnett returned it to his shoe. "And all is right in the world," Wilson said.

Garnett's playing time slowly increased as his rookie season trudged on. "You almost forget as a coach that he's going to get bigger, he's going to get stronger, he's going to grow into this body to some degree," Blair said. With Minnesota still struggling, the organization fired Blair midway through the season and named Flip Saunders as coach. Everyone talked about Garnett's bright future. Yet he had much to learn in the present. Cedric Ceballos of the Lakers dunked over him in a game and yelled, "Not ready," at Garnett during his descent. Still, Del Harris, the Lakers coach, made sure to introduce himself to Garnett after the game. Harris did that with all the players he considered to be on the cusp of greatness. He did not know he would be tutoring his own high school star the next season.

"The next day in practice, it was as if nothing happened," said Randy Wittman, a Timberwolves assistant coach who would become the head coach of the Washington Wizards. "[Garnett's] head wasn't down. He wasn't pouting, which happens to a lot of players. Forget about a high school kid. This happens to the guys that are 30 years old. That was really the first sign I really saw of, *This kid's going to be special.* By the end of his rookie year, he got through the war. He understood what the process was and then he just took off. He had things he had to work on. All you had to do is really get him and instruct him, because he was going to do the rest. He was going to work."

Garnett started under Saunders and finished his rookie season with averages of 10.4 points and 6.3 rebounds. The Timberwolves barely improved on their win total from a season earlier, but the organization and the city could see a better future evolving with Garnett.

As for Ceballos?

"I remember every time that we played those guys from then on, his intensity to play was at a different level," Saunders said. "It was one of those things where he took pride that he was going to try to dominate those guys because they questioned him when he first got into the league."

Garnett's body grew stronger. He looked like an NBA player and, other than a few eccentricities, acted like one. He wanted to learn and he listened. But if he had opened a door for other high school players to jump directly to the NBA, he did not want to be responsible for leaving it open. "I've heard that there are high school kids who are thinking about going straight to the NBA like I did," Garnett told *USA Today*. "Well, they're crazy. I'd tell them to put aside all the money, the girls and the fame . . . I'd tell them, *There's nothing easy about the NBA.* If I could have gone to college, I would have in a heartbeat."

The league wasn't a joke.

4.

John Nash and John Calipari celebrated the eve of the 1996 NBA draft by hosting Joe and Pamela Bryant for dinner. Nash and Calipari ran the New Jersey Nets, a transient franchise in the shadows of the New York Knicks. They were so new to the organization that they had yet to find housing. Calipari became coach and executive vice president after guiding UMass to the Final Four. He maintained veto power over player personnel decisions and had hired Nash as his experienced general manager. Nash had left the Washington Bullets after an extended playoff drought in one of those quit-before-being-fired deals. Like the Timberwolves a season ago, they felt that the renewal of the Nets would begin through the NBA draft. No selection process in professional sports can reinvigorate a franchise like basketball's draft. A fruitful pick enlivens an organization for years. A basketball star does not need to rely on a strong offensive line or sure-handed receivers, as a franchise NFL quarterback does. He does not need fielders to back him up, as an ace pitcher in baseball does. Basketball stars are self-sufficient. The very best can score and defend and lift a franchise nearly all by themselves. Nash and Calipari were certain they were on the verge of such an acquisition as they welcomed the Bryants inside Calipari's suite at the Radisson Suites Hotel in Secaucus, New Jersey.

They made small talk around Italian courses. Nash had coached in summer league games against Joe Bryant, a 6-foot-9-inch forward and a member of the Philadelphia 76ers when Darryl Dawkins broke into the NBA out of high school. Pamela's brother, Chubby Cox, also played briefly in the NBA. The Bryants were basketball royalty in Philadelphia. At the dinner, Calipari and Nash told the Bryants that they would draft their precocious 17-year-old son, Kobe. Calipari had hosted Kobe Bryant for three personal workouts. One stellar workout could mean that a prospect just had a good day. Three? That forecast superstardom. The Nets drew the draft's eighth selection. Bryant would surely tumble to them with a handful of established college players for the taking. Why risk passing one of them for a high school guard? All the other high school entrants—Dawkins, Moses Malone, Bill Willoughby, and Kevin Garnett—had been frontcourt players. Bryant was a slender guard. At 6 feet 6 inches, Bryant did not even reach his father's height.

Jerry West, the legendary Lakers player turned general manager of the franchise, wanted to trade for New Jersey's pick. He offered his center, Vlade Divac. "I love Divac and wish I had drafted him in 1989 when I was with the 76ers," Nash told West. Every league executive knew West's intent to shed as much salary as possible to make an earnest run at Shaquille O'Neal during the nearing free agency period, when teams could sign players once their previous contracts expired. Calipari and Nash declined. They figured they would be rebuilding, a blueprint that would take a couple of years to implement. Divac played reliably but, at 28 years old, they figured he would be on his career's downside by the time they righted the team. West would have to continue his search elsewhere if he wanted to trade Divac. Nash and Calipari wanted the pick and they wanted Bryant.

With the news divulged, the Bryants smiled and appeared eager at the prospect of Bryant beginning his professional career close to home, Nash recalled. Calipari asked Joe Bryant what he expected from Kobe during his rookie season. "I expect that he'll be a starter in his rookie year and I expect he'll make the All-Star Team in his second year," Bryant responded.

They said their good-byes for then. A bright union lay ahead for both parties. "Joe had some pretty lofty goals for Kobe right out of the box," Calipari told Nash. Nash believed in Kobe Bryant, but did not necessarily share those immediate high expectations. "Yeah," Nash rationalized, "but that's a father talking."

Nash slept that night believing the Nets would draft Bryant and be fast-tracked toward NBA relevancy. He awoke to a day he would remember in another way, one that, he said, contained "the biggest regret of my professional life."

• • •

"I've seen a better high school player than you," Debbie Lucas told her husband. She announced it in a casual tone that instantly whetted John Lucas's curiosity. Since his abbreviated stint as Moses Malone's roommate at Maryland, Lucas had become the first overall pick in the NBA's 1976 draft, by the Houston Rockets. He battled cocaine and alcohol abuse before straightening himself out and successfully counseling other substance abusers. He coached the Philadelphia 76ers in 1994 and had recently returned from a long road trip when Debbie Lucas informed him of the mystery skilled player. "Who are you talking about?" he asked. There was a kid at their daughter's high school, Lower Merion, everyone raved about, she said. "We've got to go see this guy named Kobe Bean," Debbie Lucas added.

The legend of Bryant, only 16, was already spreading. Most heard about him by word of mouth, doubting the hyperbolic description until confirming it for themselves. John Lucas became the latest convert. He attended a Lower Merion game at the Palestra, home to the University of Pennsylvania's basketball teams. Lucas immediately noticed Bryant's high skill level. Bryant started the game playing center. He ended it as a guard. *She wasn't lying,* Lucas thought of his wife's declaration when he came across a familiar face at the arena in Joe Bryant. The two had squared off during their playing days. Lucas addressed Bryant by his nickname. "Jellybean, what are you doing here?" Lucas asked.

"My son plays," Bryant answered.

"Wait," Lucas said. "I'm here to see your son?"

"I guess so," Bryant said.

Pamela Bryant gave birth to Kobe in Philadelphia a year after Joe Bryant played for Philadelphia in the 1977 NBA Finals. That appearance would be the highlight of his truncated NBA career. "Joe was a very, very talented player, and a lot like Darryl [Dawkins]," said Gene Shue, who coached both on the 76ers. "But I always felt with Joe that there was a little bit more there as well." Bryant made pit stops in San Diego and Houston before continuing his career overseas. Pamela, their two daughters, and six-year-old Kobe accompanied him. They first settled in Rieti, Italy, as Joe Bryant embarked on an eight-year European career with four different teams.

Kobe Bryant displayed the same affection for the game as his father did. John Cox, Pamela's father, mailed him videotapes of NBA games and Kobe devoured the moves of his favorite players. He attended his father's games and had to be shuffled off the court after putting on halftime shooting exhibitions. In his bedroom was a giant poster of Magic Johnson. Kobe performed basketball moves kids his age in Europe could only imagine. But his talents did not faze them. He played well in an American sport because he was American, they figured. He would be average against other American kids, they rationalized.

That would be one of the few times anyone considered Kobe Bryant average in basketball. Joe Bryant's playing career ended in 1992 and the family returned to Philadelphia.

Like Lucas later, Gregg Downer first heard of the exploits of a talented middle schooler in his district before he actually witnessed Kobe Bryant play. He attended one of Bryant's games and found it difficult to fully gauge Bryant's talent level. The coach kept yanking Bryant in and out of the game. Downer did figure out who Bryant's father was and invited the 13-year-old Bryant to work out with his varsity team at Lower Merion.

The Lower Merion gym—long before a new one would be dedicated by Bryant and named after him—creaked and groaned under the weight of the players. Wooden bleachers protruded from both sides. Wind invaded its insides, making it "drafty as hell," said Doug Young, a sophomore on the team when Bryant came to the practice. "For someone to inject some electricity in there, it required a lot," Young added.

The team noticed Joe Bryant walk in first. They tried stealing side glances between drills. Every kid in Philadelphia knew of Jellybean. Not many people of his size had ever walked into their gym. The team was not exactly nationally known. "Quite honestly, we hadn't had a guy who could really dunk in probably ten years," Young said.

Their eyes then turned to Kobe Bryant. He stood about 6 feet 2 inches tall and maybe he weighed 140 pounds, if that. "He looked [like] a lamp," said Rob Schwartz, Bryant's future Lower Merion teammate.

The team ran through some exercises. Downer divvied them up for a scrimmage. *Who is this kid?* Young wondered. He and his teammates figured they would soon put Bryant in his place.

Bryant scored once.

The team did not have to say anything, but many later agreed on their consensus thinking: *That kid's pretty good.*

Bryant peeled around the lane and nailed a jumper, displaying footwork beyond his age. "This kid is going to be a pro," Downer prophesied to one of his assistants. Bryant made a bunch of shots. He missed a bunch, too. He played defense as fervently as he played offense. "I wouldn't call it cockiness," Young recalled. "But there was this kind of sense of, *Who are you guys?* Instead of just trying to prove himself as an eighth grader."

How do you become elated and deflated at the same time? Young knew Lower Merion would never be the same again. The team would be better, much better in the years to come. But the upperclassmen would have to adjust to Bryant and not the other way around. Young left the practice with his teammate Matt Snider. "I guess Coach

Downer's going to have a ninth grader on the team next year," Young surmised.

That would be only the beginning. "He transformed that place into this really loud, really warm, really buzzing place," Young said. "People came out to the games to watch him. And you could almost feel that the first time he came into the gym, that that kind of energy was coming."

The stories of Bryant's competitiveness would become legendary. He once came over to play at Young's house and tore down the rim with a dunk only a couple of minutes into the game. "I think it's time to take these games to the playground, boys," Young's mother gently suggested. Bryant was maniacal. He often called on Rob Schwartz, a scrappy benchwarmer, to shoot with him at 5 a.m. "And when I say go shoot, I would go rebound for him for an hour," Schwartz said. Sometimes Bryant and Scwartz played halfcourt games up to 100 with each basket counting as a point. Bryant often went up by 85 points— sometimes more. Schwartz, about 5 feet 7 inches tall, swore he once scored eight points against Bryant. "He was practicing real-game situations against me," Schwartz said. "I just prayed for him to miss a jump shot every once in a while and that's the way I'd get the ball back."

Downer often paired Bryant with Schwartz in drills. Phil Jackson employed the same tactic with Michael Jordan, with the stronger player hopefully elevating the weaker one to his level. The gambit once nearly ended in Schwartz's spilled blood. Schwartz and Bryant's team had possession of the ball in a tied game as they closed out practice. Schwartz dribbled around the court as Bryant screamed and demanded the ball.

Everyone's going to think I'm going to be passing the ball to him, so I'm going to use him as a decoy, Schwartz figured. Schwartz would never make the mistake of using Bryant as a decoy again. He pump-faked a pass to Bryant and drove in for a layup. An opponent nudged him in the back. Schwartz's attempt careened out. The other team raced up court and scored the game-winning basket.

Schwartz heard Bryant slam the ball behind him. He felt him staring daggers into his back. He did not want to turn around.

"Why didn't I get the ball?" Bryant asked. "Who do you think you are?"

Schwartz had had enough and returned Bryant's volley beneath his breath. He forgot what he said, but whatever it was, it did not sit well with Bryant. Bryant chased him around the school and into the locker room. Schwartz ran until he was certain Bryant had stopped his pursuit. "That's part of the insane mentality that he had," Schwartz said. "He had to win everything. Practice, drill, game, it doesn't matter. It all falls under the same realm. I think it was just his makeup. He kind of figured out where he was going to go and what he had to do and it was all he thought about."

Jeremy Treatman was a Lower Merion assistant coach. Treatman also worked as a sportswriter and filtered Bryant's media requests. He had known Bryant for a while and had never seen Bryant act that way. *What an asshole,* he thought as he drove home from practice. *It's the meanest thing ever. Rob Schwartz, he's harmless.* Treatman stopped at a traffic light and the realization hit him. *That's what makes him great,* he thought. "He was so mad that he lost the drill and I learned later that that was the first drill he had ever lost in four years at Lower Merion," Treatman said.

Bryant averaged 31.1 points, 10.4 rebounds, and 5.2 assists per game his junior year, earning Pennsylvania's Player of the Year award. Bryant fell short of his elusive state championship in 1995. That summer, John Lucas invited Bryant to play against some of his 76ers during open scrimmages at St. Joseph's University. Lucas wanted to see if Bryant could hold up against the older, better competition. During the NBA season, Lucas had arranged for Bryant to greet Michael Jordan when the Bulls came to town. Bryant referred to him as Mr. Jordan. "You can't be calling him Mr. Jordan if you're going to be playing against him in the NBA," Lucas told Bryant. That deference was nowhere to be found in the summer's pickup games. John Nash, then still with the Bullets, checked in with Lucas and asked how the players looked. Nash was still fond of Jerry Stackhouse, the former North Carolina guard coming off his rookie year in Philadelphia.

"How's Stack doing in your workouts?" Nash asked.

"Fine, but he's the second best two-guard in the gym," Lucas said.

Nash searched his brain. He knew all the players working out. None carried Stackhouse's pedigree. He finally gave in and asked, "John, who's the best two-guard?"

"Kobe," Lucas said in the same flat, certain tone his wife had once used to announce Bryant's talents to him. "He dominates every day."

News spread that Bryant, the high schooler, had demolished Stackhouse in the pickup games. Tony DiLeo, a 76ers scout, said Lucas had to end the sessions to preserve Stackhouse's confidence. "Lies, straight lies," said Stackhouse, who enjoyed a long, distinguished NBA career. As a pro, Stackhouse insisted that he had no reason to measure himself against Bryant. Most of the time, Stackhouse said, they did not even play against each other. Instead, they lifted weights or ran on the track. "That's the allure of a great player and I understand that, but I got to make sure that it's not done at my expense," Stackhouse said. Stackhouse did recall a one-on-one matchup with Bryant that resonated two decades later. Bryant, Stackhouse, and one of Stackhouse's friends were the only people inside the gym. "I know I won, but it wasn't easy, there wasn't nothing easy about it," Stackhouse recalled. "He came in and made a move and tried to just dunk on me. It wasn't like he tried to go lay it up. He tried to dunk on me and I actually blocked it. He wasn't coming and thinking about *I'm trying to lay this up*. He was coming with the intent to do damage."

Phil Martelli, St. Joseph's coach, offered Bryant the key to the gym. He did not extend that privilege to most of his own team. Bryant showed maturity and acted appreciative, projecting tact that most college players had yet to master. The pickup games took place outside Martelli's office. Although he was not curious enough to peek his head out, he heard about Bryant's performances soon after. "Some of it became an urban myth," Martelli said. "Now there were a thousand people at a pickup game on a Saturday at St. Joseph's. None of that's true. If ten people other than the ten players were there, you'd have an enormous crowd." It did not matter if people actually witnessed

Bryant pick apart Stackhouse. "What mattered was he was so damn good that you could believe it," said Young, Bryant's Lower Merion teammate.

John Nash had to see for himself. He lived in Philadelphia and often shuttled between watching two of the area's brighter prospects the same day: Bryant at Lower Merion and Kerry Kittles, a guard at nearby Villanova University. Nash made sure to get to Lower Merion early—you had to or else you could not get in at all. He purchased his own seat instead of asking the school's athletic department for a comp ticket. Kevin Garnett was still easing his way into superstardom. Many still denounced the NBA's presence in high school gyms. Nash did not want to deal with any backlash. He also did not want any teams catching wind of his scouting expeditions. "I thought the Kobe Bryant hype was probably just that," Nash said. "Then, you see him and he was so much more than what I expected."

In Bryant's senior year of high school, Downer hired assistant coaches with college playing experience specifically to guard Bryant during practices. He sometimes mandated that Bryant scrimmage against a team with more defenders—usually adding Schwartz and Leo Stacy, another irritant, to the other team. Bryant and Stacy once dove for a ball simultaneously. Blood leaked onto the floor. The collision left Bryant with a broken nose. He walked off, stopping beyond the court's border, and requested a ball. After receiving one, Bryant calmly swished a shot with his left hand, his off hand, before seeking medical attention. *How is that possible?* Schwartz thought. *This guy— he's not human.* The training staff outfitted Bryant with a protective mask for Lower Merion's state semifinal game against Chester. The mask bothered Bryant during warm-ups and fogged his peripheral vision. Bryant ripped the mask off as Lower Merion gathered for a final pregame meeting. "It's time to go to war," he declared. He played the next two games with a broken nose. Downer would remember the incident in later years as others became accustomed to Bryant's high pain threshold. A well-placed elbow would have knocked Bryant out and derailed Lower Merion's state championship hopes. Instead, they celebrated a championship win over Cathedral Prep, 48–43. The Aces ended the season on a 27-game win streak.

Schwartz had grown accustomed to the oddness of the Bryant hoopla throughout the season. On any random day, a television crew might trail Bryant from class to class. Every college wanted him. Duke and La Salle, where Joe Bryant coached, surged as frontrunners. Some also believed that he would skip college altogether. Despite Nash's preference, other NBA scouts also frequented Lower Merion. Bryant's choice would be unique from those that came before him and many who came after. He had no compelling reason to enter the league other than his own internal drive. His family possessed money. He scored a 1080 on his SAT and would have easily met the academic requirements of any school he chose.

About 400 students, coaches, teammates, media, and family gathered inside Lower Merion's gym on April 29, 1996. A steam coursed through the gym that spring, replacing the winter's draft.

"I, Kobe Bryant, have decided to take my talents to . . . ," Bryant started.

He stopped. He merely feigned nervousness, unlike Garnett, who sincerely expressed it in his declaration. Bryant rubbed his chin and surveyed the gym as laughter filled the arena. "I have decided to skip college and take my talents to the NBA," he finished.

The criticism followed immediately. Many media members accused Joe and Pamela Bryant of trying to capitalize financially off of their son. Others in Philadelphia viewed Bryant as egotistical, donning sunglasses during the announcement and escorting singer-actress Brandy Norwood to his prom.

"He's kidding himself," declared Marty Blake, the NBA's longtime director of scouting.

Blake's job was to know and predict the talent level of each NBA prospect. "Sure, he'd like to come out. I'd like to be a movie star. He's not ready." The backlash surprised Treatman. "They were calling his parents irresponsible and that he was nowhere near ready," Treatman said. "I knew he was going to take a lot of criticism. He took more than

I thought he was going to. It drove his family to tears. It just made Kobe want it more. Kobe's obsessed about proving people wrong. He's different. The more criticism he took, the more he just wanted to go out there and be a superstar in the NBA as fast as he could."

Bryant had made his decision even before Garnett had skipped college. Garnett's decision had upset Kobe. He had wanted to be the one to reopen the doors for high schoolers to the NBA. "Kobe is a groundbreaker and I'm not sure there's ever been a player, maybe with the exception of Jordan, that has the internal confidence that Kobe has," Downer said. "I don't think Kobe really listened to Kevin Garnett. He has such an unwavering confidence that he would've done it regardless of what Garnett did."

5.

The day that would change the Nets' franchise finally arrived. John Nash pulled his car into Continental Airlines Arena at around noon on June 26, 1996. He hurried to a lunch with John Calipari and Joe Taub before the day turned hectic. A group of businessmen, dubbed the Secaucus Seven, owned the Nets. They rotated on who acted as basketball liaison—the one who dealt directly with Nash and Calipari, voicing their directives and concerns. Taub represented the seven when Nash and Calipari disclosed to him their intent to select Kobe Bryant. The disappointment seeped through in Taub's response. "We could take this high school kid, groom him, and then find out that after he completed his first contract he was going to jump ship and go somewhere else as a free agent," Taub said. Bryant, Nash told Taub, was talented enough to contribute right away. Taub asked them to reconsider drafting John Wallace, a senior forward who had recently led Syracuse University to the NCAA championship game.

Nash promised Taub that they would take Wallace's proven track record into account. They still planned to acquire Bryant as Nash returned to his office at around 2 p.m. Nash settled at his desk and fielded a phone call from Arn Tellem. Bryant had chosen Tellem, a powerful agent, to represent him. "I'm sorry," Tellem said. "This isn't going to work out."

Nash could not picture a scenario in which Bryant would not want to play for the Nets. He had just had dinner with Bryant's parents and they seemed enthralled at the prospect of him playing in New Jersey. "Arn, what changed in twenty-four hours?" an incredulous Nash asked.

Tellem explained that Bryant had had a falling-out with his family. He preferred not playing in New Jersey to avoid the pressure of performing so close to home. "He started giving me some cockamamie story about Kobe and his parents getting into a dispute," Nash recalled. "I never bought that."

He ended the call with Tellem and walked to Calipari's office. Nash did not consider Tellem's stance a deal breaker. He wanted to calmly tell Calipari about the call, while reassuring him that Bryant should remain their pick.

Calipari had his own news to share. Kobe Bryant had phoned Calipari and reiterated that he did not want to play for the Nets and, if drafted by the organization, he would instead play professionally in Italy. Calipari's concern grew. He would already be taking a risk in drafting Bryant and going against the ownership group. But taking a high school player who did not even want to play for him? He could wind up a laughingstock before ever coaching an NBA game. On top of that, he had already been mocked in the press. Some sports reporters jokingly wondered if Calipari knew he now coached in the NBA and no longer needed to recruit high school players, as he had as a college coach.

"Look, just give me a couple of hours and I'll figure out what's going on," Nash said.

Agents, Nash thought, *they live on gossip. An executive can't do his job with or without them.* Nash pledged to work the phones until he unearthed the source of Bryant's backpedaling. In the meantime, Calipari received another call. David Falk, the influential agent who helped shape Michael Jordan into a marketing heavyweight, was on the line. Falk, Nash said, had caught wind of Bryant's lack of interest in the Nets. Falk pressured Calipari to strongly consider drafting Kerry Kittles, Falk's client. He bullied and blustered.

Calipari relayed the conversation with Falk to Nash. To Nash, it was typical agent talk. Nash sensed Calipari's commitment to draft Bryant beginning to wane.

Nash returned to his office at around 4 p.m. He received a call from one of Tellem's confidants. Nash learned that the Lakers and Jerry West had arranged a deal with Charlotte for the 13th pick and wanted Bryant. Nash called Bob Bass, Charlotte's general manager, and asked if he had agreed to a trade with the Lakers. "I'm not going to talk about it," Bass said. To Nash, that reluctance to talk may as well have been a heartfelt confession.

. . .

The "Showtime" Lakers that captured five championships had long lost their luster by the summer of 1996. The Houston Rockets had jettisoned the Lakers from the playoffs' first round. The dry spell between titles grated on Jerry West. As a player, West's nickname was "Mr. Clutch," for his penchant for playing well in crunch time. His silhouette would eventually be used as the league's logo. West earned 14 All-Star selections in his playing career with the Lakers. Annually, his Lakers clashed with Bill Russell's Boston Celtics in the NBA Finals and West lost six times. West's Lakers also lost in the 1970 finals to the Knicks. His long-awaited NBA title did not arrive until the Lakers finally triumphed over the Knicks in 1972. Winning did not necessarily alleviate West's pain and the frustration that accompanied losing. But it at least stiff-armed those emotions until the next game, when winning and losing again decided his self-worth. He had a textbook jumper and played defense tenaciously, working himself into a pregame hysteria that left him physically ill. The transition to coaching when he could no longer control the games through his own play went about as smoothly as one could expect. West coached the Lakers for three short years and later turned to scouting. He became general manager prior to the 1982–1983 season, a position where he could still outmaneuver his opposition but that left him a step removed from the taxing emotions that came with being on the court.

The 1996 draft represented a second priority to West. The free agency period would have a larger leaguewide impact. Heavyweights like Alonzo Mourning, Juwan Howard, Reggie Miller, and Allan Houston were all available. West cast his line at the one whose signing would cause a seismic shift around the NBA. The league had never seen a player like Shaquille O'Neal, with his combination of size, speed, agility, and more size. O'Neal had guided the Orlando Magic to an NBA Finals appearance, but was disenchanted with the organization and, more importantly, with living in Orlando. West knew of O'Neal's interest in acting and music careers. Los Angeles resonated as the perfect locale for such pursuits. O'Neal confirmed his interest, but waited to see how large a salary West and the Lakers would offer. The Lakers needed to find a way to dump money owed on current contracts. The more contracts discarded, the more money they could offer O'Neal.

Vlade Divac had two years and $8.3 million left on his contract. He remained the biggest obstacle to extending O'Neal a gargantuan offer. West called several teams and offered Divac in trades. The cold market for a quality center—like the reaction he had received from John Nash—surprised him. "It was amazing to me that people did not have an interest in doing something like that," West recalled. "People thought something must be wrong with him. There wasn't. He's a terrific player and a better person. Having said that, our eyes were on Shaquille."

As West finagled to find a trade partner, Arn Tellem called him in the weeks leading up to the draft. Bryant had already inked a deal with Adidas and the William Morris Agency, an entertainment talent company. Bryant had yet to play a single NBA game. Still, he had a boyish exuberance and charm that corporations felt certain would appeal beyond the NBA. Bryant was in town for a commercial shoot and wanted to work out for the Lakers. The Lakers had one planned the next day with Dontae' Jones, a bruising forward who had recently lifted Mississippi State to the Final Four. West knew of Bryant, but had not paid much attention to him. The Lakers possessed the draft's 24th pick. West expected Bryant to be gone by then. He allowed Bryant to join the workout almost as an afterthought.

Jones arrived at the Inglewood YMCA shortly after sunrise with his college roommate. The court bore the scuffs from the frequent cuts and stops of previous players. One rim slanted toward the earth, the result of it bearing the weight of a dunk or several too many. Jones had studied all the draft's potential first rounders, wanting to know their tendencies should he face them in a workout. The word on Bryant? Talented, but still a high school player. Jones had bullied around college's best. "My thing was I had to go represent for college basketball, just to let him know that there are some things you must do as a young man to be prepared for the next level," Jones said. His confidence had crested to an all-time high. Jones had had one of the better college tournaments and spent the summer working out with NBA star Penny Hardaway in Memphis.

Larry Drew, a Lakers assistant coach, monitored the workout. Jones, 21, figured the Lakers brass wanted to see how Bryant physically matched up against a more developed player. "I think they got exactly what they were looking for, because he was a load," Jones said. Drew instructed the pair to first play a fullcourt game of one-on-one to four.

Bryant won.

"You could just tell," Jones remembered. "You could see what his future was going to look like. I was amazed by just playing against him. I did what I was supposed to do, but that's a seventeen-year-old kid. That dude was determined to do some of the things he couldn't do and I guess I was an obstacle right there for him to try to figure out a way to chop down."

They played one-on-one to four from halfcourt. They played one-on-one, in which the offensive player had to go right and use only three dribbles before hoisting a shot. They transferred the same rules to a game on the left side of the floor. Jones got in a point and a game here and there. Some of the drills catered to him and his size advantage over Bryant. But it was the established college player trying to hold his own against a high schooler. Bryant's footwork and finesse were already beyond those of anyone Jones had ever played in college. Bryant generally found the shot he wanted within those three dribbles. "You don't realize a seventeen-year-old could do all the things he was even attempting to do," said Jones, who became a first-round selection of the Knicks. The workout only lasted about 45 minutes. A dismayed Jones stretched out on the floor afterward. Meanwhile, West watched it all. "You saw the incredible skills that he had for a young kid," West said. "The one thing that we all saw was that he had an immense desire to compete. He just didn't want to stop competing, and in an [hour-long] workout it was something to see."

The performance piqued West's interest. He wanted another look, this one to confirm his gut feeling. He approached John Black and Raymond Ridder, members of the team's public relations staff, and asked if they wanted to attend another of Bryant's workouts. Mitch Kupchak, West's assistant general manager, piled into West's car, along with Black and Ridder. Bryant's second Lakers workout figured to be more challenging. Bryant would play against Michael Cooper at Inglewood High School. Cooper, 40, had been retired from the NBA for five years, but maintained a slim, agile frame. He was a key part of the Lakers' "Showtime" championship teams and an in-your-face defender, described by Larry Bird as the best he had ever faced. Cooper did not think much of the workout entering the gym. West had requested it, telling Cooper that he wanted to see how a high school kid named Kobe would fare against him. Cooper learned that Bryant was actually Joe Bryant's son only a couple of hours before squaring off against him. Cooper and Joe Bryant had matched up before in games. "I almost had a flashback," Cooper said. "Now, if I would have done that, it would have been a different thing."

He arrived at a dark gym, almost gloomy. No matter. Bryant lit Cooper up.

They spent nearly the whole session playing one-on-one. Cooper played defense the bulk of the time. He tried using his physicality over Bryant. Bryant scored at will. He unleashed a full repertoire of fadeaway jump shots and drives to the baskets with reverse layups and dunks.

"He was playing like he had just graduated from college, twenty-one, twenty-two years old, and I think that was the most impressive thing about it," Cooper said. "All of us were very, very impressed with him and Jerry has that innate ability to see beyond what other people see at the moment and obviously, he saw greatness."

West turned to Black and Ridder about 25 minutes into the workout. "OK, I've seen enough," he said. "Let's go. He's better than anyone we have on our team right now." The trio rose from their seats. "Best workout I've ever seen," West continued.

West walked past Cooper on his way out. "I thought you were supposed to guard him," West quipped.

The group returned to the Inglewood Forum. "We've got to do everything we can to get this guy," West said during the drive back, almost to himself.

• • •

That Jerry West also wanted Bryant only strengthened John Nash's resolve that the Nets would be mistaken in passing on him. He only had to convince John Calipari of the same. "We're holding the cards here," Nash told Calipari. "We're holding the aces. He doesn't have the ability to go back and say he wants to go to college because he lost his eligibility once he hired an agent. He's not going to go to Europe. They're not going to pay him anywhere near what we can."

He told Calipari of the proposed deal with Divac between the Hornets and the Lakers—the same one that West previously floated by them.

"Look, John, you have a five-year contract," Nash said. "They're not going to fire you after the first year. And you're going to be allowed to make a mistake. But you don't want to pass on a potential superstar."

Nash saw Calipari contemplating his options. "What if we move down to like ten and we pick up another piece of the puzzle?" he asked. The Indiana Pacers held that 10th pick and were looking to trade up. Nash believed that Calipari would have felt more comfortable drafting Bryant in that spot. Nash phoned Donnie Walsh, Indiana's president, but could not agree on a trade's parameters.

Calipari and Nash walked into a dinner with the full ownership group at around 6 p.m. Calipari addressed the group. "If Kerry Kittles is on the board at number eight, we're going to take Kerry Kittles," he announced. "If he's not at the board at number eight, we're going to take Kobe Bryant." Two owners immediately left the room, disgruntled that Bryant was still being considered at that point. Nash had worked the phones all day. He knew the likely draft picks of the first seven teams. Both Kittles and Bryant would be available to them. "When I heard that, I was devastated," Nash said. "I think David Falk scared the bejesus out of [Calipari]. I really do. If David Falk hadn't been so insistent on us taking Kittles, I think Kobe would have been drafted by the Nets and John would probably still be the coach. Who knows? Maybe I would have even survived."

· · ·

T he 1996 draft is regarded as one of the deepest in the league's history. Its results shaped the NBA for the next several years. The class featured three eventual MVPs (Bryant, Allen Iverson, and Steve Nash) and seven other future All-Stars. But it took a confluence of strategy, maneuvering, and missteps for Bryant—who evolved into the most talented player in that talented draft—to plunge all the way to the 13th pick.

NBA commissioner David Stern walked to the podium on June 26, 1996 and announced that the draft and clock would start with the Philadelphia 76ers. John Lucas had lost his coaching job with the franchise after a 64-loss season. They maintained the inside track on evaluating Bryant because of his local proximity. Their scout Tony

DiLeo had even trained Bryant in preparation for his draft workouts at Joe Bryant's behest. DiLeo had known Kobe Bryant for years and had once introduced a ninth-grade Bryant to Michael Jordan. "Kobe, the way he talked, the way he acted, he tried to mimic Michael's movements and speech patterns," DiLeo remembered. "You could tell he really looked up to Michael. He wanted to emulate him." Bryant impressed DiLeo with his relentlessness during their sessions. In one drill, DiLeo instructed Bryant to convert 300 shots without missing three in a row. Bryant struggled with it at the beginning, enough to irk him. He conquered the drill within a couple of days. DiLeo pushed for the organization to take Bryant first overall. "Here's a special player," DiLeo said. "He's right in our backyard." Brad Greenberg, Philadelphia's general manager, wanted to draft Allen Iverson, a diminutive, spirited guard from Georgetown. DiLeo then suggested trading Jerry Stackhouse for a lottery selection and using that pick on Bryant. "Because of some years where the team had traded away a high pick for a veteran, it was presented to me that we needed to keep the most recent high pick, Stackhouse, and see how he was going to develop," Greenberg wrote in an email. "That factored some into draft day strategy. Doing something with Jerry would have been the only way the team could have moved down in the first round to position for Kobe. In retrospect, it would have been a great move to do that and have both Allen and Kobe. But at the time, it wasn't something we focused on."

Iverson reinvigorated the franchise. Fans can only dream, however, of a backcourt featuring Iverson and Bryant. Philadelphia went on to trade Stackhouse shortly afterward, when he and Iverson failed to coalesce.

Toronto and Isiah Thomas possessed the second overall pick. Again, a predraft phone call, Thomas said, dissuaded him from selecting a high school player. "We had scouted Kobe and we were going to take Kobe at two and I got a call from Joe Bryant, Kobe's father, and I got a call from Jerry West," Thomas said. West explained the proposed deal with Charlotte and Joe Bryant asserted that he did not want his son playing in Canada, Thomas said. "Going to the Lakers was great for Kobe. They had a lot of endorsements riding on it, and so I told Jerry and I told [Lakers scout] Ronnie Lester that we weren't going to take Kobe and we would take Marcus Camby."

The Vancouver Grizzlies had the next selection and used it on Shareef Abdur-Rahim, a forward from California. Vancouver coveted a frontcourt player in the draft, recalled Larry Riley, the team's director of player personnel. "We were sold that that was the direction for us to go as a franchise," Riley said. "Kobe was going to be a guard and we felt that we could get guards. As you look back on it and who's had the better career, it's obvious Kobe did. Did we make a decision that wasn't the best? Probably so. We did make a decision that was a good one."

Mike Dunleavy's Milwaukee Bucks picked fourth. He had feverishly worked the phones before the draft. As a player, Dunleavy had teamed with Joe Bryant and Darryl Dawkins in Philadelphia. He turned to coaching afterward, eventually serving as Milwaukee's head coach and vice president of basketball operations. Dunleavy had a scout in Philadelphia who spoke highly of Bryant. But he originally wanted to draft Ray Allen, a smooth-shooting guard from Connecticut. Then Dunleavy erected what amounted to a pyramid scheme. He agreed to select Stephon Marbury fourth for Milwaukee and trade him to the Timberwolves for Allen, who would be selected fifth by the Timberwolves. The Bucks would receive a future first-round selection in the deal. Kevin Garnett and Marbury knew each other from the summer basketball circuit and wanted to play together. Kevin McHale decided not to tempt fate by selecting high school players in consecutive years. "We got one high school kid who was phenomenal," McHale said. "Are we going to run our luck and try to go for two or are we going to go for a guy who's a little more established? I just remember looking at Kobe, liking him a lot, and thinking, *Man, we just went through this*. We probably should have kept pushing our luck, but we didn't and took Steph." Dunleavy's plan would then take off. He wanted to trade Allen to the Celtics for Boston's sixth pick and another selection in a future draft. He had another potential deal with the Nets and Calipari in place for the sixth pick and another future pick for their eighth selection. Dunleavy said he would have taken Bryant with the eighth selection and departed with the extra three picks. He even told Joe Bryant that Kobe could live at home with him and his teenage son, Mike Jr., who would one day play in the NBA. Herb Kohl, Milwaukee's owner, quashed the idea.

"I don't get this," Kohl said, according to Dunleavy. "All I've been hearing all year long is about how Ray Allen is great. Next thing I know, now you want to trade down and take these picks and take this high school guy? What happens if the Clippers take him at number seven?" Dunleavy said he would take Kerry Kittles instead. But Arn Tellem declined Dunleavy's request for Bryant to work out (and everyone else's) once the Lakers came into focus as Bryant's potential destination. "Well, if you can't work him out, you can't pick him," Kohl said.

The Boston Celtics picked sixth and did work Bryant out prior to the draft. "He was outstanding in that workout," said Rick Weitzman, Boston's head scout. "But back then, the thinking was that high school kids, because it was so new for them to come right into the NBA, everybody thought that it would take a couple of years for them to get acclimated and be productive NBA players." Boston opted for Antoine Walker, a forward from Kentucky.

The Clippers, picking seventh, faced the same predicament. They had worked out Bryant and one drill in particular stood out in Bill Fitch's mind. The drill involved Bryant hurrying to make as many baskets as he could per minute. "He did it without even hitting the floor," said Fitch, the Clippers' coach. "The best workout that anybody ever had. He was just too young and it was the wrong club for him at the time." The Clippers took Memphis's Lorenzen Wright. The selection was a surprise to Wright. His agent scrambled to retrieve him from the bathroom, so he would be present at the announcement.

Wright was not the only one in need of a restroom at the time. Nash's stomach churned with the disclosure of Wright as the seventh selection. Kerry Kittles was still available. With the Nets on the clock,

Sonny Vaccaro, an Adidas executive and a Bryant family confidant, silently prayed that they would not draft Bryant. As promised, Calipari selected Kittles with the eighth selection. "This pick isn't about instant gratification," Calipari told reporters. "It's the best thing that we can do." Jayson Williams, the Nets' All-Star center, told the *Record* that he had expected the Nets to take Bryant, "because we had him in for about eighteen million visits," he said. "I was already figuring we'd have to put Nickelodeon on the TV in the locker room."

Time would reveal the mistakes made with the next four selections. Dallas took Samaki Walker. Indiana chose Erick Dampier. "If you're saying that I wasn't looking for high school kids in those days, you're right," said Donnie Walsh, Indiana's president. "I didn't think they could come into the league without developing for two or three years. The truth is, I was wrong on that." Golden State picked Todd Fuller. "There were some circumstances in that we had [guard Latrell] Sprewell at the time and he was actually good for [coach] Rick Adelman and Adelman was good for Spree," said Dave Twardzik, Golden State's general manager. Adelman left Golden State the next year. Sprewell, in a practice, famously choked Adelman's replacement, P. J. Carlesimo. The Cavaliers plucked Vitaly Potapenko with the 12th pick. Cleveland center Brad Daugherty had recently announced his retirement because of lingering back pain. "I definitely wanted size in the draft," said Wayne Embry, Cleveland's general manager. "As it turned out later, Zydrunas Ilgauskas was available and we got him. I could have easily taken Kobe and drafted Zydrunas." The irony is that Potapenko played only a couple of seasons in Cleveland. Ilgauskas, taken 20th overall in the same draft, stabilized Cleveland's frontcourt for years.

"I always thought a great trivia question was going to be, *Who were the twelve players that were taken ahead of this future Hall of Famer?*" Downer said.

So with some twists, turns, coincidence, and dumb luck, Bryant remained available when the Hornets selected 13th overall. David Stern walked to the draft's podium. "With the thirteenth pick in the 1996 NBA draft, the Charlotte Hornets select Kobe Bryant from Lower Merion High School in Pennsylvania," he said.

Bryant rose and hugged Pamela Bryant. Joe Bryant leaned into Downer. "It's not over yet," he said. "Something's about to go down."

He told Downer of the proposed deal between the Lakers and the Hornets. "[The Nets] could've drafted him," West said. "He would've played there. He had no choice. I was shocked that he didn't go there, to be honest." The proposal snagged when Vlade Divac threatened to retire from the NBA if it went through. Divac had embedded himself within the Los Angeles community and was a fan favorite. He did not want to leave the city. "Vlade Divac is one of the greatest people— nicest, most humble people I've ever seen," West said. "He was devastated. It was an ugly time." West tried assuring Bob Bass that Divac would eventually acquiesce. "They wanted us to take the gamble and do that," Bass said. "We weren't going to do that."

The standoff lasted nearly two tension-filled weeks. Not only did Bryant's acquisition hinge on Divac's accepting the deal, but also on whether the Lakers could land Shaquille O'Neal. In a selfless act, Divac finally relented. "I played basketball because I loved the game," he said. "I didn't play because of the money. Money is there. If you're good enough, you'll make the money. But for me to go somewhere just to play because I have a contract wasn't fun for me . . . And then I realized I'm going to screw the deal with Kobe and Shaq and [Lakers owner] Dr. Jerry Buss and went to Charlotte for a couple days and I said, 'I'll give it a chance.'"

Bass won the league's Executive of the Year award in 1996, in large part because of the trade. The move landed Charlotte an established center, upped their wins from 41 a season earlier to 54, and nudged Shaquille O'Neal out of the Eastern Conference when he accepted the Lakers' offer for seven years and $121 million. "You've got to remember that twelve other teams passed on him when we took him," Bass said of trading Bryant. "Now think about that for a minute. Twelve teams passed on him and he refused to work out for us. If we brought him in for a workout, it might have been different, it might not have been different. But why didn't another team take him if they knew he was that good?"

Danny Ainge's Phoenix Suns selected 15th in 1996. Phoenix had worked out Bryant, and Ainge predicted he would be a wonderful NBA player. Ainge, once a teammate of McHale's in Boston, spent the day trying to secure a better selection. "We were doing all we could," he said. "We thought we had a good chance at getting Kobe at fifteen." Phoenix instead settled on Steve Nash, a little-known point guard born in South Africa and raised in Canada. Nash went on to win two MVPs. The Portland Trail Blazers picked two slots later and took Jermaine O'Neal. O'Neal, from South Carolina, had also declared for the draft out of high school. He would become the final player taken in that draft who developed into an All-Star. Bob Whitsitt, the same executive who had plucked Shawn Kemp in Seattle, took O'Neal for Portland. "As a franchise, we were absolutely committed to try and develop Jermaine on and off the court," Whitsitt said. "Sometimes, if you throw these young guys into the fire too quickly, you can shatter them mentally and emotionally. The basketball part almost becomes the easier part." Bass had said O'Neal was nowhere near being NBA-ready. "He wrote the most vicious article about me," O'Neal said. "I've never met this guy a day before in my life. He never attended a game of mine, and he talked about me like he knew me personally. I told my mother; she was bitter and emotional about it. I said, 'Mom, don't worry about it. I'll take care of it.'"

As the draft closed, John Nash stood inside the tunnel that led onto the court. Rod Thorn, the NBA's executive vice president of basketball operations, walked up to him. Thorn had drafted Michael Jordan to Chicago as the Bulls' general manager. He was also close to Jerry West and was keen on West's affinity for Bryant. "Didn't have the courage to take the high school kid, huh?" Thorn teased in his West Virginia drawl.

"No, I had the courage," Nash responded. "We all didn't have the courage."

• • •

All these years later, Bob Bass is weary of being known as the executive who drafted Kobe Bryant and relinquished him. His assertion is legitimate. Team after team, some amazed by Bryant's personal workouts, passed on him for Potapenko this and Samaki that.

Nash still laments the Nets' decision. He accepts the reasoning. Garnett experienced a solid rookie season, but not one that truly projected his future stardom. Executives felt uncomfortable drafting high school players and did not want to risk their jobs for the unknown. Some declined scouting Bryant on principle alone. "It hadn't yet become apparent that high school players could come in and contribute as quickly as they began to," Nash said. "Once Garnett and Kobe started to have some success, it became much more acceptable. With each passing year, it became less of a risk if you felt a player had enough talent." Chris Wallace worked in the Miami Heat's front office in 1996 and predicted the success and future breakthrough of high school players. "As [is] the case in all sports, you have to follow the trends," Wallace said. "You have it in football with the wishbone and now the spread offense, three-point shooting in the NBA, weight lifting fifty years ago wasn't really done by anyone other than weight lifters trying to win medals. There has to be some success, some reason to get the mass of the game excited, and then everybody follows."

Predicting the future of these prodigies remained difficult in a competitive atmosphere where one missed draft pick could result in the loss of an executive's job. "It takes some real courage when your job is on the line and you only have one first-round pick each year, to say, 'I'm going to take a high school kid when our franchise is in tremendous need of help,'" Whitsitt said. High school players were not players executives wanted to stake their future on. Rick Weitzman, Boston's scout, remembers watching Bryant play in high school. He had little way to gauge Bryant's skills. "It was uncharted territory," Weitzman said. "When I first saw Kobe play in high school, he came out and played against a suburban team, all six-footers. Kobe just did whatever he wanted to do."

6.

The NBA draft's greenroom was the staging area where top prospects anxiously waited to be instantly transformed into millionaires. They were usually accompanied by those who paved their way and shaped their path: family members, coaches, and lifelong friends. In 1996, the members of Kerry Kittles's entourage momentarily stopped cheering his selection to the Nets. They had noticed people at Bryant's table also applauding the pick, particularly a stout, brown-eyed man who clapped loudly. "Just think of the logic," said Sonny Vaccaro, the man who drew the lengthiest stares. "Why the hell would we jump in the air for Kerry at number eight? There was no personal relationship there. We knew what was happening." Vaccaro's presence did not involve Bryant's past; it had to do with his corporate future and how Vaccaro would help steer it.

There is little middle ground when contemplating Vaccaro's place in basketball's hierarchy. He is either the man who provided a proper platform for phenoms, and fast-tracked them toward professionalism, fame, and fortune, or he is responsible for stagnating the growth of amateur players and corrupting high school and college basketball by infusing them with corporate money. "Look, I play by the rules," he once famously said. "What I am saying is, for God's sake, go change the rules."

The alliance of Bryant with Vaccaro and Adidas rankled Nike. Phil Knight, Nike's chief executive officer, assembled the shoe company's high school basketball representatives a few months after the draft at their headquarters in Beaverton, Oregon. The group included many of the most influential high school coaches from the country's largest cities, people with an eye for talent, charged with identifying the next Michael Jordan before he became Michael Jordan. Nike paid millions of dollars annually to support summer tournaments and camps. Knight questioned why the company had lost Kobe Bryant and Jermaine O'Neal to Adidas, forfeiting them to Vaccaro, a friend turned foe.

Nike had not dealt with strong competition in years. The company had come to dominate the athletic shoe industry. It assumed the reins from Converse behind an innovative marketing campaign. Knight originally named his company Blue Ribbon Sports, selling the product from the trunk of his car. By the 1980s, the company had grown, but still operated on professional basketball's periphery. Nike chose quantity over quality, paying a number of players about $8,000 to wear its shoes. Nike's surge came in 1984, when the company decided to allocate the bulk of its marketing resources on one player. Nike anointed Michael Jordan as that signature athlete at the urging of Vaccaro, employed as a Nike recruiter at the time. Vaccaro not only possessed a knack for being at the right place at the right time, he also knew the right thing to say to the right people.

Vaccaro entered the field of shoes and basketball by accident and coincidence. He grew up in Trafford, a steel-town borough outside of Pittsburgh, with aspirations of becoming a professional athlete. A back injury rerouted him and he turned to substitute teaching after obtaining a degree in psychology from Youngstown State University. He hustled and supplemented his income to support his family. He promoted music and gambled professionally, spending part of the year in Las Vegas. Vaccaro wanted to remain in sports somehow and, at the age of 25, he started a high school charity basketball tournament in 1965 and convinced a local newspaper to serve as the sponsor. The Dapper Dan Tournament brought the area's best college players under one roof and afforded college recruiters a central location to scout them. Joe Bryant captured the tournament's MVP award in 1972, the beginning of a beneficial relationship between him and Vaccaro. One year a representative from the athletic footwear line PRO-Keds attended the tournament. He passed out free shoes to some of the players, who wore them proudly. The image remained in Vaccaro's head in 1977 when he requested a meeting with Rob Strasser, Blue Ribbon's marketing director. Vaccaro had designed a rubber sandal, with the help of a local shoemaker in Trafford, that he wanted to pedal to the company. Strasser had an eye for characters and colorful backgrounds. He hated the sandals. He loved Vaccaro. They continued conversing, with Vaccaro's sandals discussed less and less and his ideas about the future of basketball and marketing discussed more and more. To Vaccaro, the company was wasting its limited resources by allocating them on a bunch of NBA players. "You guys are missing the playgrounds," he told Strasser. "You're missing the colleges and that's what basketball is all about." Vaccaro talked about the PRO-Keds merchant and the satisfaction the high school players took in being among the few awarded those shoes.

Strasser came around. A problem loomed on how to get their shoes onto the feet of college basketball players. NCAA amateurism rules prohibited companies from paying college kids for endorsing their products. Strasser and Vaccaro saw an opening among the coaches. The coaches could get paid by Nike and their players given the shoes for free from the company. The plan had few drawbacks. The athletic departments would not complain because they would save money on equipment. Vaccaro already maintained relationships with a number of college coaches through his tournament. Strasser added that the coaches should be part of an advisory committee and head clinics to ensure that the company would be viewed as paying the coaches for their services and not paying the players to wear their shoes.

Strasser ran the idea up Nike's chain of command. The first response was that they should conduct a background check on Vaccaro.

Knight eventually hired him as a consultant. Vaccaro hit the road with a number of contracts that stipulated that the coaches had to conduct the clinics and receive the merchandise. He left in the midst of the college basketball season and hoped to sign up influential coaches in time for March's NCAA tournament. He returned to his stomping grounds in Las Vegas and enrolled his friend UNLV coach Jerry Tarkanian. Bill Foster (Duke), Frank McGuire (South Carolina), Lefty Driesell (Maryland), and Jimmy Lynam (St. Joseph) soon followed. "Picture this," Jimmy Valvano, Iona College's coach, told *Sports Illustrated*. "Two guys named Vaccaro and Valvano meeting at La Guardia Airport. Vaccaro reaches into his briefcase. Puts a check on the table. I look at it and say, 'What's this for?' He pulls a sneaker out and puts it on the table. Like we were putting a contract out on somebody. He says, 'I would like your team to wear this shoe.' I say, 'How much?' He says, 'No, I'll give you the shoes.' You got to remember, I was at Iona. We wore a lot of seconds. They didn't even have labels on them. I say, 'This certainly can't be anything legal.'" Somehow it was. Vaccaro signed nearly all of the country's top coaches in a four-month span. "I called that my kamikaze sweep," Vaccaro told the *Washington Post*.

In 1978, the newspaper reported that Nike was paying college coaches and suggested college players would be the next to be paid by shoe companies. Converse backed away as Nike increased its efforts to sign more coaches. But Converse had gotten first to the University of North Carolina and its coach, Dean Smith. Michael Jordan did not want to wear either brand when he decided to turn pro after three college seasons. He preferred Adidas, which did not make him an offer. Converse bid similarly to what the company compensated other premier players, about $100,000 a year. Nike's revenue had jumped from $28.7 million in 1973 to $867 million by the end of 1983, according to ESPN.com. They were in search of a knockout blow. Strasser and David Falk, Jordan's agent, shared a longtime relationship and Jordan agreed to meet with Nike at the insistence of his parents. Nike executives had approached Vaccaro before the meeting. Jordan bloomed late and had slipped through Vaccaro's grasp as a high school player. Vaccaro had not invited him to his tournament. But Jordan had impressed Vaccaro with his coolness in nailing the game-winning shot in the 1982 championship game. Jordan was handsome, elegant even. Yet, he maintained a sense of authenticity. People could relate to him. Vaccaro was asked if he would risk his career on Jordan and if he preferred signing 10 players for $50,000 or one for $500,000. Vaccaro responded yes, if that one player was Jordan. That was the deal Nike struck, to be awarded to Jordan annually for five years. No other player had earned anywhere close to that for marketing shoes—a discrepancy that would cause a rift between Jordan and those who had come before him like Magic Johnson and Isiah Thomas. Jordan received a signature shoe and Falk devised the "Air Jordan" moniker. Jordan was paired with Spike Lee, a rising director. In Nike commercials, Lee played Mars Blackmon, the character from his 1986 movie, *She's Gotta Have It*. In the ads, Blackmon deduced that Jordan's athleticism stemmed from the shoes on his feet. The campaign was a smashing success, with Jordan playing the straight man and showcasing a wry smile. A corporate pitchman was born.

"I believe I made two bets in my life professionally," Vaccaro said. "Michael Jordan and Kobe Bryant."

Vaccaro bonded with Kobe Bryant at his summer camp in 1994. Vaccaro had started the Nike-ABCD Summer Basketball Camp the same year that Jordan signed with Nike. There had been other national summer basketball camps. They mostly sought to improve fundamentals through drills. None carried the cachet and importance of the ABCD (Academic Betterment and Career Development) camp. Vaccaro envisioned a platform for these young, up-and-coming athletes. They had natural talents and deserved a stage on which to display that athleticism. Vaccaro would provide it. He played gatekeeper and personally invited the players he determined worthy as the country's top 100-plus to his camp each year. "There is a committee of one," Vaccaro once said. "Me." The camp offered classroom instruction in math and English, as well as classes on drug abuse and AIDS. It became a siren to college recruiters. They flocked to the camp to view the nation's best all in one place.

Abruptly, Nike severed ties with Vaccaro in 1991. The source of the termination remained tightly guarded. Vaccaro insisted that he never fit Nike's corporate image. He aligned himself with Converse and conducted the ABCD camp at Eastern Michigan University. After Converse, Vaccaro landed at Adidas, a German sports apparel manufacturer. Nike, in large part because of Vaccaro, had cornered the college market. Vaccaro figured he had to establish Adidas with players before they even advanced that far. He no longer carried the power and allure of Nike's swoosh with him. But, he thought, he brought something better—his name. "I was Sonny from Nike," Vaccaro said. "Now, it's like ABCD superseded everything. ABCD was the turning point. The camp became synonymous with being put on a pedestal. ABCD and Sonny were the conduits for the whole thing. Forget whatever the shoe company was." Nike maintained its camp in Indianapolis and braced for competition from Vaccaro. They both scheduled camps the same week in July. The struggle for the top high school players turned personal once Nike hired George Raveling to run its grassroots program. Raveling was the best man at Vaccaro's wedding to his second wife, Pam. They had since become combatants. Raveling formerly coached at USC and believed that Vaccaro had steered Ed O'Bannon, a top recruit, to UCLA. Raveling had once been critical of Vaccaro's influence over amateur players. He now worked to gain the ears—and feet—of the same kids. "I can't stand the man," Vaccaro said flatly.

The camps became breeding grounds to unearth top players. The best played in games against the best. Throw in the talent, let them compete, and see who rises to the top. Vaccaro found a home for the camp at Fairleigh Dickinson University in Teaneck, New Jersey, in the shadows of New York City. College coaches divvied up their staffs, with some attending camp in Indianapolis and some in New Jersey. The most devoted attended both. NCAA rules forbid coaches from talking to the players. But who could avoid accidentally crossing paths with someone in the parking lot or on the way to the restroom? The ABCD participants recognized that a good camp could sway a top college in their favor and the great ones eventually realized that an excellent camp could mean forfeiting college altogether for the riches of the NBA. The attention of coaches and recruiters all in one central location made the summer tournaments more important for the players than their high school seasons.

Kobe Bryant wanted to make a name for himself in 1994 at the ABCD camp. He was about to be a high school junior—one of just four in the camp—yet believed he could outshine everyone else. His game did not stand out. Instead, he merely blended in.

A scrawny Bryant approached Vaccaro once camp broke. Bryant thanked and hugged Vaccaro.

"I'm sorry, I just couldn't quite do it," Bryant said.

"What do you mean?" Vaccaro asked.

"I wasn't the Most Valuable Player at camp," Bryant answered. "Next year, I'll be the Most Valuable Player."

Bryant returned the next summer in between scrimmaging NBA players. He averaged 21 points, 7 rebounds, and 4.5 assists, and, true to his word, captured the Most Valuable Player award. Bryant's performance validated the belief of the Lower Merion coaching staff. For two years, they had believed they possessed the next Michael Jordan on their roster. Bryant had now shown his basketball prowess on a national stage. Loren Woods, a 7-foot-1-inch center from Missouri, had a clear path for a dunk during one scrimmage. Bryant chased him down from midcourt and blocked Woods from behind. "Kobe slammed it off the backboard and the ball bounced somewhere between the top of the key and midcourt," Jeremy Treatman said. "That was just a play of athleticism that I had never really seen before." Bryant's play made Vaccaro a believer. "We signed him to the multimillion dollar contract," Vaccaro said. "It was laid out because of camp and because I thought he was better than anybody else. Going to ABCD allowed the superstar to believe that anything could happen for him. He didn't have to go to college."

"We were just starting," Vaccaro continued. "Adidas wasn't like it is today. We had nobody. So, yeah, I knew who he was. I knew how great he was going to be. No one else can say that, because if you want to be honest, if you go back and ask Nike, they could've bid for Kobe. They didn't."

That changed the next year following Phil Knight's gathering of Nike consultants. Vaccaro, like Nike, employed top amateur coaches scattered around the country. He included Alvis Smith among them. Smith was once a high school basketball player in southern California, but he did not qualify academically to play in college. He became an AAU coach and roamed Florida in search of talent. "I went out and chose the kids," Smith said. "I always targeted kids that nobody knew about. I always wanted to give them a chance because they were always hungrier."

Tracy McGrady fit the prototype. McGrady lived in Auburndale, a dot of a city between Orlando and Tampa. As a teenager, his mother birthed him and McGrady's grandmother Roberta was mostly charged with raising him. McGrady loved baseball and whipping his fastball past hitters. He was the youngest of his cousins and the group traveled to the park every Saturday. They played basketball as McGrady watched from the sidelines. He did not like the sport, but when a player suffered an injury one weekend the group needed McGrady to play in order to continue the game.

"All my cousins used to slap me upside the head and call me all kinds of names, like, 'You a punk. You a pussy. Come on and play,'" McGrady remembered. "It just got to the point where I was sick of them doing that and I went out there and started playing. And I was just good. I was just naturally talented. And from that point, I just started playing basketball." Talented, but aimless. Smith heard about McGrady from another player on his AAU team. He scouted one of McGrady's games and had witnessed enough of the 15-year-old McGrady by halftime. "I sent him some [Adidas] shoes and some gear and told him I was going to watch him play," Smith said. "I went over and watched him and that was that." McGrady began listening to each of Smith's suggestions. Smith asked him to drop baseball and football. "You're six foot eight, six foot nine, and you're lanky and long," Smith said. "You're going to get broken up on the football field. You'll probably be a good baseball player, but I want you to concentrate on basketball because I think you can make a living out of this." Smith had already started planning his route. "I felt like I needed to put him in more of a structured environment because I knew Tracy had the talent to go in the draft and I wanted him ready to go straight into the NBA," Smith said. McGrady agreed to leave his family and friends in Florida to attend Mt. Zion Christian Academy in Durham, North Carolina. Joel Hopkins, a friend of Smith's, coached the team. Nearly half of the 13 players on McGrady's team came from outside of North Carolina. Adidas supplied the school with athletic gear and Hopkins sought to transform the program into a national powerhouse. McGrady had never strayed far from home before, only going to Washington, D.C., for a family reunion. Smith told Hopkins to toughen McGrady up. "I knew if he could maintain the obstacles that I put in front of him and if he could withstand the structure that I made Joel Hopkins put on him, that he would be ready to go," Smith said. Hopkins, at their first meeting, told McGrady to remove his earrings. Rules followed rules. The team had wake-up calls and curfews. Hopkins forbid cursing, television, and girlfriends. He enforced Bible study. "I'd really never really been out of Florida," McGrady said. "It was all I knew and to leave my family and leave my friends—just up and leave like that—it was tough. It was definitely a mental adjustment, but once I got up there and got settled in, I felt real comfortable and from that point on, I felt my game start to develop because of the structured program that we were a part of. It was just basketball every day. I'd eat. I'd sleep, I'd breathe basketball when I went up there. I never really had that type of work ethic. I always got by on my athletic ability and just really never put that work in before I went to that school."

McGrady's test occurred in the spring of 1996. He had yet to take the court for Mt. Zion. ABCD camp came first. Smith had delivered solid players to Vaccaro's camp in the past. He told Vaccaro about McGrady. "Make sure you have the best in the country there because I've got one that I think is going to be the very, very best," Smith said.

Vaccaro voiced his skepticism. "We'll see," he said to Smith. "We'll see." Vaccaro knew little about McGrady. The feedback he had received painted McGrady as a problem child. McGrady had missed a key game at Auburndale for verbally arguing with a teacher. His old high school coach told Vaccaro that McGrady was not worth the trouble. But Vaccaro did not just have a committee of one, as he liked to say. Pam, his wife, often served as his conscience and tie breaker.

"Nobody could be that bad," Pam Vaccaro told her husband. "And anybody that wants to hurt a kid that bad, he's the bad person. We're the ones who are supposed to be nice and give these kids a chance."

Vaccaro relented and invited McGrady to camp. Vaccaro had staked his professional name on making two bets on Jordan and Bryant. McGrady would eventually become his third and, arguably, his most daring. At 17, McGrady was all knees, elbows, and fast-twitch-fiber muscles. He walked into the stuffy redbrick gym at Fairleigh Dickinson about a month after Kobe Bryant had been taken in the draft. The kids in the gym looked too tall to be kids. Only their faces reflected their true ages. The camp featured several players bound for the NBA in later years, Elton Brand, Quentin Richardson, and Al Harrington among them. Some were nervous. Some were excited. Middle-aged men in sweats with college logos packed the stands. But a change had occurred by 1996. NBA scouts and executives were sprinkled in among them. "As NBA talent evaluators, you go from not even going to a high school game to, after Kevin [Garnett], going to the camps with fellow scouts there," said Clarence Gaines Jr., a Bulls scout at the time. "It was good to see kids at a young age and see their development, build that book on them as they go up the ladder. But it's kind of overwhelming too because you go in there and it's just so many kids, and homing in and focusing in during that time frame is always interesting." The kids knew the stakes. Blending in meant the same as not being there at all. They eagerly sought the attention of the coaches and scouts.

McGrady wore number 175. He would have been happy if the number served as his ranking. No one had heard of him and for people wanting to make a name for themselves, anonymity was not the best place to start. Zach Marbury, the younger brother of Stephon Marbury, had already angered McGrady by questioning his talent on the bus to the gym. All the scouts wanted to see Lamar Odom, a 6-foot-10-inch stick from New York, pegged as the next Magic Johnson. No camper wanted to match up against him. Guarding Odom meant embarrassment. Embarrassment was worse than anonymity. McGrady said that he would play Odom. McGrady's eyes drooped and he appeared sleepy or uninterested on the court. But he played fluidly. He glided faster than others sprinted. McGrady not only defended Odom. He had him on a yo-yo at the other end of the court. McGrady drove past Odom when Odom guarded him too close. He rained jumpers when Odom allowed him room. Players and scouts started noticing number 175.

The camp closed with the Outstanding Seniors Game, 40 minutes of dunks, crossovers, and little defense between the camp's best players. McGrady grabbed a loose ball during the game's second half and sprinted toward the other side of the court. James Felton, one of the highest-rated big men, gave chase.

The crowd turned silent. It appeared that Felton would either block the shot or his attempt would result in a violent collision. "I had the ball on the left side coming down," McGrady said. "My initial thought was to do a windmill because I thought I was by myself. And so it happened, we jumped at the same time and I was going through my motion and he happened to be right there and I dunked right on his head. Everybody went crazy in the gym. People started running on the court."

The pair had jumped at the same instant. McGrady brought the ball down to his waist, then grabbed it with his left hand before windmill-dunking it into the basket. "I'll never forget it," Vaccaro said. "If you ask me [to list] the seminal moments of my life, that's one of them. That dunk, if that was on YouTube, it would've gotten billions of hits. Some of these things are frauds, compared to what Tracy did to that kid." Few people in the world could display that type of athleticism. The ones who could already played in the NBA. "I had no inclination of what might transpire out of this," McGrady said. "Not at all. I had no clue because that was really the first camp I had ever been to." Jeremy Treatman watched from the stands. He had seen that type of athleticism from Kobe Bryant a year earlier. "His elevation was so high that anyone who can do that is such a freakish athlete that he's bound for instant stardom," Treatman said. "Unlike Kobe, nobody knew who he was until he walked into that camp."

McGrady entered the camp wearing number 175. He left as the country's top-ranked player. "I brought him out of nowhere," Smith said. McGrady returned to Mt. Zion. He was months away from becoming a multimillionaire. Yet, he slept in a bunk bed and woke up before 5 a.m. Joel Hopkins likened himself to a high school Bobby Knight. Hopkins and McGrady physically fought during one practice. Surprisingly, their relationship improved afterward and emotions softened. They realized they needed each other. At the time, McGrady figured he would have his pick of colleges. He wanted to attend the University of Kentucky. But he noticed more and more NBA scouts attending his games throughout his year at Mt. Zion. Craig Neal, Toronto's scout, watched McGrady play seven straight times. Neal gave McGrady rave reviews when he reported back to Isiah Thomas and insisted the Raptors find a way to draft him. "A lot of people didn't do as much homework as we did," Neal said. "They didn't see him enough. Once it came out that he was going to come out, everybody was scrambling to try to see him and there really weren't a lot of places to do that."

Hopkins declined to let scouts watch McGrady up close, in case they unearthed any weaknesses. He brought McGrady into his office after the season. Hopkins and Smith had already escorted McGrady to an Orlando Magic game to see the athletes up close. McGrady had doubts and they wanted him to see that he matched their athleticism. McGrady knew that Hopkins would offer more of the same talk during the meeting in his office. "You're going to the NBA," Hopkins told him. "There's not too many players who can say they can come out of high school and go to the NBA. You'll be a first-round draft pick." The decision between college and the NBA kept ping-ponging in McGrady's head. *I'm not really trying to hear this shit, man,* he thought. *I don't know if I'm ready for this jump. I'm seventeen years old. I don't know if I'm ready for this.*

"By the end of that day, I was like, forget it. Let's do it," McGrady said. "I'm going to the league. I made my decision to go to the league. It was a tough situation for me to make myself eligible, knowing that, *Damn. I could be the first in my family to go to college. But then, I could be the first to play professional basketball from my area.* Am I ready still? I had doubts within myself whether I made the right decision."

Vaccaro wanted to sign McGrady. But Nike had caught on to Vaccaro's pattern of signing the top high school players. "Tracy, by then, was on the open market, so I competed," Vaccaro said. "There was competition for Tracy. He was an unbelievable bet, because, for the first time, Nike got into the war with me." McGrady had established a bond with Vaccaro. But he had grown up wearing Nikes and idolized Penny Hardaway, an Orlando Magic player and one of the company's signature athletes. Nike hosted McGrady at its headquarters, inviting him to take anything he wanted at the campus store. "I was leaning toward Nike," McGrady said. "But obviously money talks, right? I went shopping on their campus and I went in. I went in on that campus up in Portland and got all types of stuff like the new Penny foamposites. I was the first to have those. I was walking around thinking I was the man."

Nike and Adidas both bid for McGrady. Smith and Hopkins, McGrady's advisers, worked for Adidas. Arn Tellem, McGrady's agent, had just negotiated deals with Adidas for Kobe Bryant and Jermaine O'Neal. Nike offered McGrady a multiyear deal worth $1.85 million annually. The bid topped that of Bryant's agreement of five years and $8 million and O'Neal's of five years, $500,000. As Tellem negotiated in his Brentwood office with Nike, Vaccaro fielded a phone call from Smith some 100-plus miles away in the desert resort city of Palm Springs. Smith wondered how it would affect his relationship with Vaccaro and Adidas if McGrady signed with Nike. "I love you, Tracy loves you," Smith said. "If you can come close, we stay with you." Vaccaro decided to end the negotiations. Raveling operated with a larger amateur budget than Vaccaro. But Adidas had started to loosen Nike's stranglehold on the $12 billion industry. After signing Bryant, Adidas had risen to third in the country's shoe market, trailing Nike and Reebok. Vaccaro offered McGrady a six-year deal for $12 million. "Adidas didn't give him twelve million," Smith said. "Sonny Vaccaro gave him twelve million. Sonny Vaccaro believed in Tracy McGrady. He gave Tracy more money than he gave Kobe the year before. He believed in Tracy. I convinced him. I convinced Sonny and Sonny believed in me." McGrady accepted the deal. The Nike spending spree had nearly swayed him. "I was walking around thinking I was the man and a couple of weeks later, I signed the Adidas contract and had to give all that shit away," McGrady said.

The contract stipulated that Hopkins and Smith would receive $150,000 annually over the deal's life span. "I don't know if they always had my best interest," McGrady said with a laugh. "I think they may have had my best interest, but it was in their best interest as well. I don't know. I was going to get something out of it, but they were also going to receive something."

McGrady's deal represented a landmark moment in the developing, symbiotic relationship between the NBA, shoe companies, and amateur sports. Shoe company bidding wars might never have happened had Vaccaro and Nike never split. Likewise, Vaccaro never would have fully turned his attention to younger players had he remained with Nike. The split spawned the future windfall that McGrady, Smith, and Hopkins all benefited from. McGrady, the nobody from Auburndale, became the next Michael Jordan as the modern-day sneaker pitchman.

The agreement also shifted the attention of some amateur coaches. Some—though not all—operated in the background and looked to direct the career of a prodigy in search of a future payday. Smith and Hopkins proved that the lottery could be struck without waiting all that long after all. They became father figures to kids who needed those kinds of paternal role models, mostly black kids whose biological fathers had long ago vanished from the family picture. Here lay the conflict faced by McGrady and others who followed him. McGrady needed Smith and Hopkins more than they needed him at the time. They took his talent, molded it, and directed him to the right people, who further advanced his career. Would McGrady have been a washed-up relief pitcher somewhere had he never met Smith? "Probably worse than that, because Tracy was having all types of problems in school," Smith said. They also financially benefited once McGrady signed his shoe contract with the company they had been affiliated with for years. Their actions were not completely altruistic, but McGrady stayed on track, in part, because of them.

That give-and-take is not lost on McGrady. His relationship with Smith and Hopkins fizzled as his NBA career took off. The more they inserted themselves into McGrady's professional life, the more he realized he was no longer the kid who had once relied on them. "I don't fault them at all," McGrady said. "I wasn't old enough to recognize what was going on. I was young and too naive, too blind to see at the time and understand. But as I got older, I knew what was going on. That's why we don't really have a relationship today. They gained some financials off of me, which was understandable because they made some things happen in my life that probably wouldn't have happened if I didn't establish that relationship with them. I'm not tripping on them. I'm not greedy. They put me in some great situations. Their greed also, I think, caused them their downfall as well."

McGrady prepared for the NBA Finals with the San Antonio Spurs in 2013, nearly two decades after he had broken into the league. He was closing a remarkable career as a dazzling scorer, but one who fell short of any meaningful playoff wins. Reporters crowded him. They wanted his thoughts on his playing career, even though his last impact on a game of importance had occurred years ago. A reporter asked McGrady what the determining factor was in his decision to declare for the NBA out of high school.

"Well, let's see," McGrady said. "Adidas gave me a twelve-million-dollar contract. Shit, enough said."

7.

The prospect of drafting high school players—and outscouting, outwitting, and outmaneuvering his opponents—deeply intrigued Jerry Krause. Their ceiling was predicated on potential, and few gauged ceilings more accurately than Krause. "It created a new avenue," he said. Krause crafted the Chicago Bulls and possessed a baseball background. He was a native Chicagoan and the son of a shoe salesman. He was a dedicated, relentless worker who did everything he could to throw other NBA personnel off his scent. Krause was also perennially disheveled, short, stout, abrupt, and opinionated. Michael Jordan mockingly called Krause "Crumbs" for the doughnut fragments that somehow seemed to find a permanent home on his shirt. Teams occasionally enter weight clauses into players' contracts and either award them bonuses for making a certain weight or fine them for crossing over it. Jerry Reinsdorf, Chicago's owner, once inserted one into Krause's contract—"Not so much for his looks," he told the *New York Times*, "but for his health." But it was Krause who pieced together the Bulls' dynasty team. In 1987, he shrewdly traded for the little-known Scottie Pippen, originally a walk-on at the University of

Central Arkansas. Krause insisted that Phil Jackson, considered a radical with no NBA coaching experience, become an assistant coach on Doug Collins's staff and later elevated Jackson to Chicago's head position. In all, Krause obtained each and every one of Chicago's dynasty mainstays with the exception of Jordan, drafted third overall by Rod Thorn in 1984.

The Bulls had just captured consecutive titles in the summer of 1997 when the contracts of Jordan, Jackson, and Dennis Rodman were set to expire. Pippen was unhappy, having played for years under a contract below his market value. Part of Krause longed to rebuild, to show that he could again develop another championship core—one without the expanding egos of Jordan, Pippen, and Jackson. As the 1997 draft loomed, Krause planned for such a scenario. He had scouted a few of Tracy McGrady's games. Clarence Gaines Jr., one of his key scouts, had trailed McGrady closely during McGrady's final year of high school. Krause was still upset that he had passed on Shawn Kemp, who never played collegiately, several years earlier. Krause had hosted Kemp for a workout and left highly impressed by his athleticism. But he worried about the influence that Kemp's inner circle had over him and that playing so close to Kemp's Indiana roots would prove distracting. Krause drafted Stacey King sixth overall instead and selected B. J. Armstrong one pick after Seattle took Kemp. Kemp developed into one of the league's most devastating, athletic forces. "We pushed really hard for Shawn and Jerry was just not going to do it," said Jim Stack, Chicago's assistant general manager. "He just thought there were too many factors of being home at that young of an age that would cause a problem for a young man. I don't know if that would have been right in hindsight."

Krause did not want to repeat the same mistake. He envisioned McGrady as a younger Pippen. "He was Scottie," Krause said. "He was quick and active and a better shooter than Scottie was and Tracy McGrady was one of the better high school players I've ever seen and a very, very mature kid at that age." The Bulls scheduled a predraft workout with McGrady. Gaines Jr. picked him up from the airport and brought him to the Berto Center, the team's training facility in suburban Illinois. A McGrady Bulls jersey awaited him on his arrival. "He put it on and you could just see the kid light up in terms of him really visualizing and seeing himself in a Bulls uniform," Gaines Jr. recalled. "I'll just never forget when that jersey hit his body and the lights were on in the Berto Center." Krause entertained several trade offers for Pippen that would have allowed the Bulls a draft pick to take McGrady and kick-start their rebuilding efforts. Krause even secretly arranged a late-night physical for McGrady a couple of days before the draft. "Jerry Krause was famous for those clandestine last-minute physicals," Stack said. Questions had arisen about the durability of McGrady's back and if Krause was going to end the Bulls' dynasty, he wanted to be damn sure he would inherit a healthy player. The Boston Celtics dangled the draft's third and sixth picks before Krause. He deliberated about that all the way up to the draft. "Jerry Krause was receiving death threats because he wanted to trade Scottie Pippen," said Alvis Smith, McGrady's youth coach. "He wanted to trade Scottie Pippen to draft Tracy. Jerry Krause wanted to do that. Jordan called him up and said that if he drafted Tracy he [Jordan] was going to retire. That's a true story. That happened." Stack said that Jordan definitely voiced his opposition to a Pippen trade. "I don't think he would have retired, but he would have been very, very upset if we would have done that and he voiced that to us and you could understand," Stack said. "Scottie had been his running mate since '87 and they had done a lot of good things and won a lot of championships and Michael just felt that loyalty with Scottie and felt that we could continue to win." After much debate, Krause held on to Pippen. "If you're going to trade for a player the magnitude of Scottie Pippen, then you've got to knock somebody out," Krause told reporters. "It can't win by a decision. We just didn't feel the packages we were offered were strong enough to be a knockout." The rest of the pieces fell in line following the decision. Jordan signed for another season, this time for $33 million. Dennis Rodman and Phil Jackson also returned. The Bulls held off breaking the team apart for another year. "You always wonder," Stack said. "What if we had Tracy?

Would we have been able to sustain it longer? We would have had him on a rookie-scale contract. It would have allowed us to maybe add another piece or two and Scottie had a balky back at the time. He had had a couple surgeries. But we were very loyal to our players."

Instead, Isiah Thomas finally landed his high school prospect in Toronto after willingly passing on Kevin Garnett and Kobe Bryant. He sensed that he had purged his roster of enough misfits and malcontents to allow a high school player to develop and grow. "Had Garnett come that first year, I don't know if he would have had as much success as he had in Minnesota, and if Kobe would've come that second year, those guys' careers would've been totally different than they turned out to be," Thomas said. "We didn't have the infrastructure to really support what they were bringing to the table as young high school players." Thomas interviewed two prospects in the middle of June who could not have come from more disparate backgrounds, but represented the draft's fast-changing face. Adonal Foyle was a 22-year-old academic All-American from Colgate University. His guardians taught at Colgate. McGrady, meanwhile, was a teenager who attended the meeting with his agent and AAU adviser fresh from signing his huge Adidas deal. Thomas informed them that he would draft McGrady if he lasted until their ninth pick. On draft night, Thomas was shocked that the Bulls declined the offers to move up and selected McGrady, while deflecting trade offers. "He reminded me a lot of George Gervin at that time in terms of his ease, in terms of being able to always get it done very easily without looking like he was working too hard to do it," Thomas said.

McGrady smiled warmly as he met Canada's media the next day. The Raptors ensured that McGrady would at least have familiar food at his introductory press conference. They held it at a downtown Toronto steakhouse. "He's an exceptional talent, a great kid, and I think all of Toronto is going to look forward to knowing him in the years to come," Thomas said at the beginning of McGrady's introductory press conference. "And I must say he's a fine dresser, too." Thomas motioned to McGrady, clad in a black shirt and a bright yellow suit. He had celebrated his selection until the early-morning hours and admitted to being tired after traveling. "I'm glad I hung around to the ninth pick to be here in Toronto," McGrady said to the media. "I thank Isiah for picking me for this team. I think I'll enjoy my career here."

The initial Toronto trip proved brief. McGrady spent most of the summer in California and a good portion with Kobe Bryant, coming off his rookie season. Bryant had purchased a six-bedroom hilltop house in the affluent neighborhood of Pacific Palisades. The manor offered a glistening view of the Pacific Ocean, an indoor Jacuzzi, Italian marble floors, a pool, and six bathrooms. Joe Bryant had quit his coaching gig at La Salle. He, Pamela, and their daughter Shaya moved into the house with Kobe Bryant. Bryant's other sister, Sharia, stayed in Pennsylvania for her senior year at Temple. "He held his own, won the Slam Dunk Contest," McGrady said of Bryant. "He was not as successful as he wanted to be his rookie year and I wasn't either . . . It was a work in progress for us." McGrady stayed a couple of weeks at Bryant's home—the two were not just linked through basketball, after all, but also to Adidas and Sonny Vaccaro. The teenagers trained and watched plenty of karate movies. Between films, Bryant advised McGrady to remain patient early in his career and his playing time would follow. Bryant spoke from his own experience. His rookie season landed flat if judged by the lofty predictions that Joe Bryant foretold to John Nash and John Calipari.

With his white-topped head and glasses, Del Harris looked more the part of a science professor than an NBA coach. But he had an encyclopedic knowledge of the game. Harris worked his way up to coach the Lakers after beginning as a high school coach in Tennessee. In the NBA, he had spent time coaching Moses Malone, Bill Willoughby, and Joe Bryant. Harris had quickly burst Kobe Bryant's dreams of immediate stardom and success. He told Kobe that he had joined a quality team that had just gone 53–29 and added Shaquille O'Neal. They were built to win then and not develop players by spoon-feeding anyone playing time. Besides, the Lakers already possessed Eddie Jones, a soon-to-be All-Star, at Bryant's position. Any minutes Bryant received would have to be earned.

"You decided not to go on to college, but to join a man's world and I will be treating you like a man and not a kid," Harris said to Bryant. "You will be dealt [with] like the other players with the same expectations. We already have a good team and you will have to earn playing time. We are going to try to win every game. The other players will be watching to see if you get special treatment and will resent it if you do, because this is a competitive business and playing time is essential in it. They will respect you more when they see that you have earned what you get. You have a chance to be great, but you will not be able to be a starter on the team until you knock out a starter. You will not be given the decision on a draw."

Bryant nodded knowingly, not at Harris's words, but in his belief that he could usurp any starter. "It was not as easy as he expected," Harris said. "Still, he worked hard and never doubted [himself]."

Wrist and hip injuries prevented Bryant from playing in the Lakers' 1996–1997 season opener against the Phoenix Suns. Bryant made his NBA debut against Garnett and the Timberwolves, of all people and teams. Garnett served as a barometer for how far a high school player could progress within one short year. He quickly jumped from being developed slowly by Bill Blair to being pushed to the forefront by Flip Saunders. Garnett started the final half of his rookie season averaging 14.0 points and 8.4 rebounds. He scored a season-high 33 points in a late-season game against Boston, while playing 43 minutes. Afterward, he placed his arm around Saunders. "Coach, thanks for believing in me and trusting me and playing me that much," Garnett said. "Believe me, son, you're going to be playing a lot of minutes in this league," Saunders responded. That fall night, a Sunday, at the Great Western Forum in 1996, Garnett played 39 minutes in front of pockets of empty seats and spent much of his night being bullied by Shaquille O'Neal. Bryant, meanwhile, subbed for Cedric Ceballos, becoming the youngest player to appear in an NBA game at 18 years and 72 days old.

Bryant's mind moved faster than his body. He tried driving the lane the first time he touched the ball and traveled. Officials whistled Bryant for playing illegal defense a couple of possessions later. Garnett reminisced about how painfully slowly that aspect of the game had come to him. Cherokee Parks got a finger on Bryant's lone shot attempt of the night, a three-pointer. Bryant returned to the bench a few minutes into the second quarter. The score tightened and so did Harris's rotation. Bryant remained on the bench for the rest of the game as O'Neal helped the Lakers pull away. "It was a struggle for him because he knew that he had this exceptional talent," Jerry West said of Bryant's early professional days. "In practice, he would do a lot of things you see him doing today, but he made so many mistakes. From a team perspective, mistakes kill you. It was never talent with him, it was just finding a way."

The Lakers did not own their own practice facility and held training sessions at various colleges and gyms. That caused Bryant's development to stagnate at times, Harris said. "Kobe did find places to work out on his own, but had he had a facility where our players could have been coached beyond the two hours we had rented at any one of the four to six different sites we used during any given season, he would have progressed even faster," he said. Still, Bryant did little beyond play, practice, and think about basketball. He did not go out on the road carousing, let alone deal with his teammates much at all outside the gym. Some viewed him as aloof, but even those players gave him the ball at practice once they saw what he could do. "He was very individually orientated and he isolated himself," said Kurt Rambis, a Lakers assistant coach. "He didn't assimilate himself with his teammates and team at that young age. But his talent level was clear and there were no ifs, ands, or buts about that. Once you saw him compete against men, you could see that the sky was the limit with him. He was obsessed." In a time before DVDs, Bryant frequently traveled with video of Michael Jordan's highlights. "He never paid attention to any outside activities that I could tell," Harris said. "The flight attendants could have been topless for all he cared. He never looked at them."

But the games ran into one another, dragging on. Bryant's minutes had still not increased enough for his liking. He would receive five minutes one game and maybe seven the next. The Lakers kept winning and Harris refused to alter his lineup. In a moment of mounting frustration, Bryant told Harris at one practice that he could beat anybody in the league one-on-one if Harris would just clear out the post for him.

"I'm not going to move Shaq out of the low post so you can go one-on-one," Harris said. "That day will come, but you cannot beat guys one-on-one at a high enough percentage for that moment to be now."

Bryant proved he could dazzle a crowd in February. At Cleveland's Gund Arena, Bryant played center stage at All-Star Weekend without even earning an invitation to the marquee game. Bryant poured in 31 points in the rookie All-Star Game. Allen Iverson was named the game's MVP with his 19 points and 9 assists as boos cascaded down from fans who thought Bryant deserved the award. He captured the slam-dunk contest by rotating the ball through his legs and toma-hawking the ball through the rim. The dunk brought Julius Erving, the contest's innovator, out of his seat.

Bryant's talent was undeniable. Harris slowly started increasing Bryant's playing time. By the end of the regular season, Bryant had become one of his first substitutions off the bench.

The Lakers cruised past Portland in the playoffs' first round, advancing 3–1 in the best-of-five series. Bryant sparkled in the third game with 22 points. A veteran Utah team awaited the Lakers. Behind John Stockton and Karl Malone, Utah quickly jumped to a 3–1 lead in the best-of-seven series. Meanwhile, Bryon Russell stifled and harassed Bryant. The Lakers appeared primed to unravel at any moment. O'Neal was a force inside, but Harris and his point guard, Nick Van Exel, engaged in a heated argument near the end of Game 4.

The series reverted to Utah for the next game, with the momentum awarded to the aggressor. The Jazz sprinted to lead by as many as 16 points in the third quarter before Van Exel charged a comeback, dizzying Stockton with his drives to the basket. The Lakers gained possession with 11 seconds remaining in the game, tied 89–89. Harris motioned for a time-out. Van Exel, he thought, would be the logical choice for a final shot. He had the hot hand, having already scored 26 points. Harris knew and believed that Van Exel could shake Stockton for a decent look at the basket.

He decided to gamble. Harris thought Bryant could free himself for a better shot. *Hit or miss, we win or tie,* Harris thought, *but Kobe will know his coach had confidence in him to give him that shot in his rookie year. Either way, he will benefit from it.*

Bryant received the ball near the right elbow, with Russell shadowing him. The 14-footer felt good off his hands, but fell far short. The overtime session proved worse. Bryant lofted up two more air balls from beyond the three-point arc and the Lakers succumbed to Utah, 98–93.

As they walked back to the locker room dejectedly, Shaquille O'Neal stopped Bryant. They huddled for about 15 seconds and O'Neal later said that Bryant was the only player on the team who wanted to take those crucial shots.

"Tonight, I just didn't come through," Bryant told reporters. "But play the game again and I want the ball again."

Most teenagers would wonder why a coach would entrust them with the season on the line at that pivotal moment. Not Bryant—even after failing. Rambis was an NBA veteran who had been in drag-it-out playoff contests many times over the years when his Lakers played Boston. He knew the look of a player who shied away from shots in a game's waning moments. "You never saw that in Kobe," Rambis said. "It was almost indifference. It was like, *Yeah, Fuck it.* You just knew that it wasn't going to bother him." Had the Bryant heroics actually happened, they would not have changed much. A new, younger guard had yet to topple the league's old power. The Bulls still dominated the NBA. Jordan's champagne swig and cigar puff had become something of an annual tradition that continued into the summer of 1998 with another championship, in spite of Chicago's internal strife.

8.

Silence loomed a couple beats too long for Eric Fleisher's comfort. Fleisher had phoned Kevin Garnett in the fall of 1997 to notify him that an agreement on his contract extension had finally been consummated. The Timberwolves were set to hand Garnett, at a time when he would have been midway through college, the most lucrative contract not only in basketball but in all of sports. All Fleisher needed was Garnett to come to his hotel and sign the contract before the deadline. They had just one hour.

Garnett finally responded. He was at the Lake Minnetonka home of his friend, music producer Jimmy Jam. They were busy.

"We're listening to Janet's album," Garnett said. Jam was previewing a copy of Janet Jackson's *The Velvet Rope* for Garnett. "Could we do it a little later?" he asked Fleisher.

Fleisher sighed. He wasn't surprised that he faced one more hurdle in finalizing an extension where talks had occasionally turned acrimonious and frequently went cold.

"It was pretty clear how good he was and, even more importantly, how good he was going to become," Fleisher recalled. "The important part of understanding that deal is that it came a year in advance of him becoming a free agent. It was strategically timed because the collective bargaining agreement was coming to an end a year later. Nobody knew what the new rules were going to be, but it was a safe bet that they were going to be significantly more prohibitive and restrictive than the current collective bargaining agreement, so it became a timing issue. In my mind, it was absolutely imperative to do everything possible to try and push for an agreement the summer before and the only way to do that was to have a great deal of leverage. It's hard to have leverage when you're not a free agent."

Negotiations between Fleisher and Glen Taylor, Minnesota's owner, and Kevin McHale began in July. Garnett's development had continued its acceleration during his sophomore season when he faced a rookie Kobe Bryant. Garnett averaged 17 points and 8 rebounds, guiding Minnesota to its first playoff appearance in franchise history. His potential had blossomed into productivity. Garnett would be paid. The question remained how handsomely. He was a marvelously gifted athlete who practiced mercilessly to better himself. Still, he had yet to make a true dent in the league. Garnett would become next in line to benefit from talent and, more importantly, timing. Before him, Michael Jordan had certainly prospered from his gifts and drive. He also benefited because of the period when he played. Jordan received economic endorsement opportunities unavailable to players only a few years his elder, like Magic Johnson and Larry Bird. Likewise, Tracy McGrady's Adidas contract came not only because of his promising future, but also because of external factors—the success of Garnett, the popularity of Bryant, and the burgeoning shoe war to lure the best, youngest stars. Conversely, Scottie Pippen gambled at the wrong moment by accepting a long-term contract before salaries exploded. He continued as the league's poster boy of an athlete and his agents misgauging time and opportunity. "What we want to avoid with Kevin is that he doesn't find himself in a situation Scottie Pippen is in, where he's in a contract in which he's vastly underpaid," Fleisher said to the *Minneapolis Star Tribune* in the fall of 1997.

Fleisher knew that timing would be crucial in brokering a deal before the labor agreement between the league and the players union expired in the summer of 1998. The NBA tried correcting a broken system in 1995 when rookies held underperforming teams captive so the rookies could land large contracts. They closed that loophole with the implementation of the rookie wage scale but, in doing so, created another giant, gaping problem. Rookies could become unrestricted free agents after three years in the NBA and the league had no salary ceiling on individual players. Teams had to deliver huge extensions to their rising stars, trade them away, or risk losing them to free agency for nothing in return. Eight of the top 10 picks of the 1995 draft (Joe Smith, Antonio McDyess, Jerry Stackhouse, Rasheed Wallace, Damon Stoudamire, Shawn Respert, Kurt Thomas, and Ed O'Bannon) were traded early in their NBA careers. Losing Garnett would be disastrous for the Timberwolves and possibly fatal to the franchise's future in Minnesota. Minnesota possessed no history, no brand, and little following. The mere possibility of Garnett leaving offered Fleisher the leverage he needed. If the sides could not reach an agreement by October 1, Garnett would play out the final season of his rookie contract and become a free agent, allowed to sign with any team that could afford him.

In their initial meetings, Fleisher relayed the importance of a long-term bond between Garnett and the Timberwolves. He pointed out how much more in endorsements Garnett would earn by playing in bigger cities like Los Angeles and Chicago, instead of Minnesota. Glen Taylor was a self-made millionaire and a former state senator who earned his fortune through his printing business. He led a group that purchased the NBA franchise for $90 million in 1994 out of fear that another ownership group would relocate the team to New Orleans. The Timberwolves, to him, represented a source of civic pride, and the responsibility for the team's success and rewards for its failures were to be shared throughout the organization. Taylor originally suggested to the *Star Tribune* that he was unwilling to give an enormous salary to just one player. He bemoaned the increasingly soaring salaries across the NBA. Shaquille O'Neal had just signed a humongous deal with the Lakers. Alonzo Mourning and Juwan Howard had also both recently signed contracts that topped $100 million. "That doesn't make sense," he told the paper in July 1997. "You have twelve players, five coaches, sixty people in the franchise doing the work to keep it going and you can have one or two people so out of proportion. That bothers me about the whole league and where the league is going. We had more players last season by far making five million than ever before. But, on the other hand, we had more players at the minimum salary. That doesn't make sense, even for the players, that one player should take so much more salary that they have to surround that player with other players at lower playing skills."

Taylor eventually came to his senses. Garnett *was* the organization. He wanted to keep him. He figured Garnett wanted to stay. Why waste time? The Timberwolves opened the bargaining with hopes of ending it swiftly. Taylor offered a contract extension worth a whopping $103.5 million over six years. "We made sure that this one was even more than [Shaquille O'Neal's]," Taylor told the *Star Tribune*. "We did that so that he, his agent, and everybody else could say that we made the biggest offer. We thought it would give him and his agent some leverage, where people could say, 'They really did a super job.'"

It was a great offer, an otherworldly one. Fleisher had negotiated most of his life. Anyone who brokered a trade in an elementary school cafeteria knew never to accept the first offer. A better one always loomed around the corner. "Even though we had had all kinds of dialogue prior to the first offer and even though it was a very, very significant, precedent-setting first offer, it was still their first offer," Fleisher said. They declined, holding out for a contract they hoped would stretch upwards of $120 million. The entire franchise was worth only $127 million, according to *Financial World* magazine. The declining of the initial offer shocked Taylor, but it also upset the league's veteran players, establishing a chalk line within the NBA fraternity. It served as confirmation that this younger generation of players had not scrapped and clawed before striking it rich, as the players before them had. They had received too much too soon, without any sacrifice, and gained the fruits of others' labor. Pippen had played underpaid for years, lifting Chicago to championship after championship. What had Garnett done beyond nudging Minnesota to one playoff's swift exit? "Don't give the guys who don't deserve it the money," said Charles Barkley, the outspoken veteran forward. "How about that? When Kevin Garnett was offered twenty million and he turned it down, I wouldn't have given him a contract on principle alone. What right does he have to turn down twenty million?"

His words echoed similar thoughts throughout the league. Beyond Garnett, the initial prep-to-pro players experienced growing pains while assimilating into the NBA. Yet, they were still multimillionaires. Bryant, while spectacular at times, was often regarded as cocky by his elder peers. He carried the confidence he gained when Harris awarded him those shots at the end of his rookie season into his second. Bryant more than doubled his scoring average and, although he was a sixth man on the Lakers, was voted to start the 1998 All-Star Game. He became the youngest All-Star in NBA history and occasionally matched up against Michael Jordan under Madison Square Garden's bright lights. Jordan was 34, battling the flu that night, and fairly certain he was in his final season and making his last All-Star appearance. It came in an arena that, as a visitor, he had transformed into a second home. New York fans appreciated the game's beauty and, for them, Jordan with the ball was like Mozart at the piano—no matter how many times Jordan had placed a dagger and twisted it into the heart of their beloved Knicks. In 1995, Jordan established a scoring record in the arena with 55 points. Back then, Bryant was just a high schooler fresh off referring to him as "Mr. Jordan." In 1998, fans and media speculated about whether the All-Star Game would mark a passing of the torch. Bryant wanted to be master instead of apprentice that night—time, talent, and waiting in line be damned. Midway through the third quarter, Jordan faked a shot along the baseline, ducked under Bryant, and scored. Bryant responded with a beautiful flip of the ball into the basket on the baseline. "He came at me pretty early," Jordan told reporters of Bryant. "I would if I was him. If I see someone that's maybe sick or whatever, you've got to attack him. He attacked. You know, I liked his attitude." Jordan took 23 points, the MVP trophy, and the win. Bryant scored a team-high 18 points and wowed the crowd at times. That was the good. With Bryant in those early days, his growing pains ensured that a dose of bad accompanied the positives. Bryant had infuriated Karl Malone during the game. Malone was also 34, and the evening marked his 11th straight All-Star Game. Malone arrived to set a pick for Bryant and establish himself in the post as he had done a million times for John Stockton, his Utah teammate. Bryant did not even look at Malone. He simply waved Malone away, caught up in the game. "Malone was so incensed that he said he didn't ever want to play in another All-Star Game if he was going to be chased out of the post by a kid," Del Harris said.

Meanwhile, Bryant's contemporary Jermaine O'Neal could only dream of appearing in an All-Star Game. O'Neal had joined the NBA the same year as Bryant and spent the first 17 games of his career on the injured list, waiting, watching, and wishing he was still the man, as he had been just a year ago. It seemed as if he had just begun to grasp one set of plays when the coaching staff came up with new ones. He had wanted to lift his mother from poverty. He did. He thought he had been ready for the NBA. He was not. He signed his first contract before turning 18 and moved to Portland with his brother Clifford and his cousin LeVar. "If I had it to do over again, I would have thought about it a lot more and I would have gone to college," O'Neal told the *Fort Worth Star-Telegram* in 1997. "There's a lot of other things than basketball you have to deal with. Mentally, I think the NBA is a little too much for seventeen- and eighteen-year-olds to deal with . . . I miss the college experience. In high school, I was able to do whatever I wanted to do. There weren't that many big bodies or guys bigger than me to play against. Now I'm up against a lot of bigger, stronger guys, and I'm lacking that experience of playing against guys like that . . . [Kevin Garnett] kind of opened the doors for guys like Kobe [Bryant] and me. I just thought I would be able to do it. Now that three people have done it, everybody thinks they can do it. It's going to take one person to fail for everybody to realize that everybody's not ready for the NBA." O'Neal recently recalled the experience of trying to break into the NBA at such a tender age. "I was very blessed to go to an organization like the Portland Trail Blazers, who really were prepared to draft an inexperienced, immature, underdeveloped high school kid," he said. "I was every bit of that—you had guys pick me up from the airport right away. They always made sure they had people around me. If I needed to talk to a therapist, they had that in place. The city took to me like I was their adopted child, so it was perfect for me. Obviously, I didn't get an opportunity to play my first four years as much as I wanted to, but it was a perfect chance for me to go and really develop not only physically, but emotionally and mentally."

Tracy McGrady began his NBA career in much the same way as he arrived on the league's radar in the first place. The Toronto Raptors trained at Buffalo's Erie Community College in the fall of 1997. Doubts still coursed through his body. "Up until that point, I really never played against any NBA talent," McGrady said. "Then once I got to training camp and it was just all NBA guys and I was holding my own, I was like, *Oh, shit. We're good*." McGrady drove the baseline during one scrimmage and tomahawk-dunked over Sharone Wright. "It was one of the nastiest dunks nobody ever seen," said Damon Stoudamire, McGrady's teammate in Toronto. Darrell Walker, Toronto's coach, decided to end practice after the dunk. It was all anyone could talk about. "It was one of the most incredible things I have ever seen," Walker said. "I've been in the league a long time. I've played against Michael. I've played against Dr. J. I've played against some high fliers and that was just unbelievable."

That moment, for a while, provided the highlight of McGrady's early NBA career. A left ankle sprain hindered McGrady's debut. He seldom saw the court once healed and when he did, he played erratic minutes. Walker told him that he would not unseat any of the veterans in front of him. McGrady no longer even had Isiah Thomas as a mentor. Thomas's attempt to purchase more of a stake in the franchise failed and he resigned to become a television commentator. The

Raptors slogged through the season, at one point losing 17 straight games. "Adapting from being the man in high school to not really playing at all was difficult," McGrady said. "I played ten, fifteen minutes one night, then I probably wouldn't see the court for two or three games. It was a lot of adjustments that I had to really adapt to and then my coach—he was tough. He was an old-school guy. He felt like I wasn't working hard enough and any little show-off thing that I did, I got benched for it." Walker requested meetings with each of his players after Washington thrashed Toronto on New Year's Eve. In the meeting with McGrady, Walker relayed his doubts as to whether McGrady would make it in the NBA. He called McGrady a floater and said the team was sick of him coasting by. "The problem that I had with Tracy was his work habits," Walker recalled. "We clashed about that. That definitely hasn't been a secret. I was on him because I saw so much in him, but also saw that if he didn't put in work, he had a chance to be out of the league."

Glen Taylor only concerned himself with one prep-to-pro player: Kevin Garnett. Hoping to gain public support and possibly reach Garnett (Fleisher had made sure Garnett was unavailable to Minnesota management and dispatched him back to Mauldin and Fleisher's home in New York's Westchester County), Taylor made the generous offer known to the public. "Glen felt people were questioning him on what kind of deal we were putting out there," McHale told reporters. "If Glen Taylor doesn't have the right to make a statement—he's the owner of the team and we made a good offer—who does?" The disclosure infuriated Fleisher, who declared that Garnett would play the final season of his current contract in Minnesota and not entertain their offers the following summer when other NBA teams could and would bid for his services. "It was totally contradictory to what we discussed when we sat down the first time," Fleisher said. "It was a decision that they made at the time because things didn't go the way that they had hoped. They had made a very, very significant offer and it was an offer that was rejected, which they didn't expect."

The sides went weeks without any dialogue and barreled toward the deadline. Taylor did not want the organization to start from scratch. He began to come around on Fleisher's demands. Fleisher convened with Taylor, McHale, Flip Saunders, and Rob Moor, the team's president, the day before the deadline. They agreed that too much of the negotiations had unraveled in the media. Everyone had Garnett's best interest at heart. Garnett attended the final two hours of the meetings and Taylor discussed with him the pressures an enormous contract would place on him and the responsibilities he would inherit in becoming the franchise's face for the long term. McHale loved Garnett. Still, he advised Taylor not to extend such a lucrative contract to him. Not only did he worry about the precedent in allowing a young, talented player to hold that much leverage over a small-market team, but he worried about the burden that accompanied the deal. "It's such a huge contract," McHale told Taylor. "It's going to be a game changer in the NBA." Taylor responded that the organization could not afford to lose Garnett. "I was really afraid of that contract," McHale recalled. "I just didn't know . . . I know his agent's job is to get him every last nickel, which they did, but I was uncomfortable for Kevin with that contract just because I knew all the stuff that would come with it. A lot of my feelings were Kevin-driven, like, man, this is going to be a hard thing for a young guy to live up to."

In the hours leading up to the deadline, Taylor decided to offer Garnett a contract extension for six years, $126 million, an offer that sent shock waves through the NBA. "Kevin, you need to come over now," Fleisher insisted after Garnett told him he wanted to listen to Janet Jackson's album. "The deadline is almost here and this needs to get signed."

"OK," Garnett said, leaving grudgingly to make history.

The signing was major news in Minneapolis. Reporters had staked out Garnett's brief appearance at the meeting a day earlier. A helicopter hovered above them as they left Fleisher's hotel and made their way to the arena to sign the contract. Garnett had not spoken to the media in months. "I told my agent that my comfort level was in Minnesota and that is where I wanted to be," Garnett said in the conference

announcing the deal. "You know, it is not only about money. I hope
people understand that, even though I turned down the first deal . . .
Money doesn't always make you happy. It solves some problems. But
mentally and sometimes socially, it's not everything." This was supposed to be a joyous day for the franchise. Instead, it felt as though
they had been hostages freed from captivity. "All the Bulls had to do
was to sign Michael Jordan for about $2 million for next year and then
make it up the next season," Taylor told the *Star Tribune*. "Once they
signed Garnett, [the Bulls] could then pay Jordan any amount the next
year because you are not limited in what you can pay your own players. Denver is in a great position from a salary cap position. They had
the money to sign Garnett." Heat coach Pat Riley simply told Miami's
media that Garnett "got paid out of fear."

The contract sparked an uproar. Garnett made $2.1 million
in 1997–1998, the final year of his rookie contract, before his salary jumped to $14 million the following season. Teams and players
targeted him. Garnett's demeanor did not change. "I was never concerned," Flip Saunders recalled. "Kevin was never a guy that money
was going to change what he did and how he prepared and played on
the court. I wasn't really worried about that being an issue. From the
league's perspective, I mean, that was what the league was about. If
you could pay guys, you pay them. There wasn't a max on what guys
could make. Did it change the league? Yeah, but it probably changed
the league from a perspective of everyone, probably for the best."

The NBA arrived at a crossroads and threatened to implode. The
league had never been more popular or marketable, thanks largely to
Jordan's crossover appeal. His feathery jumper over Utah's Bryon Russell in the 1998 NBA Finals appeared to be a fitting final image of
him as a player. Jordan leaned toward retirement and would leave few
heirs to walk in his air as the league's new face. A series of television
deals had recently netted the league $2.6 billion, but rising player sala-
ries threatened to negate any profit. The league locked out its players
in the summer of 1998, with NBA owners clamoring for more economic restrictions on contracts. Garnett's deal became a rallying cry

for most owners. Taylor defended himself. Other owners turned irate that a relatively new owner from a small market could so easily influence the entire league. "I feel no fault for the lockout," Garnett said to the media. "It's all about how you take advantage of the options you have once they're given to you." *Washington Post* sportswriter Tony Kornheiser categorized the rift as an argument "between tall millionaires and short millionaires." He was wrong. Twelve majority owners were billionaires. They were adept businessmen and few derived the bulk of their earnings from professional basketball. They united in wanting to curtail salaries and prepared to lock out the players for the long haul.

"I think the league was building up to that point and [Garnett's contract] was the straw that broke the camel's back," McHale said. David Stern and Billy Hunter, the executive director of the players union, both refused to budge. "We had gotten ourselves into a spiral where it didn't matter what somebody had actually done," Stern said. "It's not about Kevin. It's about other players who say there's a pecking order. If somebody thinks that he's as good as Kevin Garnett, then all of a sudden he's being underpaid, undervalued, underappreciated, and you wind up having an unhappy and underproductive player. And that's a bad thing. So we were trying to bring some more order." As fall turned to winter, the NBA hurdled toward becoming the first major sports league to lose an entire season because of a labor dispute. Both owners and players suffered losses that totaled in the hundreds of millions of dollars. In early January 1999, nearly 200 players packed into the GM Building on New York's Fifth Avenue. Stern had rejected the union's latest proposal. Hunter put the owners' offer to the players who opted overwhelmingly, 179–5, to accept the deal just hours before the owners would vote on whether to cancel the rest of the season. The sides scrambled to cobble together a shortened season of 50 games that birthed new governing rules. The players had acquiesced to the majority of the demands from the owners. The NBA became the first major sports league to cap individual player salaries and introduced the limits on a sliding scale. Players with less than six years of NBA experience could not sign a contract worth more than $9 million in its first year.

Players with existing contracts could re-sign with their current team for a contract similar to their previous deals. A player would be subject to the new rules if he signed with another team. The agreement also lengthened the time a team controlled the rights of a drafted player before he could enter free agency by granting organizations an option for the fourth year and the right of first refusal the following year.

The league would face no more contracts like Garnett's. In the end, his contract had less of an impact on him and more on the group that trailed him. Stephon Marbury, Minnesota's point guard, had once been Garnett's close friend and ally. As a rookie in 1996–1997, Marbury averaged 15.8 points and 7.8 assists per game and teamed with Garnett to lead Minnesota to the playoffs. "[Celtics legendary point guard] Bob Cousy and those guys must be sick to their stomachs," Marbury said to reporters upon learning about Garnett's contract. Still, Marbury viewed himself as Garnett's peer. "After Kevin's deal, he was never going to be able to get paid the same as Kevin and he thought he was worth every bit that Kevin was able to receive," said Fleisher, who also served as Marbury's agent. The relationship between Marbury and Garnett soured. Marbury occasionally refused to pass the basketball to Garnett. He represented a young, entitled class of players who judged themselves in comparison to the paychecks of others more than by their play on the court. Garnett had not done much in the league, but had displayed the promise for more. Players of lesser caliber and potential still clamored for what had been deemed "Garnett money." "Steph had a tough time dealing with the fact that Kevin was maybe going to be making twice as much money as him, yet they were basically equals on the court with what they did for the team," Saunders said. "Ultimately, the contract alienated Stephon."

9.

Most of them started with the same dream. The thought could have been rooted in watching Michael Jordan plant his feet and rise on television. It could have spread by wanting to lift themselves or their families out of poverty. The dream of one day making it to the NBA was like one day winning the lottery. The odds were ridiculously minuscule. The payoff was laughingly lucrative. But Kevin Garnett proved everyone wrong. His success provided a blueprint for a new generation. If he could do it, others could also beat the odds, forsake college, and become instantaneous millionaires.

They became the favored few, the ones who experienced that huge growth spurt and towered over their peers. They could dribble a basketball, shoot, pass, and jump from an early age. They were the prodigies and phenoms allegedly bound for greatness. National magazines wrote glowing profiles about them. Ranking analysts placed them high on their lists from an early age, sometimes right around puberty, sometimes even before it. The competition had their eye out for them now. But they could handle it. Their skills topped those of every other teenager. The dream was sustained, nurtured, and encouraged. They were special. They focused their energy and time on basketball: playing it, practicing it. Why not? It was fun. It was a game. Schoolwork and social integration got pushed to the background. *They were the lottery winners, the ones in a million, the needles in the haystack. The best since Wilt Chamberlain.* A lot of slick-talking people lobbied for their ears. They made promises about the future and how they were the best equipped to steer these young athletes toward that payday. The advice may have come from a friend, an uncle, or a coach. It could have come from all of them and, sometimes, even more people came to comprise their inner circle. They got whispered to by runners and agents who sought the next Michael Jordan with the same fervor exhibited by the sneaker companies. The high school coach, a pillar of the community for years at a lot of high schools, was once the guiding conscience for prep athletes. After McGrady's contract, summer league coaches gained more credibility and influence. Those were the hot months when players would get ranked and pad their budding resumes, while traveling the country and receiving the attention and adulation of the shoe companies. The idea of delayed gratification evaporated after Garnett. The path of least resistance to the riches and fame of the NBA became the preferred route.

The system weeded out the weaker players, the ones who did not develop, who hit that early growth spurt and did not continue to sprout. As Kevin Garnett, Kobe Bryant, and others assimilated into the NBA, the few failures who tried leaping into the NBA from high school became nearly as widely known as the players who successfully made the transition. While still in high school, Garnett played in a summer league game against a teenager named Taj McDavid. Garnett casually told McDavid afterward that he was "a player," a compliment McDavid took to heart. McDavid was a rail-thin 6 feet 6 inches who did it all for the Palmetto High Mustangs in their red-and-white jerseys. He scored. He rebounded. He defended. But the Mustangs played in the second-smallest classification in South Carolina. He was unknown even within the state. Jermaine O'Neal, the state's premier player in McDavid's class, had not heard of him. Neither had most college coaches or NBA personnel.

McDavid was a good high school player who ignored his school-work. He may have even become a decent lower-level college player. Still, McDavid entered his name right alongside O'Neal and Bryant into the draft class of 1996. Marty Blake ran the NBA's scouting service. He could not have been more off base in his prediction about Kobe Bryant. He was dead accurate when asked about McDavid, however. Blake had to phone his sources in South Carolina when he first heard the name. He had feared that a quality player, a premier prospect, had somehow slipped beneath his radar. Nope. "He can't play," Blake told the *Boston Globe*. "Who is filling these kids with these dreams?" The decision stunned McDavid's principal and high school coach. They counseled against the decision. "What's wrong with dreaming?" Mc-David told the *Globe*. "My day will come. I know that. I know that it's going to come. People around here don't think I'm crazy." An uncle told the newspaper that no one in the NBA could stop McDavid, that his stock was low only because he had played at a small school.

Framed basketball certificates covered every corner of McDavid's room at the mobile home he shared with his uncle and his mother. Pictures of the Bulls and Michael Jordan also decorated his wall. The family waited and watched on draft night. John Nash was not the only one who had his bubble burst during the 1996 draft. McDavid, to no one's surprise except that of his family, went undrafted, caught between a kid's dream and an adult's reality.

At the time, Steve Lytton coached at Anderson College, a junior college transitioning to play in Division II athletics. He had awakened one morning and read an article in the *Anderson Independent-Mail* headlined, "Palmetto's McDavid Takes Shot at Draft." Anderson College stood roughly 20 minutes from Palmetto High. Lytton had watched McDavid play a handful of times. McDavid had a future somewhere in the college game. That, Lytton was sure of. McDavid was athletic. He did not shoot particularly well, but was quick and cagey enough to often field his own miss and lay the ball home. Years around the game had taught Lytton the wonders of how just a couple of months playing against stiffer college competition could improve and toughen a high school kid. He worried that McDavid had received tainted advice and would be hurt by missing a crucial step in the maturation of a player, but he did not think it was his place to go out and give him his opinion.

Instead, Lytton wished McDavid the best. "I know you have some things going for you and I know you have some aspirations," Lytton told McDavid. "I just want you to know that if you have a problem with that and you don't get the offer you're looking for, let me have the chance to work with you."

McDavid remembered the talk when he went undrafted. He decided to attend Anderson with his college eligibility still in limbo. He did not bother informing Lytton, who learned of McDavid's enrollment from a member of his team. He brought McDavid into his office. "You need to get into the weight room," Lytton told him. "You need to get started working on your basketball drills and I'll help with some of the things when the season's over. You need to get in here and play with our guys and go through the workouts with them. That's going to help you as far as where you go from here and what you're going to do with your basketball future."

That ended up being the last meaningful conversation Lytton had with McDavid. McDavid petitioned and regained his college eligibility from the NCAA, but never played for Anderson and mostly vanished from sight. Every once in a while, Lytton would hear that McDavid had visited the gym, but never on a regular basis. Lytton soon accepted an assistant coaching position at Virginia Tech and was never even sure if McDavid had finished out the semester at the school. Lytton had always liked McDavid during their brief interactions and sometimes wondered if he could have helped McDavid reach his ultimate goal. "There were some bad decisions, perhaps some inaccurate advice," Lytton said. "But a lot of people make bad decisions in their lives, myself included. But rarely do we pay the type of price he did in this particular instance."

As McDavid tried restarting his career, he made his way out to Los Angeles and played against a high schooler named Ellis Richardson.

McDavid passed down the same compliment to Richardson that Garnett had once awarded him. While McDavid was the linchpin of his high school team, Richardson did not even really fit into the dynamic of his squad at Sun Valley's Polytechnic High School in California. Richardson had changed high schools and spent most of his junior season sidelined with an ankle sprain. His teammates were a tight unit and could do with or without him. Richardson would often tell them about how he was congregating with other stars like Schea Cotton, another phenom, during his off time. He was aloof and his own coach considered him strange.

"Ellis, do you want to play or do you not want to play?" Sun Valley's coach Jay Werner would ask. Werner could have gone either way.

Werner went on vacation during the late spring of 1998. Upon his return he was shocked to learn that Richardson had faxed his name to the NBA as an early draft applicant. But Garnett had applied to the NBA when Richardson was a high school freshman and he had decided at that impressionable age that, one day in the future, he would do the same. Richardson had called the league, asked what he needed to do to apply for the draft, and filed the required paperwork. A couple of NBA teams called and inquired about him, just to cover their bases. They found out that Richardson was not ranked among the top 100 high school players in California.

"He was an athletic kid—there's no doubt about it," Werner said. "But the NBA? Even Division I?" They had talked about the process briefly, once. Werner had advised him to attend a junior college. "You're not ready," Werner said. "You can go there and work on your game."

"But he got some advice from other people," Werner recalled. "I kind of just said, 'You have to be kidding me.'"

Richardson's name went uncalled in the 1998 draft. The *Los Angeles Times* caught up with Richardson two years after his NBA declaration. By then, Richardson had served eight months in prison after being convicted of a robbery in the San Fernando Valley.

"After the draft was over, that's when I realized I made a mistake," Richardson told the paper. "What I've learned over the past two and a half years is a lot. I've learned the people I was dealing with, who were telling me I was going to get drafted, were bogus people. I should have waited."

In prison, he prayed, did push-ups, and tried to steer clear of the surrounding violence. He played at a park upon his release, telling anyone who would listen that he had a tryout with the Dallas Mavericks or the Los Angeles Clippers coming any day now. That day never arrived and he relocated to Florida.

The stories of McDavid and Richardson serve as cautionary tales for those opposed to the inclusion of high school players in the NBA draft. The league was a huge carrot that many kids would aspire to and few would reach. Skeptics predicted more flameouts on the horizon and that those kids would ruin their chances of playing college basketball and gaining an education. But McDavid and Richardson would have struggled against college competition, let alone professional players.

The legitimate next wave of high school superstars, the ones who had tested themselves at Sonny Vaccaro's camp and drew recognition from the shoe companies, would provide a tougher case study for the NBA. They would blossom into many NBA success stories. But, occasionally, others diverged from the path to stardom. The combination of youth and potential often proved toxic. The media overestimated the mix. What a prospect may become was more tantalizing than what had been established. The ending only sometimes synced with the prediction. Yes, they got drafted—the ones who did—by an NBA team. They lived the dream, but it did not feel like one anymore. Basketball became work. It involved sweating hard, bending over and tugging at shorts, puffing-for-air–type work. Kevin Garnett knew this. So did Kobe Bryant. But some of the other kids who attempted to jump to the NBA in their shadows remained clueless. The transition was tougher than anyone ever told them it would be. They encountered men on the court who fought to feed their families. In high school, they had never played against someone at that level. In the NBA, everyone was better than they were. They could no longer get their shot off as easily

as they once had. Someone jumped higher for the rebound that had
fallen in their lap in high school. The offenses were complicated. The
defensive assignments may as well have been a foreign language. Their
coaches had mandates to win now. Those coaches had little time to
develop players who would probably only reach their physical maturity
once the coach had been fired or had moved on. The games came one
after another. In high school, they played about 30-something games
in a season. In the NBA, teams played almost every other night. They
were constantly traveling and adjusting to new beds. They were always
tired, even though they hardly played. They lost more games in their
first couple of months as professionals than they had in their entire
lives. The media built them up, they thought, just to tear them down.
They wondered why the kid they had written about for years was not
playing like the next Jordan. The fans had their expectations inflated
and now constantly derided them. Their confidence slipped.

Those were just some of the on-court adjustments they had to deal
with. Off the court, the kids swore they had not changed. Everyone
and everything around them did. A friend or a few usually accompanied them to the big, new city. But they were just as directionless
as the players themselves. Balance a checkbook? They had never had
a bank account until their first NBA paycheck. But they had made
it, so their family made it. If the family made it, the extended family
made it. If the extended family made it, the newfound cousins made
it. Everyone needed something. If the athlete bought them clothes,
they wanted cars. If he bought them cars, they wanted houses. Yes, the
money was nice. But they burned through it. The peripheral benefits—
the women, the adulation, the fame, the respect, and more women—
were nice, too. But they had two feet in the adult world with no clue
as to what it meant to be a man and to truly dedicate themselves to
developing their talents. They needed more ears for all the people who
tried lending advice or gaining their favor, only they never had the opportunity to find out who they actually were and what they stood for.
The 32-year-old man with the locker next to them did not want to be
a friend or a mentor. That man wanted the scant minutes of playing

time the kids did receive, so he could furnish his family with the same lifestyle for a couple more years. Opponents would not provide any favors or tips, either. They wanted their contracts. Why should these kids come into the league as millionaires with a guaranteed three years of job security without having done anything to earn it?

In a year or two, their NBA careers were close to ending. They never had a chance. They were individuals with stellar talent and stunted growth. They needed to continually work on their game for it to advance. Like a blooming plant that receives no water, sun, or manicuring, their careers withered without that sustenance. Most NBA coaches and executives advised that the real dream, the one with substance, was not to make it to the NBA. That was just the beginning. The goal was to make a mark in the league, one worthy enough to receive a second and third contract. Instead, their 15 minutes of fame may have lasted a couple of years, maybe three. The rest of their lives, which they had never bothered concerning themselves with, now loomed.

No matter. On to the next phenom. So-and-so was a flop, a bust, a dud. But this next kid? Why, he was the best since Jordan.

10.

The shifting demographic of younger players entering the NBA troubled Jerry Colangelo. Colangelo was self-made, an athlete turned sports tycoon, revered and respected in Phoenix. He was general manager of the Phoenix Suns until 1987 when he led a group of investors that purchased the organization for $44.5 million. The team had sold out every game since downtown's America West Arena first opened in 1992. That season, Charles Barkley propelled the Suns to the NBA championship against his close friend Michael Jordan. Chicago bested Phoenix in six games, capping its third of three straight championships.

If it was sports and Phoenix, Colangelo had his hands in it. By 1994, he had been named the NBA's Executive of the Year four different times. He spearheaded a group that brought a baseball expansion team, the Arizona Diamondbacks, into existence. Football? He held a financial stake in the Arena Football League's Arizona Rattlers. Hockey? Colangelo headed investors who brought the Winnipeg Jets to Phoenix in 1996. In transforming the sports landscape, he also revitalized the downtown, parking his teams there and breathing life into the area's economy.

Colangelo had been around the NBA for decades, watching it grow from its humble infancy into a sport where players commanded millions in salary. He worried about floodgates being opened, about high school failures outweighing the successes, and about the NBA being saturated by emotionally stunted kids. The longer someone stayed in school, Colangelo believed, the more he would be exposed to as a basketball player and a person and the better prepared he would be to become a professional. Colangelo raised his concerns during the 1998–1999 lockout. But the league had more pressing concerns in corralling skyrocketing player salaries. Colangelo had predicted such a showdown between the league and the players union years ago. In 1989, the death of union chief Larry Fleisher, the father of agent Eric Fleisher, brought about a change in the dynamic between the players and the owners. Larry Fleisher was tough, in Colangelo's estimation. He knew when to push, but he also knew when to pull back, a tactful tool for a negotiator, Colangelo thought, and pivotal in ending any arbitration amicably. The new heads of the union wanted more and more as the owners claimed to be financially suffering. The owners dug in, united, and ended the lockout with, Colangelo believed, a more economically stable structure moving forward.

Many around the league shared Colangelo's concerns over the league harboring recent high school players. Russ Granik served as the league's deputy commissioner under David Stern. He thought the process would take care of itself. He believed it would take only one drastic failure to curtail others from trying to make the same jump. But, at the time, the rules were the rules. High school players were not barred from entering the draft. "The view, even after Kevin [Garnett] was in the league, was that he probably would be the exception," Granik remembered. "I think we were wrong about predicting how many players were likely to try and follow his example." Most NBA personnel did not share Jerry Krause's view of high schoolers as a new pool of talent. They were reserved and reluctant to scout in high school gyms. It was nearly impossible to predict how a teenager's body would develop and how his outlook would shift once exposed to previously unimaginable riches. "I saw Michael Jordan play in high school," said Keith Drum, a scout for the Sacramento Kings. "Had he come out of high school as a player, our whole opinion of Michael Jordan would be different. He might've developed into a very nice player, but he wouldn't have come into the league and become a star right away." Kevin McHale and Flip Saunders were applauded for gambling on Kevin Garnett, but even they were reluctant to draft high schoolers in successive years and passed on Kobe Bryant. Jerry West, the executive who went out on a limb to secure Bryant, expected him to eventually mature into a star. Bryant had the work ethic and the tools. He also knew Bryant was an outlier. "Potential is sometimes like if you don't take care of a nice car," West said. "If you don't take good care of it and nurture it, pretty soon it's going to be a pretty bad car. These young kids really need a lot of attention in trying to steer them into areas that will help them achieve their goals, and many don't make it." Meanwhile, David Stern and Granik viewed the issue with the league's overall well-being in mind. The draft was aimed at restocking the weaker teams. It was obvious soon after the 1995 draft that Garnett was the premier player of his draft class. He would have been the number one pick had he played in college just one season and allowed teams to better measure his ceiling. But Washington's Abe Pollin had urged John Nash not to further scout Garnett simply because he was a high schooler. "Four teams that had a pick better than Minnesota's didn't feel they had enough faith," Granik said. "Everybody knew by then who he was and that he was coming out. What we'd like to think was that the teams that had the best picks have a better shot of making a good judgment and that was hard to do in this case."

Colangelo did not arrive at his stance without due consideration. He ran a baseball franchise in a league where hundreds of players are taken in just one draft. But they progressed through the minor leagues—more like a graduate program than the big leagues. The fame, attention, riches, and adulation would arrive later if they advanced and proved themselves through a myriad of bus rides to cities like Visalia and Macon and hard hotel beds. Colangelo himself was once a hotshot pitcher who was scouted by several teams out of Bloom Township High School in Chicago Heights. But he was not offered a signing bonus large enough for his liking, so he enrolled to play basketball at the University of Kansas in 1957. Colangelo planned to pair with the great Wilt Chamberlain and win a national championship. Instead, he saw Chamberlain, an athlete before his time who helped modernize the game, serve as one of the first basketball players to enter professional basketball and forgo his remaining college eligibility.

Chamberlain confided to Colangelo that he was leaving college prematurely to play professionally after his junior season. The college games were no longer enjoyable. Opposing fans had hurled racial insults at him throughout his college career. He played before the shot-clock era, and more and more opposing teams employed delaying tactics to hold on to their possession, while sending three players to guard him whenever Kansas did have the ball. Chamberlain could not join the NBA until his college class had graduated. Chamberlain did not try to circumvent that mandate. He would join the Harlem Globetrotters and play with the barnstorming troupe for a year before entering the NBA. He sold the story of his decision to *Look* magazine for $10,000, a sum more than most NBA players earned in a season. "I need money to help my family," he wrote. "There are nine of us, six boys and three girls, and we've always had a struggle to get along. My father, fifty-seven, still has to work as a handyman for sixty dollars a week. My mother, fifty-six, has to go out as a domestic. I want to fix it so they can stop working and enjoy life more." His Globetrotters contract was for $65,000, an unheard-of salary for a basketball player at the time.

Soon, Colangelo joined the professional ranks as well, but not as a player. He was instrumental in starting the Chicago Bulls in 1966, joining the NBA at an opportune time. Basketball was displaying its first signs of joining baseball and football as a major sports league. Attendance topped 2.5 million and ABC's contract awarded the league $4 million over five years. The NBA expanded further, adding teams in San Diego and Seattle in 1967 and in Milwaukee and Phoenix the following year. Both Milwaukee and Phoenix asked Colangelo to join their nascent franchises as general manager. Colangelo thought Milwaukee was too close to home, more of a northern suburb of Chicago than a fresh beginning. He decided to go to Phoenix, becoming the youngest general manager in professional sports at the age of 28.

• • •

Colangelo's stance on high schoolers entering the NBA was clear. Still, he evolved with the new era. Colangelo, like Jerry West, prized the athleticism and drive of a young Kobe Bryant. The Suns had hosted Bryant, who performed magnificently for them in a workout. Colangelo and his coach, Danny Ainge, worked diligently to move up from their 15th pick in the draft in order to take Bryant. But they found no takers, stayed in place, and took Steve Nash instead.

Six years later, Colangelo had another decision to make regarding a high school player.

Amar'e Stoudemire was ranked at the top of his high school class in 2002. His body was similar to Darryl Dawkins's, in that he resembled more man than teenager at 6 feet 10 inches and 240 pounds. It was not difficult to project how his body would develop as he matured. At 19 years of age, he was already sculpted. Stoudemire was commonly referred to as a freak, an athlete with absurd genetic blessings who could run, jump, and rattle the rim. But he had a difficult path in even getting to the NBA's doorstep. Stoudemire grew up outside of Orlando and his parents divorced when he was young. His father, Hazell Stoudemire, died when Amar'e was 12. His mother, Carrie, was in and out of jail for crimes ranging from theft to forgery to drugs. His older brother, Hazell Jr., served a prison stint on drug and sexual abuse convictions. Amar'e Stoudemire was often left to fend for himself at a tender age. There always seemed to be a coach willing to take in the talented player, who grew like a weed. But because of eligibility issues and family drama, Stoudemire ended up attending six different high schools, one in a basement, and playing only two seasons—all while helping to raise his younger half-brother, Marwan. Stoudemire was about the only athlete who could raise questions after averaging 29 points, 15 rebounds, and 6 blocks in his final prep season at Florida's Cypress Creek High School. Yes, he put up monster numbers. But his team had lost 13 of its 29 games.

"It was a problem for me because of how I thought about this issue," Colangelo recalled. "I kept saying, 'We're not drafting a kid out of high school.' And then my team of people said, 'You've got to look at this tape.' Then I saw Amar'e in the McDonald's [All-American] Game, and he looked like a man against boys."

The Suns decided to bring in Stoudemire for a workout, supervised by Bryan Colangelo, Jerry's son. Bryan had attended Cornell University before his father brought him into the business, eventually naming him the team's general manager. Nearly half of Stoudemire's shots in the workout were air balls. "He wasn't drawing iron," Bryan Colangelo recalled. "We were trying to figure out if it's nerves, technique— what could it be? What it came down to was he had never really been coached or taught or put through the rigors of a true, fundamental exercise on his shot and technique." But his athleticism was evident. Stoudemire impressed Bryan Colangelo and the scouting department, but they were split on whether to gamble on the high schooler. "Amar'e was definitely one of the guys that, talentwise alone, he was ready for the NBA," Bryan Colangelo recalled. "The question was, Was he ready for the NBA mentally? Did he have enough of a clear path to success that it was worth the risk?" Jerry Colangelo walked in near the end of the workout and watched Stoudemire for a few minutes. "He's our pick," Jerry Colangelo said. The Suns gave Stoudemire a psychological test and its results hinted at a deeply motivated person. Colangelo thought of his own meager beginnings, strengthening his conviction to secure Stoudemire. Stoudemire still had to fall to the Suns with the ninth pick. The Clippers, selecting eighth, loomed in the way. A Clippers executive phoned Bryan Colangelo shortly before the draft. The Clippers had been unable to secure a workout with Stoudemire or, for that matter, to get in touch with him at all. The Clippers executive accused the Suns of stashing Stoudemire away, hoping that he would fall to them in a prearranged deal.

"No, we haven't," Bryan Colangelo responded. The Clippers said they would take Stoudemire, workout or not. "Well, take him," Colangelo responded. "You're drafting ahead of us. Take whoever you wish." But the Clippers took Maryland's Chris Wilcox with the eighth pick, allowing Phoenix to draft Stoudemire.

Stoudemire progressed to become the first high school draftee to win the NBA's Rookie of the Year award and combined with Steve Nash through the years to become one of the league's more devastating inside-outside combinations. A dozen years later, Jerry Colangelo recalled his dilemma in choosing between Stoudemire and sticking with his druthers. "I had to make an exception to the rule for Amar'e Stoudemire," Colangelo said.

11.

That a drastically different NBA loomed in the summer of 1998, through a probable lockout and the likely retirement of Michael Jordan, did little to dissuade the high school–to–pro hopefuls. Al Harrington had made reaching the NBA from New Jersey's St. Patrick High School Academy a priority during his senior year. The thought would have been laughable just four years earlier. Growing up, he preferred football. Mona Lawton, Harrington's mother, always beat him in basketball whenever they played one-on-one. He was short, clumsy, and chubby, until one summer it seemed as if he had been stretched out like a rubber band, turning tall and elastic. His game developed quickly and he became capable, but not exceptional, in most aspects of basketball. He could jump, but was not considered a jumper. He could shoot, but was not considered a shooter. He could defend, but was not considered a defender. Rather than excelling at any singular aspect of the game, he was well regarded as solid in all categories, an athlete and a diligent worker who would only improve with time.

For a while, Mona Lawton thought that her son's ears had been filled with wild fantasies when she heard about him jumping straight to the NBA. She was happy with him receiving a college scholarship. Lawton wanted Harrington to attend the University of North Carolina and even phoned their coaches to make sure they had room for him. To her dismay, they had already received a commitment from a player at Harrington's position. "Mom, for me to go to college would be for what?" Harrington asked one day.

"For an education," Lawton answered. "To get a good job when you're done."

"For me to go to the NBA right now would be for me to get that job," Harrington said, adding that he could still take classes during the summer. Lawton found the logic hard to argue with. He would elect for the NBA. The decision eased Harrington's burden. He had college after college recruiting him. He developed close relationships with some of the coaches. It made it easier to say no to all of them, rather than yes to just one. The choice also eased the pressure Harrington faced from friends he had played with in AAU and high school ball, who had wanted to team with him in college. His old high school running mate, Shaheen Holloway, played at Seton Hall. Once, the school had lost a game in Hawaii and Holloway phoned Harrington back in New Jersey. Harrington, because of the time difference, had already been asleep for a few hours. "Just commit, commit," Holloway kept saying, trying to get a half-asleep Harrington to pledge his loyalty to Seton Hall then and there.

The feedback Harrington received from the NBA had him pegged to be selected anywhere between 8th and 15th. The range made him cautious enough to stay home from the draft, held that year in Vancouver, where only the top handful of selections would greet David Stern. Instead, several dozen family members, friends, teammates, and coaches gathered with Harrington at Niecy's Southern Cuisine Restaurant in South Orange, New Jersey. They ate, settling into the night on the big screen. Stern opened the draft by announcing that the Clippers had chosen Michael Olowokandi, a big man from the University of the Pacific, who had only started playing the game a few years earlier. Stern called name after name, welcoming them into the

NBA's fraternity. Harrington was sure that he would be called when the Hornets selected 21st. They instead opted for Ricky Davis, a guard from Iowa. The hope and optimism that he had started out the night with dissipated. "Al, you're going to be big," Tiffany, Harrington's sister, said while offering a hug. "Just keep your head up."

In Wichita, Kansas, Korleone Young prayed as the draft continued. *Oh God,* he thought. *Let me get drafted in the first round.* He knew that the difference between being drafted in the first round and the second round was substantial. First rounders were awarded guaranteed contracts of at least three years. Second rounders had to make the roster to get any real money and risked being cut loose on a whim at any time. Young had declared for the draft out of Virginia's Hargrave Military Academy, the boarding school he attended. He had spent his high school years bulldozing through and above opponents. His shoulders were especially broad for a high schooler, as if he always wore football shoulder pads. A neighbor threw a party in his honor at a bar the night of the draft. It seemed as if half of Wichita had showed up. They had expected about 100 people. The crowd soon swelled to at least twice that. They watched on a television screen. The first round continued to progress without Young's name being called. His future, one way or another, would be decided that evening. The music blared. There was food to be eaten and drinks to be downed. *Fuck it,* Young thought. *Whether I get drafted or not, we are kicking it tonight.*

At some point in the evening, Young's father, largely a stranger to him until then, even though they both lived in Wichita, showed up. One of Young's friends asked him to leave, Young recalled. If he was there now, he would expect something later. A wave of shock washed over Young. The sensation soon evaporated. Young had envisioned this day for years. He wanted to celebrate with no distractions. Young agreed to send his father off and settled into the party.

Of the three high school players with pro potential (Ellis Richardson also misguidedly declared for the draft that spring), only Rashard Lewis showed up in Vancouver with the rest of the top prospects. Lewis was raised in Houston. He had not originally planned to attend, but his hometown Rockets possessed three first-round selections. He had been assured that the organization would use one of the picks on him. Instead, Houston selected Michael Dickerson (14), Bryce Drew (16), and Mirsad Türkcan (18) with their first-round selections. Lewis felt as though he had sat in the draft's greenroom for days. Celebrations burst out like fireworks all around him as others heard their names called, their dreams realized. It was as though he was witnessing the slow death of his own dream. He felt weak and dizzy. *I already hired my agents, so I can't go back to school,* he thought. As the first round wore on, Lewis dreaded being guaranteed nothing if the round ended without his name being called. *No contract, no nothing,* he thought. He squirmed. He would have to struggle just to make a team or end up playing somewhere overseas. That scenario, in particular, frightened him, as it would most teenagers.

Lewis first planned to play at the University of Houston, where he would team up with his childhood friends. But the university had recently fired Alvin Brooks, scuttling plans for Lewis to attend the school with Brooks's son, Alvin III, and others. Lewis was elegantly tall and slender. He stood about 6 feet 10 inches tall and could play inside or outside. NBA scouts had come to his games at Alief Elsik High School, but only after Brooks's firing did Lewis start seriously considering declaring for the NBA. "Not only that, I could stay home," Lewis remembered. "I could get drafted by the Houston Rockets, so I'd still be there under my mom's wing, so that made me more interested in making that jump, because, hell, I'll be right here in my backyard." Juanita Brown sat next to her son at the draft. She had grown up a sports fan, watching as many games as she could with her brother. She worried about her son making this choice. She did what she could to educate him about those who had failed before him and stressed the importance of being humble and becoming a diligent worker. She ultimately left the choice to him. He was on the precipice of manhood and she believed he might potentially harbor resentment if she wrested such an important decision away from him. Now, she worried if she herself had made the right decision. She shared in his agony as he waited at the draft. She had first hoped that he would be drafted away from Houston, to live on his own and be fast-tracked on his way to manhood. She now desperately wanted some team, any team, to draft him and end their collective agony. She looked at her son's face and knew they shared the same frustration and pain from not knowing. Lewis had always been quiet. He talked when he was ready to talk. Otherwise, there was no use in initiating the conversation. "It's going to happen, Rashard," she said, trying to keep his spirits up. "You're going to get drafted." At one point, Lewis rose and left the greenroom. He silently sobbed in the bathroom. She prayed.

The evening inched on. Other players celebrated. The high schoolers with a toe gingerly stepping into adulthood waited.

• • •

That the three had entered that year's draft was no coincidence. All year, they had used the others as a measuring stick, playing against one another in the summer at AAU tournaments and during their high school seasons. The shoe companies regularly arranged the anticipated matchups, a sign of their growing interest and power in the amateur game. Nike sponsored a meeting between Al Harrington and Korleone Young in January 1998, a showcase named the Nike Super Six that highlighted three matchups and six high schools.

Harrington, in particular, looked forward to the game. The two had traded off as the number-one-ranked player all year. Harrington figured that if he played well and proved himself against Young, he could jump straight to the NBA. About 5,000 people attended the game, with college coaches and representatives from the Clippers, Kings, Trail Blazers, Knicks, and Spurs mixed among them. The total paled when compared with Madison Square Garden's capacity of nearly 20,000. But the setting provided an intimate view and a classic backdrop at an arena where an aging Michael Jordan would square off against a youthful Kobe Bryant in less than a month. Harrington felt good during the warm-ups, confident that his jumper would not betray him once the game began. He started strong, scoring 18 points in the first half. In the second quarter, Harrington sank a three-pointer. He smiled at Young. "Why don't you get one of those?" he teased. Young answered by draining his own long shot. "I love it when you talk to me," Young said as the two made their way back up court. Harrington responded by dunking home an offensive rebound. The two rarely guarded each other, but the offensive square off everyone wanted to see appeared to be materializing.

For Harrington, just playing in Madison Square Garden was a huge deal. He had grown up in the area, across the Hudson River in northern New Jersey. Unlike most NBA prospects, Harrington arrived to the spotlight late. He was anything but a spoiled athlete, having performed as Frank Butler in his high school's performance of *Annie Get Your Gun*, serving as a church usher, and maintaining a 3.4 grade point average.

Harrington's ascension in high school basketball was meteoric. His father, Albert Harrington Sr., was once an amateur boxer who had died suddenly a decade earlier. The tragedy drew the family closer and Mona Lawton, a toll collector at the Lincoln Tunnel, worked diligently to provide for Al and his three siblings. Al Harrington did not even start for his freshman basketball team, but was tutored that summer by Sandy Pyonin, an AAU coach in Union, New Jersey. Pyonin had once guided the career of Edgar Jones, one of the state's dominant players in the mid-1970s. The Milwaukee Bucks drafted Jones out of the University of Nevada at Reno and Pyonin continued coaching AAU in New Jersey, racking up mileage on his Dodge Charger, and acquiring the state's best amateur talent for his team. He saw talent in Harrington when few others did. "He could hardly make a layup," Pyonin remembered. But Harrington's growth spurt soon hit and he traveled up and down the coast with Pyonin, starring for the team. Harrington played well at Sonny Vaccaro's ABCD camp in 1996, but everyone and everything had been overshadowed by Tracy McGrady's performance that year. The following summer, Kevin Boyle, Harrington's high school coach, switched shoe allegiances and Harrington skipped Adidas's camp in favor of Nike's in Indianapolis. The colleges came calling shortly afterward. Tommy Amaker of Seton Hall phoned at 12:01 a.m. on the first day coaches could make contact with prospects. The family kept the thousands of recruiting letters he received stacked in a few shoeboxes. But Pyonin had told him that he could jump straight to the NBA if he trained hard enough and obtained the country's number one ranking. Harrington believed it. He trained. He worked. He regarded the decision in business terms and believed that this route would surely and quickly secure his best future. He was close to being considered the number one player in his class, as determined by the country's prep basketball analysts. All he had to do was prove himself against Young.

He was now doing so. While Harrington starred in the first half, Young seemed overtaken by the moment. He had walked the bowels of Madison Square Garden before the game, amazed at the framed photographs of all the athletes and performers who had held the same stage before him. He turned the ball over several times in the first half as St. Patrick's assumed a 31–26 edge at halftime. Myron Piggie Sr., a mentor of Young's who had no official capacity with the team yet moved in and out as he pleased, came into the locker room at halftime, imploring the team to play better and stave off embarrassment. Over the next few years, the relationship between Young and Piggie would be heavily scrutinized and criticized as an example of amateur basketball's burgeoning problems.

• • •

K orleone Young was raised in a modest house in Wichita at 24th Street and Lorraine Avenue in a neighborhood with piercing sirens that warned of impending tornadoes. Young's mother, Kim Young, had read *The Godfather* shortly before her only child's birth and named him Suntino Korleone Young, after the book's fiery eldest son, Santino Corleone. Young knew his father was a former high school track star named Juan Johnson. He occasionally saw Johnson hanging around

Wichita, but his father never acknowledged him. Young was always getting into fights—with his cousin Antoine and neighborhood kids who incessantly teased him about his stuttering. Kim Young did not view her son as a magnet for trouble. Instead, she saw an active young boy and sought ways to harness that energy. She enrolled Korleone in extracurricular activities—"keeping busy," she would call it. So Young tap-danced. He gave football a shot. But basketball evolved into the sport he truly loved and completely devoured. He fashioned a hoop out of a bike's wheel by removing the spokes. The more modest the bike, the smaller the wheel, the truer the shot. His grandfather Charles Young, who played a stint with the Harlem Globetrotters in the 1960s, later erected a real hoop for Korleone.

Young shot up fast, towering over other kids. When Young turned 10 years old, he began playing with the talented Wichita Blazers. The program was elite and rigorous; players attended church every Sunday and were expected to earn high marks in school. Young quickly became the team's star, dunking for the first time in sixth grade. Word of his unique blend of height and athleticism quickly spread to Kansas City's bigger AAU scene. In 1992, Young joined the Children's Mercy Hospital 76ers, a Kansas City team coached by John Walker. The team featured several future NBA players, but its best athlete was JaRon Rush, a silky forward who had started receiving attention for his basketball prowess at a young age. Rush found a benefactor in Tom Grant, a local millionaire, chief executive officer of LabOne Inc., and University of Kansas alumnus. Grant paid for Rush's high school tuition at a private high school and bankrolled the 76ers, a team that soon featured JaRon's best friend, Myron Piggie Jr.

During one summer practice in 1995, the team convened and Grant introduced a new head coach: Myron Piggie Sr., a former crack dealer and convicted felon who had been sentenced to a year in jail for shooting at a Kansas City police officer in 1989. Grant was familiar with JaRon Rush's bond with the Piggie family and sought a connection to keep his prized player happy and satisfied. Piggie, a charming conversationalist, had talked his way up the organization's ladder until he found himself at the top. "We were like, 'What? Myron ain't no coach,'" Young recalled. "Keep in mind, he didn't coach us. We had coaches. He just wanted to be in control. All Piggie did was look tough, sit at the end of the bench, and scare all the other AAU coaches."

Piggie's rise within the program coincided with Nike's interest in securing the best high school talent to perform in its shoes and keeping them away from Sonny Vaccaro and Adidas. To counteract the incursion, Nike hired Piggie as one of the company's consultants. The Children's Mercy Hospital 76ers quickly became a traveling All-Star team loaded with soon-to-be Division I players. They traveled around the country first class, and stayed in luxury hotels.

"We messed it up for everybody," Young said. "Shit, it became the war. We started the Nike-Adidas war. Me, Corey [Maggette], JaRon, Al [Harrington], and Rashard [Lewis]."

Both Grant and Nike eventually upped Piggie's salary. "We hooked up with Nike and it was lovely," Young recalled whimsically. "Me and my mom had a '96 Altima in '96. I got my '82 Impala. Never wore nothing but Nikes. Nike care packages every couple of months. Bags full of stuff. The influence of Nike is the ultimate influence. Why do you think all the kids wear Jordans?" Piggie doled out money to his top players—Young; Rush and his younger brother, Kareem; Maggette; and eventually Andre Williams. According to a later federal indictment, Piggie angled for a payoff similar to the one Alvis Smith and Joel Hopkins had received for steering the beginning of Tracy McGrady's career.

During the summers, Young's life revolved around AAU. But during the school year, he belonged to Ron Allen, Young's high school coach at Wichita East. The tough-minded Allen had heard about Young's talents since Young began dominating sixth graders. He promoted him to varsity as a freshman, with a plan to bring him along slowly. That unraveled the moment the 14-year-old forward left the bench in his first game. Young lit things up, pouring home 27 points in his first varsity appearance. Allen recalled Young as a fledgling Charles Barkley, an athlete who played bigger and longer than his frame. He tried keeping his star grounded. Allen was an old-school coach, having played at the University of Arizona in the early 1970s, and refused to cater to Young when he turned petulant. He regularly kicked Young out of practice to make his point. "Today's not a good day," Allen would say. "Try again tomorrow."

But Allen was naive about the burgeoning power of the AAU circuit. Once the summer began, he relinquished Young to Piggie. While visiting the AAU outfit one day before Young's junior year, Allen remembered being struck by the scope of the program—the sneakers, the jerseys, the crowd, the sheer magnitude of everything. "That was like a brand-new day for me," he recalled.

Then, later that summer, Young disappeared from Kansas. A *USA Today* reporter phoned Allen in August 1997 and asked him to confirm that Young had transferred to Hargrave, a private boarding school in Chatham, Virginia. The news blindsided Allen. He called Young's mother, Kim. "Coach, Korleone hasn't talked to you?" she asked.

Allen knew that Young didn't want to admit that he'd planned to transfer. But Kim forced her son to take the call. "What's happening?" Allen asked.

"I'm just going to stay up here," Young replied.

"For what?" Allen asked. "For what reason?"

Young turned silent.

"Look, if this is what you want to do, if this is really your decision, I'll support you," Allen said. "But if you are doing this for somebody else or for somebody else's purpose, I've got a problem with that. We'll leave this conversation here and when you come back to Wichita, when AAU's over with, I want you to come back and we'll grab a hamburger and sit and talk about this."

When he returned to Wichita, Young met with Allen and revealed his commitment to change high schools. He'd outgrown the city, he said. The intense media scrutiny that followed an underage drinking incident had confirmed it in his mind. Earlier that year, Young, a few other players, and some cheerleaders had sneaked alcohol into a hotel room during a trip to Topeka for a tournament. After they were caught, Young lied about his involvement. When it was revealed that he had indeed been there, he felt he had been singled out as the only one to draw a one-game suspension. Local television stations camped outside his mother's doorstep. He had contemplated transferring then. But then he heard about Hargrave's loaded roster; that was where Myron Jr. also planned to attend. Allen begged him to reconsider. Young remained steadfast.

"I didn't lose any love for the kid," Allen recalled. "I still cared for him as a person. He has a great heart. He'd do anything for you. He was just that way. But he was too young to be off by himself. That ultimately came back to haunt him."

The transition to Hargrave did not come easily. Young often did as he pleased in Wichita. Back then, recruiters called so often that his mother installed a second phone line in the house. Young tied it up talking to girls. But Hargrave specialized in instilling discipline in teenage boys. Colonel John W. Ripley, a decorated Marine, presided over the school. Young was not allowed to own a phone or a television. He woke up at 6 a.m. every morning and was in bed promptly at 10 p.m. He spent the first few weeks crying to his mother whenever he could get near a phone. Still, the school had its advantages. With its prestige and national profile, Young had his choice of colleges. He nearly went to the University of Kansas. He almost joined JaRon Rush at UCLA. "The crazy thing about it is, Hargrave, as a coaching staff, we never talked about him jumping and going directly to the NBA," said Kevin Keatts, then an assistant at Hargrave. "Everything was about college and recruitment and where he wanted to go."

Young had wanted more exposure against better competition. He was receiving it from Harrington. After halftime of their matchup, St. Patrick led by seven points with less than five minutes remaining in the game. Hargrave rallied and Young tied the game, 56–56, with 2:23 remaining. Young fouled out of the game shortly after that, but Lavar Hemphill's three-pointer for Hargrave broke the deadlock. St. Patrick could have tied the game, but turned the ball over while trying to free up Harrington for an isolation play. Hargrave prevailed in a 63–59 victory.

Harrington had the better game, finishing with 28 points on 9-for-15 shooting and 7 rebounds. Young overcame his slow start to end with 20 points and 8 rebounds. Hargrave escaped with the win, but Harrington left even more confident that he was the nation's best high school player.

• • •

Al Harrington went first. The Indiana Pacers grabbed him 25th overall. Harrington leapt in the air at his name being called and raised his arms toward the ceiling. He walked into a corner of the restaurant and cried.

He looked up to see a giant cake being wheeled out. "The sky's the limit, Big Al," it read.

Harrington would be joining one of the league's better organizations, a veteran team coming off a 58–24 season. They had stretched the Bulls to seven games in the Eastern Conference Finals. Donnie Walsh, the team's architect, had once figured that high schoolers would not have a profound influence on the league. But he had seen the impact of Kevin Garnett and the potential of Kobe Bryant. Walsh still did not think that teenagers could immediately improve a team; rather, he hoped that Harrington could apprentice for a couple of years under the stable of veterans and assume a larger role as he matured and the older players phased out. Larry Bird, the Celtics legend, had returned to his home state to coach the Pacers. Bird had always figured that if someone could play, he would receive playing time—no matter what his age. As a player, Bird could have joined the NBA early out of Indiana State. Boston had drafted him sixth overall in 1978. Instead, Bird finished out his final college season, deepening his rivalry against Magic Johnson and helping revitalize interest in the college game. "I think these kids should stay in school," Bird said of Harrington to reporters. "But he made a choice to come out. We'll let him come along slowly. In two or three years, he probably would have been in the top five of the draft, but he thinks he can play now. We'll find out."

The first round of the draft ended. Rashard Lewis slouched. He knew that his high school teammates had gathered at his coach's ranch back home to watch the draft and was utterly embarrassed to be the last remaining prospect in the greenroom.

Seattle ended Lewis's grief by taking him seven picks after Harrington with the second round's third selection. Seattle was another strong team, having gone 61–21 the previous season. Lewis had not even worked out for the organization prior to the draft. He did not care. The weight had been lifted off his shoulders. He turned to his mother. "Well, Mom, I'm going to have to make the team," Lewis said. "First round is different from the second round, nothing is guaranteed."

"Yeah, I know it, but you can do it," Brown responded. "You can make the team."

"Yeah, I know I can," Lewis said.

The party raged on in Wichita. The Detroit Pistons finally took Korleone Young with the 40th overall selection. Rick Sund, Detroit's general manager, had watched Young participate in Chicago's predraft camp that summer. He was intrigued by Young's already developed body. The hardest aspect of trying to draft high school kids, Sund figured, was how their bodies would develop after being drafted and whether they could withstand the game's physicality. He viewed Young as a cost-free project, someone with a high ceiling and low risk whom the organization could sever ties with if he did not progress as hoped. Such an outcome seemed unlikely for a player who had star potential written all over him only a short time before. "It was a good gamble," Sund remembered. "You don't take those type of gambles in the first round."

12.

The rain, Rashard Lewis wondered, was it ever going to stop? In Seattle, the gray skies cried endlessly and heavily, seemingly every day. The weather matched his mood. He was not necessarily depressed, but he had taken stock of everything in his life that had shifted so dramatically, so drastically. The climate difference from Texas was just another significant factor in the complete totality of the change. After the draft, Lewis had remained in Texas, practicing in the sweltering heat and humidity in a cramped gym with his high school coach, Jerrel Hartfield. There was familiarity and comfort in being home, although Lewis remained nervous about his own uncertain future and the NBA's overall unsettledness. When it seemed as if the NBA was on the verge of ending its lockout, Lewis hurried to Seattle and moved into an apartment. His mother, Juanita Brown, offered to move to Seattle with him. In the end, they decided that she should remain in Texas, at her job and near Lewis's siblings.

Lewis was excited to receive an invitation to play in a pickup game with some of Seattle's veteran players, who now scrambled to work themselves back into shape. He hopped in a car with Jelani McCoy, a fellow rookie who had played at UCLA. Their driver took a wrong turn and the duo arrived in the middle of a game that had already started. Gary Payton, the team's star point guard, savvy and outspoken, stopped dribbling up the court when he noticed the pair's late arrival. "What the hell are you doing?" Payton yelled. "Y'all are late. Y'all are supposed to be here on time." All eyes shifted toward Lewis and McCoy. They were not, Lewis noted, unlike schoolboys tardy to class. They pointed at their driver. "It's his fault," Lewis said. "He was late and didn't know where he was going."

For Payton, their lateness exemplified the mind-set of the NBA's new generation of players. Payton was 30 years old and had been in Seattle for almost a decade. The SuperSonics were one of the league's premier teams and their future success or failure hinged on Payton's play and ability to lead. Seattle was one of the teams expected to vie for a championship with Michael Jordan's probable retirement, having already been thwarted by Jordan and the Bulls in the 1996 finals. Payton was now one of the league's marquee players, as Jordan and his generation of superstar peers—Magic Johnson, Larry Bird, Patrick Ewing, Charles Barkley, Karl Malone, and others—were retired or nearing their final seasons. Payton was part of the group that rose to prominence after Jordan's. Still, he had learned from those players. He had earned what he received and nothing had been handed to him. The new players expected to be millionaires first and learn the game's intricacies later. Payton felt he had to immediately receive respect from Lewis and McCoy. *So what, you're a rookie?* he thought. *So what, you got drafted? Those other people who got drafted on this team before you are just as good or better. You're coming in here like a regular job. Respect the job. If everybody else is on time, why should you be late?*

"I don't give a damn," Payton yelled at the rookies. "Call one of my homeboys. They'll come pick you up. But you gotta be here. You've got to put the work in."

The admonishment took Lewis by surprise. Maybe he had wanted too much too fast. He had realized early on that his life span as a professional athlete came with an expiration date. He wanted to be an NBA player, sign a contract, and secure his future before suffering some freak injury. Only a few weeks earlier, he had been a teenager, or, more accurately, a boy, grateful for his mother to stir him in the morning, pack his lunch, and send him off to school. He had still not signed a contract and taken out an insurance policy for $2.5 million. While it was a safe assumption that he would earn money by playing basketball somewhere, Juanita Brown was certainly not about to allow her son to spend money he had yet to make. She took him to open his first bank account and they passed over purchasing the flashier items he preferred, like a big-screen television. She did allow him to buy a new cell phone and a car, and finally relented on letting him get a tattoo on his biceps. He now realized, almost as an epiphany, that he would be accountable for waking himself up, paying his own bills, and being disciplined enough to refrain from eating fast food every day.

That he remained mute, listened to his coaches, and stayed mindful of not stepping on the toes of any veteran teammates was natural for Rashard Lewis. Payton's scolding did provide motivation. He entered the game and played as hard as he could. Dwane Casey, a veteran Seattle assistant coach, watched the action. Lewis, he noticed, did not say more than a couple of words to anyone. He just went about his business on the court and blended in. Lewis then showed his potential in a flash. He stole the ball from Payton and reversed the court's action. Payton scrambled to catch up and leaped in an attempt to block Lewis's shot. Lewis dunked on top of Payton and released a primal scream. Casey believed at that time that Lewis could develop into a star. Payton was one of the game's better trash talkers. His jaw was in constant motion even in matchups against Jordan. In that instance, Payton simply asked for the inbounds pass and made his way back up court, mindful, this time, of where Lewis was so as not to have his pocket picked twice.

Because of the lockout, NBA personnel were prohibited from contacting players. The league canceled rookie camp, training camp, exhibition games, and the season's start. Suddenly, when it looked as if the entire season would be missed, the sides announced their agreement.

Players had lost nearly $500 million in salary. There would be a hurried schedule, one consisting of 50 games instead of the regular 82. Teams would occasionally play three games in three nights. Jordan indeed retired, saying he had accomplished everything he wanted to in the game. The league would have to deal with fan apathy and the loss of not just the most popular basketball player but one of the most recognizable people on the planet. Truncated training camps and exhibition schedules were announced. How individual teams developed their younger players was now more important than ever. High schoolers, more than any other rookies, needed molding and mentoring. Too often a bright prospect drafted by a bad organization proved to be a bust. But a gifted coach and his staff could sometimes push a player to advance beyond his potential. Rashard Lewis, Al Harrington, and Korleone Young would all be tended to differently, reflecting not only their own worth, but their respective organizations as well.

The Seattle coaches agreed to bring Lewis along slowly. Rushing toward the season hurt most of the league's players. It worked for Lewis, however. The SuperSonics presented Lewis with a two-year guaranteed contract shortly after his dunk over Payton. They did not have to offer him a contract at all or they could have signed him to a make-good deal. Instead, they showed their commitment to Lewis and put his racing mind at ease. The lockout had allowed him more time to measure himself against professional players outside the spotlight. It built his confidence. Later, Lewis wondered if he would have ever made the team if not for the lockout. Everything happened so quickly once the season started that he did not have time to overthink things. Brown still worried about her son. They talked on the phone nearly every day, but Payton and some of the other team members eased her mind to some degree by vowing to watch over Lewis. He hardly, if ever, played. Still, the fewer number of overall games served as an ideal transition between the high school season of around 30 games and the pros. Sometimes, Lewis would be jealous when he talked to his twin sister and she spoke of the college experience she was having. Occasionally, he played pickup basketball over at the University of

Washington and spent time on their campus, "almost like I was trying to live a college life, while I was an NBA player," Lewis recalled. "I was trying to catch up to speed with them."

Over the next few years, Lewis would develop into a dependable inside-out threat and eventually an All-Star. In 2007, he signed a contract with Orlando for $118 million. He did not hesitate when asked which contract meant more to him. "The first deal," he said. "Being a young kid, dreaming of being in the NBA, signing that first contract, I don't care if it was $100 or $100,000. I just felt so good about signing a deal in the NBA and being able to play and compete in the NBA. The dollars didn't even matter to me. I just wanted to be in the NBA and when I signed that deal, I was calling everybody. It was the minimum. It wasn't for that much and it was prorated [because of the games missed because of the lockout]. I made $100,000 or less than that that first season, but I felt like a millionaire. I didn't care."

• • •

The Indiana Pacers were another team looking to take advantage of the dismantling of the Chicago Bulls dynasty. For years, Reggie Miller, their star, was a constant nemesis to Michael Jordan, but also a constant runner-up to the superior Bulls. With Jordan gone, the Pacers were prepped to peak, propped up by Miller and a strong core of Mark Jackson, Chris Mullin, Rik Smits, and Antonio and Dale Davis. They were a powerful, united group that had played together for years. Al Harrington had spent the beginning of the lockout waiting for his dream to materialize and flying between New Jersey, Indiana, and Atlanta to find the best pickup games. Because he was drafted in the first round, his immediate future was assured and he took out loans to pay for the flights and hotels.

The veteran Pacers, like Seattle, organized pickup games to stay prepared for a season that could begin at the snap of a finger, or more accurately, the signatures of David Stern and Billy Hunter. Harrington played in the pickup games but, unlike Lewis, the matchups diminished his confidence. He had been able to declare for the NBA because of his strong mind-set. He had believed he was the best high school player and willed himself to play like it. It was impossible to convince himself he was the best against the professionals. Even the most menial tasks, like fighting through a screen, was a herculean task in Harrington's estimation. Meanwhile, the wily older players slipped through screens set by burly players as though they were ghosts. *I've got to start from scratch,* Harrington thought. *I've got to start all over again just to get respect and be a player in this league.*

Harrington also received veteran mentorship, but of a different sort than Payton offered Rashard Lewis. Antonio Davis was a fan favorite in Indianapolis. The Pacers had drafted him in the second round of the 1990 draft from the University of Texas at El Paso, but Davis began his professional career in Greece before moving on to Italy. He finally joined the NBA in 1993 and entrenched himself in Indiana's rotation, providing scoring and rebounding as a reliable power forward. Because of his circuitous professional beginnings, he appreciated his NBA standing and remained cognizant of the nourishment that a young player needed. Davis had confidence in Donnie Walsh and Larry Bird. If the Pacers believed in Harrington and felt that he could help the team in the future, then Davis would do all he could to help bring him along in the present. Harrington had yet to secure permanent housing in Indiana and was staying with a trainer. He asked to stay at Davis's home one weekend. Davis called his wife, Kendra, who agreed to the request.

Davis could not imagine transitioning into professionalism after high school. Harrington stayed a weekend at his house. The weekend turned into a week and then a month. Before long, Harrington had become both family member and tenant. Davis was 30 years old and half-teammate, half–father figure to Harrington. He hoped to teach Harrington what being a professional entailed. "No one is saying not to go out there and have fun," Davis told Harrington. "But when practice starts, we're there an hour ahead of time. When practice starts, we've already been sweating and ready to go. After practice, we're getting better every day. This is not something you do when you feel like it. This is a job, and if someone's going to be paying you to do this and you want to do it for a long time, hard work is not an option."

At home, Harrington enjoyed playing with Davis's twins, Antonio Jr. and Kaela. Harrington lived in the basement and often played video games. At first, he had a lot of free time, which was new and exciting to him. In high school, everything was planned out with his school and practice. Now, he could practice for six hours and still have much of the day to kill. Antonio Davis had his wife and kids, so he could not constantly watch over Harrington. He told Harrington that even though he had free time, he did not have to fill it all. "Just because you're 18, doesn't make you have to act like you're eighteen," Davis would say. Sometimes Davis still caught himself smiling. Whenever they attended a high school football game together, Harrington would become lost in a sea of high schoolers, mixing and mingling. *Well,* Davis would think. *Those are his peers.* The Davises paid a housekeeper and Kendra Davis's parents lived around the corner and often helped with the twins. They still wanted to assign Harrington some responsibilities to help round out his day. They would ask him to take out the trash and do the dishes and occasionally retrieve the three-year-old twins from day care. It was Harrington's job to drive Antonio Davis to practice every day. Harrington mostly adhered to the rule of no guest visitors of his own at the home. Davis tried to find the middle ground between being a father figure and a teammate. He did not particularly want Harrington to stay out late, but cautioned that it was his decision, with the only caveat being that he alert the family of his location.

It did not take Davis or the organization long to realize that the reputation Harrington had carved out in high school was accurate. He worked hard and wanted to improve. Harrington was grateful. He was not on his own and lived with a family who cared about him, an arrangement that helped him stave off homesickness. Mona Lawton visited her son and found comfort in the Davises. They called her son "Baby Al." She still asked that Harrington return home until the lockout ended. Antonio Davis insisted that returning home would stunt Harrington's basketball growth. "We're going to be working out every day, keeping busy, and staying in shape," he told her. "He'll be fine, Mama Mona." Lawton planned to move her family to Indianapolis after the lockout ended. Of all the arrangements, she thought, having her son stay with a grounded family seemed like one of the better ones and she allowed him to stay.

Davis was the Pacers' player representative, at the front line of the labor negotiations, and Harrington figured he would be one of the first to know whenever a deal to end the lockout was reached. He was overjoyed when there finally was an agreement. He still needed to find a place to stay. The season would be starting soon. "It's going to start soon, but there's only another couple of months before it's going to end," Davis said to Harrington. "Why don't you just stay here?" Harrington did.

The Pacers, in those days, had another advantage over other organizations in helping players adjust to the NBA. Her name was Kathy Jordan. Jordan was just out of college when she married a player named Walter Jordan, who was about to embark on his own professional basketball career. The couple lived in minor league cities before Walter played briefly with the Cavaliers in Cleveland. At every stop, Kathy found little support awaiting a couple who knew nothing about the practicalities of that city—where to live and eat and how to get around. To her, that did not make sense. The players were treated more like movable commodities than human beings. Wives, she believed, were viewed in an even dimmer light. She felt like a piece of baggage carried to whatever new city her husband landed in. An injury derailed Walter's career and the couple eventually separated. Kathy accepted a job with the Pacers as a promotions assistant. She developed into a jack-of-all-trades, influencing nearly every corner of the organization. The Pacers drafted Vern Fleming in 1984, the first year she worked for the Pacers. Fleming was from New York City and had a wife and a young child. Jordan thought how foreign everything had been for her when she was young and introduced to professional basketball, how no one had reached out to bridge that uneasiness. She phoned Fleming and his family and asked if they had any questions concerning the transition and living in Indianapolis. The job developed from there. Donnie Walsh heard of her work when he became the team's general manager in 1987 and asked her to keep it up. She was one of the first from the organization to meet and greet a new player's family and offered the information she herself had earlier lacked. She directed families on where to live and the best schools for younger siblings. Harrington came to call Jordan his second mother and Reggie Miller referred to her as his aunt.

At first, Jordan simply welcomed the drafted player and his family to the city. They were mostly four-year graduates and largely prepared for the NBA. Jordan's role evolved as the league drafted more and more teenagers. The "Mother of the Pacers" was how people outside the organization described her, but she thought of herself more as a mentor than a mother. She began working with other organizations and gave presentations about the healthy relationships a franchise should develop with their younger players and their families. Her work tied in with that of the NBA/NBPA Rookie Transition Program, which began in 1986. The retreat was mandatory for all rookies. The new players enjoyed the company of some of the league's pioneers—Tom "Satch" Sanders, the Boston Celtics legend ran the program—and included seminars from professionals about dealing with the media, image building, gambling, financial management, and HIV and AIDS awareness. The players could not learn about all the trapdoors that could ruin their career in a few short days, but it was a start.

• • •

Korleone Young found no safety net like the ones Rashard Lewis and Al Harrington landed on in Seattle and Indiana. Young had people around him. More often than not, they pitched the wrong opinions and dispensed the wrong advice. Young had been coddled throughout his life as a superstar athlete and while he had developed as a high school basketball star, he was ill suited to face every other aspect of adulthood. The Detroit Pistons were another solid team and featured Grant Hill, a young player who had spent four years at Duke. Hill burst onto the scene in 1994 as an immediate sensation and appeared uniquely equipped to step into the league's superstar void left in Michael Jordan's absence. The Pistons were not nearly as invested in Young's future or development as the SuperSonics and Pacers were in Lewis's and Harrington's. Young signed a one-year contract with an option for a second year held by the team. Kim Young remained in Wichita and kept her job at Cessna Aircraft Company. Korleone Young's pro career had a suspect beginning. Young split with his agent, Jerome Stanley, soon after the draft. Stanley had secured a $500,000 deal with Nike for Young, but the lockout loomed and that was not the kind of shoe money that Myron Piggie had envisioned. "I declined," Young remembered. "I had people decline half a million dollars. That's the truth. That's a fact. Nike was gonna give me half a million my rookie year, just for nothing." With Stanley removed, brothers Carl and Kevin Poston became Young's representatives. The Postons counted NFL Pro Bowlers Charles Woodson, Orlando Pace, and Champ Bailey among their clients. "We went with bigger agents," Young recalled ruefully. "That was the worst move I could've made."

Young still had to prove himself on the court when the NBA reconvened. Joe Dumars, at the end of his stellar playing career, recalled listening to Young speak during one early practice. "When he got on the court, you could see he had talent, but you knew the process was going to be hard because he was just so young for the league," Dumars said. "He sounded like a young high school kid all of a sudden thrown into the NBA world." But the Detroit staff still held out hope that Young's size and skill set would make him an asset for the team. John Hammond, who had worked out Kevin Garnett before scouts a couple years earlier, watched when Young sometimes matched up against Grant Hill in practice. No one in the league could capably contain Hill at that time. Young was among the closest, Hammond thought. Still, Alvin Gentry, Detroit's coach, had doubts about whether Young would ever mature as a player. Young dominated in the paint in high school. Though he was strong, his height of 6 feet 7 inches did not allow him to dominate the game from the interior as he had done in high school—he would need to develop a perimeter game if he ever hoped to succeed in the NBA. "I just thought that his game needed so much improvement," Gentry recalled. "Needed improvement in ball handling, needed improvement in transitioning from an inside player in high school to being a wing player. Defensively, guarding guys on the floor. I just thought he needed a ton of improvement." Young, Gentry said, was the beneficiary of unusual sympathy in a normally cutthroat business. "We kept him for a year, really, because we just felt sorry for the kid," he said. As time went on, Young's role with the team turned hazy. On a few occasions, the organization sent him to attend community events while the team practiced, according to Young. *Am I even on the team?* he wondered. Meanwhile, the combination of money, idle time, and an introduction to the local nightlife proved destructive. He traveled from Auburn Hills, the suburb where the Pistons played, to downtown Detroit's strip clubs and nightclubs. Even though he was just 19 years old, Young knew that he would not be carded if he arrived with a teammate. Some players looked out for him. Young fondly recalled spending time with Christian Laettner. Bison Dele taught him how to drive a stick shift. But Young spent most of the season on the injured list with back spasms. When he did finally dress, the Pistons veterans asked him to lead them onto the court. An excited Young rushed out ahead as the crowd began to cheer. Young looked back and noticed something horrifying: he was all by himself. His teammates stood waiting in the tunnel, giggling at the perfectly played prank on the rookie. The joke, Young later said, represented one of the best and worst moments of his life. He played in just three games that season and totaled 15 minutes on the court. Detroit declined to pick up the second year of Young's option. He spent the next fall trying to catch on in Philadelphia's training camp. (Larry Brown, Philadelphia's coach at the time, had also graduated from Hargrave.) One morning, as he walked in Philadelphia's Center City, two men struck Young from behind and robbed him of his cash and jewelry. Philadelphia cut him before the season started.

He had burned through two organizations, but Young was just 20. He still anticipated an NBA future. Then, the past caught up to Myron Piggie, Young, and the rest of the paid AAU players. In April 2000, a federal indictment accused Piggie of paying $35,550 to players, including $14,000 to Young. One of the players, Andre Williams, told Tom Grant that he felt uneasy about the money Piggie had given him. When asked about the payments by Grant, Piggie denied them. Grant then delivered a secretly recorded audio tape of Piggie discussing the payments with Williams to federal investigators.

"This is not a case of fifty dollars, a pair of shoes, and a prom corsage," U.S. Attorney Stephen L. Hill Jr. said. "He paid these players with the expectation that he would be paid later." Piggie pleaded guilty to a conspiracy charge for defrauding four universities and the NCAA by paying players and affecting their eligibility. A federal judge sentenced him to 37 months in prison. "[The kids] know my heart, and I know their hearts. They know I didn't intentionally set out to hurt anyone," Piggie said at the sentencing. "And I'm sorry for the way it all went down."

Young's view of Piggie remained conflicted. Yes, Piggie tried to profit from Young's talent. But it was also in Piggie's interest for Young to succeed. Piggie didn't just hand off duffel bags stuffed full of cash. He would chip in the extra $50 for a tournament registration or even the box of pencils Young needed for school. Piggie became the father figure Young had always sought. "He was my consigliere," Young explained. "If he told me to do it, then I did it. So to throw anyone under the bus for the decisions that I made is tough. But when you're a child, you got a lot of different people influencing you."

For years, Young toiled in basketball's lower echelons. His first layover was with the Rockford Lightning in the Continental Basketball Association, where he averaged 18.3 points and 7.3 rebounds under former Bull Stacey King. He had mostly stopped talking to reporters during this period. "My dream is to play in the NBA again," he told the *Wichita Eagle* in a rare interview in June 2001. "That's where I belong." Stacey King ran the triangle offense and Young's knowledge of the system eventually earned him an invitation to the Lakers' summer league team in 2001. "The most intriguing thing right now, in addition to the things that got him drafted three years ago, is his age," Lakers general manager Mitch Kupchak told the *Los Angeles Daily News*. But he failed to make the roster and spent that fall with the Canberra Cannons of Australia's National Basketball League. His career went downhill from there. He ruptured his Achilles tendon in his first Australian game. The following January, Young crashed his car while driving in Canberra, Australia's capital city. He had been at a club, drinking. A friend offered to drive him and teammate Emmanuel D'Cress home. "Man, I got it," Young replied. In his haze, Young drove as though he were in the United States and not Australia. He drove the wrong way on a roundabout. He avoided hitting another car, but swerved his Holden into a ravine. Young's airbag deployed and knocked him out. The radio had been tuned to a fast beat before the crash. Young awoke to the radio playing in slow motion. He believed his seat belt saved his life and still carries the scar it left across his neck. When he regained consciousness, his senses slowly returned. He looked at D'Cress, still knocked out. Young said he carried D'Cress nearly two miles back to his apartment. D'Cress sustained a broken neck. Doctors, Young said, later told him that if he had carried D'Cress much farther, D'Cress would have never walked again. The Cannons and Young agreed to terminate his contract after the accident—with Young's visa now void. He contemplated retirement. Instead, Young embarked on a self-destructive cycle. Though waning interest in him remained from overseas teams, Young slipped out of shape. He treated the tryouts with foreign squads like paid vacations. Young did stints in Australia, Russia, China, and Israel from 1999 to 2006. The farther he traveled, the further he got from his dream of returning to the NBA. He thought of himself as a victim. He drank. He smoked. He partied. He struggled with depression, racked by the mistakes he had made. "Shit, I was so dumb," Young said. "I leased shit then. I had a Ford Explorer. I had a Chevy Corvette. I had a couple mopeds. I was a big kid. I had toys, man. Kids have toys."

During this time, Young employed a financial adviser to oversee his affairs. But he would sabotage himself by telling the adviser that he planned to visit his daughters in Houston for a couple of weeks. The adviser would give him the money he needed for the trip, then Young would leave Houston after a couple of days, return home, and burn through the surplus on more cars and clubs, and on fronting more money to more friends and more family. His father asked for money every once in a while. Young said he gave what he could when he could. The cycle continued until Young could no longer secure a roster spot on a team overseas. Back in Wichita, police arrested him for missing a hearing over child-support payments.

Rashard Lewis and Al Harrington both carved out successful NBA careers as reliable professionals. Neither had heard Young's name for a while. "I always ask about him," Harrington said to a journalist. "Have you heard about him?"

"Me, him, and Al Harrington played against each other," Lewis said as his Miami Heat prepared to play in the 2013 NBA Finals. "Al is still in the NBA. He had a successful career. But Korleone Young coming out of high school that year was the best player in our draft out of the high school kids. He was by far the most dominant player in our era. After Detroit, I don't know what really happened to him. It seemed like he just kind of disappeared."

• • •

The NBA faced an assortment of problems by the end of the lockout-shortened season. Television ratings had plummeted without Jordan. Players rushed to work themselves into shape at the season's start and were made weary by the relentless onslaught of games. The Super-Sonics, Pacers, and Pistons all had aspirations of replacing the fractured Bulls on the throne. Seattle hit turbulence and missed the playoffs completely. Detroit fell in the first round against Atlanta. The Pacers advanced to the conference finals, but could not get past the Knicks. The 1999 finals featured the Knicks against the San Antonio Spurs.

It became obvious that Tim Duncan, San Antonio's young center, had been one of the most complete players to enter the NBA in years. He was efficient and well coached, a tower who nailed his bank shot from all angles on the court, an impossible shot to guard, and he always made the right play. He linked with David Robinson in San Antonio's post as a connection to two generations. Duncan could have probably left Wake Forest at the end of his sophomore year in 1995 and been the league's top draft pick. He certainly could have departed at the end of his junior year and been swiped first overall. But Dave Odom, Wake Forest's coach, never thought his star would prematurely leave college. Duncan's mother died before his 14th birthday and had stressed the importance of college and an education. *I've never seen a kid enjoy college life more than Tim,* Odom occasionally thought to himself. What had cemented Odom's belief was a trip he and Duncan took to Los Angeles to attend a banquet for the John R. Wooden Award. "Out here, there's going to be some different writers and television people," Odom told him. "They don't know you well. They know you're a great player, but they don't know you. They're going to ask you why you stayed for another year when you could have gone number one and that's a lot of money for you and your family. You're going to need an answer. I don't know what that answer is, but you're going to need one." "Coach, it's not really hard," Duncan said. "I've always thought why should I try to do today what I'll be better prepared to do a year from now?" Odom could not have thought of a better answer.

Television ratings for the finals dropped 39 percent in the first two games of a finals San Antonio would win, compared with a season earlier when Jordan battled the Jazz. The NBA was inferior that season. Teams averaged just 91.6 points—down 4 points from a season earlier—the lowest since the inclusion of the shot clock in 1954. The perception—more than the frantic schedule, out-of-shape players, and the aging of a previous generation of superstars—was that the league had gotten too young, too fast. It was being overrun by players unprepared for the NBA. For the first time, David Stern gave serious thought to how he would logistically implement an age minimum of

20 years for new players. "I am prepared to go forward and try to put some rule in that would have the effect of raising the beginning age at which players can come into the NBA," Stern said to reporters. In Indiana, Antonio Davis did not think it was necessarily a bad idea. He again thought about his own fragile mental state when he had left high school. For that reason, he had helped and mentored Harrington, and was kind and nurturing. The Pacers traded Davis to the Toronto Raptors after the NBA Finals, gaining the fifth overall pick in the approaching draft. The Pacers used the selection on Jonathan Bender, another high school prodigy, from the small city of Picayune in Mississippi. Stern still needed a groundswell of support to implement an age rule. There were not enough cautionary tales. Kevin Garnett, Kobe Bryant, and Tracy McGrady were developing into stars. Taj McDavid and Ellis Richardson were not heavily recruited by colleges, let alone ready for the NBA. Korleone Young had yet to become a full bust. But the approaching case and sad story of Leon Smith would offer Stern support in his burgeoning cause.

13.

Bill Peterson felt helpless as he watched doctors and medical personnel scramble to save Leon Smith at Parkland Memorial Hospital in Dallas. Peterson was there to check on Smith, a Dallas Mavericks rookie drafted out of high school, who had tried to take his own life. He was far outside the realm of his job as an assistant coach for the Dallas Mavericks. With the team, he was a new breed of tutor, hired from the college ranks in 1998. An infant NBA once featured a single coach who presided over an entire team and occasionally doubled as a player. By 1999, coaching staffs stretched four or five deep and the Mavericks gave Peterson a wide-ranging job description that included developmental duties. Not only was he charged with advancing a player's basketball skills, but, as the league annually introduced more teenagers, his portfolio included helping them acclimate themselves to adulthood and their new lifestyle. Because NBA teams were investing millions of dollars in young players largely based on potential, it became more financially responsible, even essential, to cultivate and extract that potential. The pool from which teams now drafted was vast. The NBA draft had expanded globally, with scouts spanning the world for premier talent. They were not to be disappointed. Dirk Nowitzki was part of a young, talented crop of players influenced in 1992 by watching Michael Jordan and his Olympic teammates tear through their competition in Barcelona. Nowitzki was tall and scrawny, a pure shooter who immediately drew comparisons to Larry Bird. The Milwaukee Bucks drafted him from Germany in 1998 after he had played three and a half years of professional ball there, then traded him for Robert "Tractor" Traylor on draft night to the Mavericks, who assigned him to Peterson's watch. Peterson was patient, a useful trait developed in his days coaching at small junior and community colleges. In Nowitzki, Peterson found a willing and energetic worker who needed educating not only about the NBA, but also about American customs. Nowitzki was still learning English. The two often ran errands together. Peterson would take Nowitzki shopping for supplies and essentials like groceries and a bed. Nowitzki struggled on the court that first season. He barely played. When he did, he was often physically outmatched. "I'm going to fight this," Nowitzki promised Peterson. "You watch. I'm not going to let those guys dunk on me and push me around. They ain't going to push me around next year. I'm going to spend time in the weight room. I'm going to get after it." True to his vow, Nowitzki returned with a larger build and a better shooting stroke the following season after regular visits by his German coach, Holger Geschwindner. He was on his way to stardom. "I knew he was going to be successful," Peterson recalled. "It didn't matter how he started when he first got here. With him, you just knew."

In all, it had been a good experience, one worth repeating, Peterson thought. The Mavericks were ahead of the curve in drafting international players. Donnie Nelson, another assistant and the coach's son, also helped coach the Lithuanian national basketball team and was well known within international basketball circles. The Mavericks took pride in developing other lesser-known prospects and Peterson had been integral in boosting Steve Nash's early career. Peterson hoped to have a similar experience, like the one he had shared with Nowitzki and Nash, when the Mavericks drafted Leon Smith. Smith was an unpolished player with imposing physical attributes. Dallas took Smith in

Left: At the age of 14, Moses Malone scribbled in the back of his Bible that he wanted to be a professional athlete. He turned pro in 1974 after an ABA team recruited him from Virginia's Petersburg High, becoming the first player to play professional basketball straight out of high school. Shortly after, Malone joined the NBA and became a three-time MVP and one of the league's 50 greatest players of all time.

Above: Bill Willoughby never experienced the NBA stardom he had hoped for, although blocking Kareem Abdul-Jabbar's shot in the 1981 playoffs qualified as a memorable moment. Many regarded Willoughby's struggles to assimilate from high school to the NBA as a primary reason why no one else made the jump for another two decades. Willoughby went on to obtain his college degree and now hopes to counsel young players.

Left: Even with Kevin Garnett's name on the tip of every NBA executive's tongue, his mother, Shirley Irby, wanted Garnett to attend college, after gaining his diploma from Chicago's Farragut Academy.

Left: Kevin Garnett reopened the door for prep players to join the NBA in 1995 when he declared for the draft out of high school. Garnett became a superstar, but still did not want others to follow in his wake. He knew the transition had been difficult.

Below: Kobe Bryant dazzled while attending Lower Merion. Gregg Downer, his high school coach, believes Bryant would have declared for the NBA even if Kevin Garnett had not made the same decision a year prior.

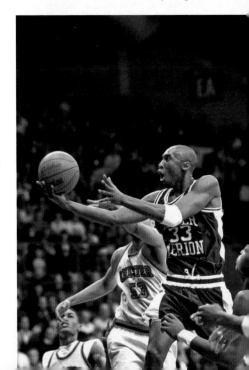

Players routinely signed Arn Tellem to represent them after declaring for the NBA from high school. Tellem represented Kobe Bryant, Tracy McGrady, Eddy Curry, and Kwame Brown. He navigated Bryant's route to Los Angeles in 1996, refusing to allow him to work out for several teams and helping to orchestrate his trade from Charlotte. In 2015, Tellem left his agency to become an executive for Palace Sports & Entertainment, which owns the Detroit Pistons.

Sonny Vaccaro's ABCD camp became a launching pad for talented high school players to showcase themselves and bypass college. Players like Kobe Bryant, Tracy McGrady, and LeBron James first gained national acclaim following their performances at the camp.

Above: Kobe Bryant looked to make his mark quickly in the NBA. Del Harris, his first NBA coach, realized that Bryant was different from most of his players. He was obsessed.

Left: Kevin Garnett works for position against Kobe Bryant. In 1995, Garnett became the first player in two decades to join the NBA out of high school. Bryant jumped straight to the NBA the following season. Both experienced bumpy introductions but quickly blossomed into dominant players, reopening the door for an influx of high schoolers to follow in their footsteps.

Above: Jermaine O'Neal made the transition all the way from South Carolina to Oregon when he joined the NBA from high school in 1996. O'Neal's career started slowly in Portland, where he seldom departed the bench. But with the Indiana Pacers he evolved into a frontcourt force and a regular all-star.

No team executive placed more faith in high schoolers entering the NBA than did Chicago Bulls general manager Jerry Krause, who confers here with Bulls chairman Jerry Reinsdorf. Krause believed he could gain a step ahead of his NBA peers by drafting high school players. In the wake of Michael Jordan's second retirement from the Bulls, Krause drafted Eddy Curry and traded for Tyson Chandler, both fresh from high school, in 2001. Neither performed to expectations, and Krause departed the Bulls in 2003.

Right: As a high schooler in Illinois, Eddy Curry had been projected as the second coming of Shaquille O'Neal. Curry's hometown Bulls plucked him out of high school with the fourth pick in the 2001 draft. Curry had his moments in the NBA, but his career was ultimately a disappointment.

Right: Tyson Chandler was known among pro personnel at an early age before ultimately joining the NBA out of a Southern California high school in 2001. He essentially skipped adolescence. Said Chandler, "My life was accelerated because I had to learn how to protect myself and use people who thought they were using me and do all of that to get to where I wanted to get to."

Left: Kwame Brown became the first high schooler drafted first overall when Michael Jordan handpicked Brown to join the Washington Wizards in 2001. The stress and expectations of being not only the top pick but also the player chosen by Jordan derailed Brown's career. He evolved into a role player, never developing into the superstar that many had predicted he'd be.

No one knew Tracy McGrady before his performance at the ABCD camp. A devastating dunk landed him on the radar of college recruiters. But McGrady skipped college to declare for the 1997 NBA draft.

Left: Tracy McGrady began his first NBA training camp in the fall of 1997. He drove the baseline during one scrimmage and tomahawk-dunked over Sharone Wright. "It was one of the nastiest dunks nobody ever seen," said Damon Stoudamire, McGrady's teammate in Toronto.

Leon Smith became one of the poster figures for skeptics of the idea that high schoolers could be ready for the fast-paced world of the NBA. The Dallas Mavericks selected Smith in the first round of 1999's draft without working him out. Smith never played a game for Dallas, while suffering from psychological issues.

Rashard Lewis sat through the entire first round of the draft waiting for his dream to be realized and a team to call his name after declaring for the 1998 draft out of high school. The Seattle SuperSonics finally summoned him in the second round, with the 32nd overall pick. Lewis, unlike those selected in the first round, did not start off with a guaranteed NBA contract. But he matured into a dependable inside-outside threat and signed a deal in 2007 with the Orlando Magic worth nearly $120 million.

Right: LeBron James supported a burgeoning economy that his talent and work had created as a high schooler in Ohio. Several of his games were even carried on national television. *USA Today* estimated that James generated $1.5 million his senior year of high school for his school, promoters, and others. Yet under amateur rules, he could not profit off himself at the time.

Below: LeBron James sits next to Carmelo Anthony before the 2004 Rookie Challenge game. No high school player seemed as ready for the NBA as James. But even he experienced growing pains as a teenage professional and was met with jealousy from veteran Cavalier players when he joined the NBA in 2003.

Many predicted years of high-soaring exploits from Jonathan Bender when he joined the Pacers in 1999 out of high school in Picayune, Mississippi. But knee injuries severely truncated his professional career. Bender, whom Toronto chose with the fifth overall selection before trading him to the Pacers, started just 28 games as an NBA pro. He found a second calling as an entrepreneur by starting a nonprofit and inventing a resistance-training device.

Left: In 2003, as a member of the Phoenix Suns, Amar'e Stoudemire became the first player who joined the NBA out of high school to win the league's Rookie of the Year Award. Stoudemire overcame a difficult upbringing to make an immediate impact in the league. Jerry Colangelo, who ran the Phoenix Suns, had been reluctant to draft high school players. But Colangelo realized he had to adapt to the times if he wanted to remain competitive and accrue talent.

Above: Sebastian Telfair, Dwight Howard, Rudy Gay, and Josh Smith sit on the bench at the 2004 McDonald's High School All American Game in Oklahoma City. A solid performance in the game can drastically raise a player's stock in the minds of NBA front-office personnel. Ultimately Telfair, Howard, and Smith all bypassed college to enter the NBA. Gay spent two seasons at the University of Connecticut before declaring for the NBA.

Right: Dwight Howard embraced Stern when his name was called as the first pick in the 2004 draft after he decided to forgo college for the NBA. For Stern, the trickle of players who entered the league out of high school turned into a steady procession. In 2004, 8 of the first 19 players selected were high schoolers. Change arrived when the NBA began disallowing players from entering straight from high school following the 2005 draft.

1999 out of a high school in Chicago. But from the beginning nothing had gone right. In life and on his quick ascent to the NBA, Smith had been let down in every conceivable manner by nearly everyone close to him. Everyone said they had helped, accepting praise for his rise. No one took responsibility for his downfall. Now Peterson found himself in the hospital with Smith. The young basketball player had attempted suicide by ingesting 250 aspirin tablets. He had painted his face, telling paramedics that he was an Indian fighting Christopher Columbus. Peterson was summoned to the hospital and unsure of what to do amid the frenzy. He suggested that a nurse remove an intravenous line from his right arm because that was Smith's shooting hand. He did not know what else to offer and thought of all the other people who were supposed to be in Smith's life, yet were absent in his time of need.

. . .

Leon Smith had never seen anything so new, so clean. He did not want to leave the police station, with its revolving doors and shiny benches. Smith was about five years old and accompanied by his younger brother, Jerry. Living in Chicago, the brothers were often on their own. Sometimes, they rummaged through trash cans for food. Sometimes, they stole candy from convenience stores, a tactic of survival they practiced skillfully for some time because they were not being fed at home, wherever home happened to be at that moment. But this time they had been caught. The cop asked the brothers where their mother was. They responded that they did not know. That was enough for the cop. They were named wards of the state, their mother losing custody of them, their father long out of their lives, and sent to the Lydia Home Association. The boys' home was founded in 1913, originally to house the city's orphaned children. Doris Bauer, the home's executive director, recognized the look when the young brothers arrived. It was the same mix of caution and confusion that she had seen in other children. The boys were surprised that they could now eat whenever they wanted and, for the first time, had their own clean beds. Leon Smith still suffered from a lack of love. He wanted it desperately. But he had most other essentials met, a step up for him in his young life. One day, a lady approached him and Jerry in the park and asked if the boys knew who she was. They said they did not and the woman said she was their mother. The reunion was short-lived.

Smith was put in another home after eighth grade to start the transition from boyhood to adulthood. He was without his brother and felt like a stranger. He occasionally tried to return to Lydia, only to be turned away. Sometimes, he opted to sleep on park benches instead. Carl Bauer, Doris's son, heard of Smith's new predicament and Smith again changed homes, this time to the Sullivan House on the city's South Side. Smith did not like his first high school and asked to transfer to King College Prep, one of the city's powerhouse basketball programs. He had not played basketball beyond pickup games until a five-inch growth spurt the summer before eighth grade made him perfect for the sport. Meanwhile, he continued visiting psychiatrists. They could see his problems—anyone could spot the root of his pain as the lack of ever feeling loved. But he did not like to take medication. At King, Smith would become a moldable player for its coach, Landon "Sonny" Cox. Cox took over the school's basketball program in 1981 and would produce 15 All-State players and more than 500 wins. But his success brought scrutiny. Opponents complained that he recruited players and the Illinois High School Association always seemed to be investigating him and the King program. Many of Cox's players went on to college, but few graduated. "I can't control their lives after high school," Cox once told a reporter from the Associated Press. "They got a college experience and went on from there."

Smith would not get that experience. To Doris Bauer, Smith was often laid back and lethargic. Yet he seemed to harness an unseen energy when he stepped onto the basketball court. It was as if nothing else mattered, the court a safe haven where he could block out all of life's woes and release his pent-up frustration. At King, it took him more than a year to feel comfortable enough to eat lunch in the cafeteria with his peers. Oftentimes, he ate with an assistant coach in the basketball office. His basketball progression was initially slow, but by his junior season, his potential seemed limitless. Smith was not just adept at powering through opponents on offense. He also blocked shots with impeccable timing, draining an opponent's will to drive the ball toward the basket. Smith soon drew the attention of Mac Irvin, a well-known power broker of an AAU coach in Chicago, and joined Irvin's summer team. Irvin was an Adidas coach, so Smith earned an invitation to the ABCD Camp and won MVP honors. Later, at another of Sonny Vaccaro's camps, Vaccaro called Smith over. The two talked for hours and Vaccaro found Smith to be fascinating. Smith recited random definitions from the dictionary to Vaccaro and quoted the famed poet Langston Hughes. Vaccaro asked Smith what he wanted to do with his future. "I want to go pro," Smith responded. Vaccaro asked how he had done on his college entrance examinations. Smith said he had not taken any and actually was unsure of his own grades in school. Still, Vaccaro liked the kid. "I'm going to help you," he promised. "I'm going to get you drafted."

Then, in November 1998, Smith disappeared from school and the Sullivan House. Reports surfaced that Smith planned to transfer all the way to Centennial High School in Compton, California. Over the summer, he had befriended George Borthwell, a volunteer coach at Centennial, at a basketball camp in Las Vegas. Borthwell had watched Smith get the better of Tyson Chandler, a tower of a prospect known throughout California coaching circles for years. A member of the Sullivan House filed a police report about the missing Smith. Smith had just turned 18, but still had to petition to gain emancipation as an adult.

Years later when he discussed Smith, Borthwell said he was on the verge of crying over the memories. "The kid had no one to talk to," Borthwell said. "No one cared about the kid. No one gave a shit about that kid. Nobody. They were using that kid." Borthwell had promised Smith that he could join the team and that he would get an education. But just a season earlier, six of the team's players had been ruled academically ineligible. Borthwell took issue with being characterized as someone who attempted to lead Smith astray. "They put it in the paper like I kidnapped the kid," Borthwell said. "Like I met him on the AAU circuit and kidnapped the kid. I'm like, '*What the hell?* This kid is seven feet, two hundred seventy-five pounds. I'm like five feet seven, one seventy. And I kidnapped him? . . . The only problem with Leon is that I did not understand the law at the time. We were waiting for him to be emancipated as an adult, but the process takes a little while and instead of starting the process earlier, we didn't."

Smith returned to King, scoring 25 points a game as a senior and averaging 15 rebounds and 8 blocked shots. He left the Sullivan House, drifting from place to place, eventually moving in with his friend Steve Brown, an associate of the agents Carl and Kevin Poston. Smith and Brown had a falling-out and Doris Bauer found Smith temporary housing. "He had a mattress on the floor that we brought him and a couple of chairs and not much else," Bauer remembered. "He had no money, of course, so I would give him twenty dollars or whatever every week. And then a month or two later, he signed his contract for over a million."

In the end, despite whispers of agents, runners, and other influences, Smith decided for himself to jump straight to the NBA. All his life, he had felt that others had made decisions for him. Rarely, by his estimation, had they helped. "I'm young enough to make a mistake," Smith told the *Chicago Tribune*. "I don't want to wait until I'm twenty-one or twenty-two and then finally figure out that's what I want to do. I already know what I want to do with my life. People nowadays don't want to accept who they are and their roles in life. This is my role in life." Now, he would be in charge of his own destiny and this small declaration would allow him to realize his dream. "I hear these fools on the radio and in the paper saying he's stupid for doing this," Landon Cox told the *Tribune*. "Listen, if [NBA teams] are going to give him the money, he has to take the money. Until you've walked a mile in his shoes, you should keep your mouth shut. This kid's life has been a horror story." It was doubtful Smith would have been eligible for college anyway. Few schools recruited him, due to his shaky academic record. He went through a new principal seemingly every year at King and was allowed to coast through school.

Smith was not pegged to be drafted in the first round. But the Dallas Mavericks decided to trade two second-round picks for San Antonio's pick at the end of the first round and used it on Smith. Don Nelson, a member of the Celtics dynasty as a player and an outside-the-box thinker as an innovative coach, was at Dallas's helm. Neither he nor his son Donnie had seen Smith play. But they had heard of his size and potential and feared that the rival Lakers would take him with the first pick of the second round, thus getting bigger, stronger, and deeper, already having Shaquille O'Neal on the roster. They asked Smith to play overseas for a year and develop, but Smith refused. To Smith, someone asking him to play anywhere other than the NBA was just somebody else trying to get in the way of his dream. As a first-round pick, his contract was guaranteed. Dallas signed him for three years and $1.45 million. Doris Bauer took him to open his first bank account. Smith arrived in Dallas with just a bag of dirty clothes.

Bill Peterson met with Don Nelson and Donnie Nelson after the organization selected Smith. "Spend some extra time with Leon," Don Nelson advised Peterson. "He's got a long way to go, but he's got a lot of raw skills." They soon encountered trouble with Smith. At one of his first practices, Donnie Nelson told the team to run another set of sprints because a player had finished too slowly. "You run it," Smith shouted right back, removing his jersey and heading toward the locker room. *He's not ready for the NBA yet,* Peterson thought. *He's got a long way to go.* Smith returned to Chicago, where his girlfriend, also a budding basketball player, broke up with him. He was arrested for throwing a rock through the car window of his girlfriend's mother—a vehicle that he had purchased for her. Peterson realized that Smith had trouble handling pressure. It built and bubbled up quickly inside him before bursting out. Peterson often picked Smith up from his apartment and drove him to practice. He found a player who wanted to do well, but had little clue as to the effort and diligent work needed to arrive at that destination. The pace of the NBA's games and practices was fast and unrelenting. A player could not allow his emotions to rise too high or dip too low. He had to play and forget, not allowing a bad play to affect the next one. Too often, Peterson found, Smith was incapable of that. A bad play led to a bad day and affected his mood the next day, turning one misstep into a bad week. Away from basketball, Peterson tried to help Smith grasp life's practicalities. "You've got to eat," he would tell him. "You've got to go downstairs to the restaurant or order room service. You can't just go to 7-Eleven and buy a bunch of junk food and eat it all the time." Peterson was a religious man. *Everyone makes mistakes in life*, he thought. He prayed that Smith would come around. But he could not be with Smith all the time. No one could. "He's not a baby, you know," Peterson said. "He still gets to make his own decisions. He's just trying to be a man in a man's league." The Mavericks deemed Smith unready for the NBA. Smith turned down their request that he play in the minor leagues. With the sides at an impasse, they told Smith to stay away from the team and work with Peterson and a couple of other coaches on his own time. He was placed on injured reserve with a phantom back injury. Smith felt he had fulfilled his dream, only to have it unfairly ripped away from him.

The pressure around him kept mounting. Doris Bauer's children visited Smith in Dallas and could not believe the number of phone calls he received during the visit from people in Chicago asking for money. Bauer thought she could help him save his new fortune. "Leon, you know I've known you for all these years," she said. "You can trust me. You can give me some money and I'll put it aside for you. When this is over with, you'll have money to buy a new house or apartment or something in the end that you can call your own." But Smith, she knew, could be strong-willed, and he declined the offer.

Bauer was in Dallas with Smith at the time of his suicide attempt in November 1999, having driven his car for him from Chicago to Dallas. She left the apartment when Smith started acting strange. He had painted his face and was more withdrawn than usual, even for him. She later rushed to the hospital and said that medical personnel originally prevented her from seeing him. After handing a social worker her business card, Bauer said she was finally allowed to enter his room. Smith was upset and crying. Doctors had pumped his stomach. Everyone, even people he did not know, had wanted something from him. He once felt like he had no family. Now, he had too many, people who always had their hands out. He saw his NBA career as already being taken away. That, capped with the ending of the relationship with his girlfriend, proved too much. "I was trying to get rid of the pain," Smith later told a Houston television station. "There are plenty of ways to commit suicide, but I thought that would be the least painful because I was already in pain from the inside. There was no need to have it from the outside." Smith had left two suicide notes, one for his ex-girlfriend and one for the Nelsons. "We went down there then and I think he was so overwhelmed that he just tried to end it all," Doris Bauer said. Afterward she found her contact with Smith limited. She said the NBA and the Dallas Mavericks were practicing "damage control." She saw her role as altruistic. "They knew I was white," she said. "They asked, 'What do you have to do with this person? Why do you care?' I said, 'He's one of my kids. I loved him since he was five years old.' 'Course everybody thinks we're getting rich. We never got a penny. We just wanted to do for him whatever we could."

The players union helped Smith enter a psychiatric care center in Atlanta, but he landed in more trouble by threatening his ex-girlfriend. Don Nelson said Smith needed help and had for quite some time. Landon Cox said that the Mavericks had treated Smith like garbage. No one took responsibility. Smith and Doris Bauer rebuilt their relationship as Smith tried resuscitating his career, Bauer said. Smith played in the minor leagues in St. Louis, Sioux Falls, and Gary, Indiana. He performed in 14 games with the Atlanta Hawks in 2002 and in a game for the Seattle SuperSonics in 2004. In Seattle, Smith one day looked admiringly at Robert Swift, who was at a practice with his father, Bruce. The SuperSonics had drafted Robert Swift in the first round, fresh out of high school in California. "I think it's really great that his father's around, watching everything that's going on and taking steps with him," Smith told Steve Kelley, a veteran basketball writer. By then, Smith was 23, long past the age where he had wanted to decide what he would do with his life, still struggling to figure it out. "He's still a kid and he still needs that fatherly advice."

Smith would never come close to realizing that tantalizing potential he had so briefly flashed and, more devastatingly, never appeared settled in life. To Jack Sikma, an assistant coach with the Seattle SuperSonics, Smith was talented, yet disconnected. "I'm not so sure Leon was comfortable at that time after being burned or making bad decisions on trusting people," Sikma recalled. "He just threw in the white flag one day." Smith moved around, drifting from place to place. Every once in a while, Bauer heard that he was sleeping on one of her daughter's couches. She last heard from Smith a few Christmases ago. "He has since kind of gone off the grid," Bauer said. "I've heard that his brother doesn't even know where he is. It's a very sad story in my mind because how many people get to live a dream and get a chance to play in the NBA? I wondered, How do you go from sleeping on a mattress to this classy, upscale apartment in a matter of weeks or months? It just breaks my heart that he's not successful in life. I don't mean that he's not a millionaire. I just mean that he's not comfortable."

Few, even today, accept blame for Smith's sad trajectory. "Dallas didn't do anything wrong," Sonny Vaccaro said. "They drafted him because of his ability. No one, including me, knew he had mental problems . . . No one failed him other than his school district and his coaches in Chicago. That's who failed him. They allowed it. It wasn't going pro. That had nothing to do with it. He was allowed to play high school basketball . . . It was there for everybody to see. But no one wanted to see because they just wanted him to play. Don't blame Leon Smith and say he was a failure. He did everything he could to the best of his ability. He just shouldn't have been put in that position. He needed help long before he got to camp and the Dallas Mavericks."

Years later, Robert Swift's career would also collapse. He won Seattle's starting center job in 2006, but landed awkwardly, twisting his right knee in a preseason game against Sacramento and tearing his anterior cruciate ligament. Swift's NBA career ended three years later.

In 2013, his home in Sammamish, just outside of Seattle, was fore-closed upon. For weeks, Swift ignored orders to vacate the property until one day he simply left without most of his belongings. Jon Humbert, a reporter for KOMO, a television station in Seattle, wrote about the home's utter disarray: *Animal feces clog the deck. Walls are punched out on different levels of the house. One even has an autograph. Pizza boxes and beer bottles are piled on the kitchen granite. Multiple guns were found in the home . . . A box of letters from colleges around the nation sat pushed against a downstairs wall. It looked like another trash box. Crests and logos of UCLA, Arizona, UConn and others are jammed together as untold memories of what could have been for Swift.* In 2015, Swift was arrested for his involvement in an armed home-robbery attempt.

Those once close to Robert Swift labeled his parents as a road-block toward his maturation in trying to steer his professional ca-reer. Though both are tragic cautionary tales, Smith was not better off than Swift without parental guidance and Swift was not better off than Smith with parental influence. That is why one blanket rule in either allowing or disallowing high school players entrance into the league was difficult to forge. The separation between a high schooler who succeeded in the NBA, like Amar'e Stoudemire, and one who vanished, like Leon Smith, could oftentimes be small, despite their similarly difficult upbringings. Bryan Colangelo, Phoenix's general manager, accurately pinpointed the source of Stoudemire's problems as external factors beyond the teenager's control. The same could be said of the root of Smith's troubles. Stoudemire succeeded. Smith did not. The ones who developed into great players were united in viewing the NBA as a starting point toward achieving their goals, not the end point, a pursuit that Kobe Bryant took to the extreme in his maniacal pursuit of championships and accolades.

• • •

Kobe Bryant raised his arms to the sky. He then brought his left hand to his right, and pointed to his ring finger. He had just calmly sunk two free throws, cementing the Lakers championship win—his first of five—over the Indiana Pacers in Game 6 of the 2000 finals. "Can't wait to do it again," an exuberant Bryant told NBC's Ahmad Rashad as purple-and-gold confetti drifted from the Staples Center rafters. Bryant was 21 and concluding his fourth NBA season. He had continued to simultaneously amaze and frustrate teammates and coaches with his talent and perceived selfishness. He was like a boxer with a devastating knockout blow who went for such a punch at every opportunity he could. The same gift that led him on a path to greatness also ostracized him within the organization. But everything came together that season. Phil Jackson had arrived to coach the Lakers, the organization providing a soft landing for him after the nasty breakup of Chicago's dynasty. Jackson immediately saw the similarities between Bryant and Michael Jordan. Jordan had already come into his own by the time Jackson became Chicago's head coach and was a reluctant but willing member of a participatory offense. In Bryant, Jackson saw an immense talent who still wanted to do too much on his own too often. Jordan also never had an interior force, like Shaquille O'Neal, to play alongside, one who needed the ball and his own space to be effective. Jackson spent much of that season tutoring Bryant on when and where to pick his points of attack.

Bryant was marvelous throughout the playoffs. Against Phoenix in the second round, his last-second jumper lifted the Lakers to a Game 2 victory. His lob to O'Neal capped a frantic comeback in Game 7 of the Western Conference Finals over Portland. But his coming-of-age moment arrived in a pivotal Game 4 against the Pacers in the championship. The game stretched to overtime, where O'Neal fouled out. Jackson finally offered Bryant what he had yearned for since the debacle against Utah—a green light on a big stage. "In a situation like this, Jordan wouldn't let his team lose," Bryant told his teammates. "I'm not going to, either." Bryant scored 6 of the Lakers' final 8 points for a total of 28 and the Lakers pulled away from Indiana and assumed a commanding 3–1 lead in the series. On the sidelines, Pacers coach Larry Bird watched. He was set to retire after that season and it seemed as if

Bryant, a legend in the making, had hurried another into retirement. "Every shot was all net," Bird told reporters. "I mean, it wasn't even close. He made big play after big play. I thought Reggie [Miller] came back and made some big plays, but we knew Kobe was just going to take over. It's just that we didn't stop him . . . And it was awesome."

As Bryant closed in on his first title with the free throws, Mark Heisler watched from the Staples Center's press row. Heisler was a veteran journalist who covered the NBA for the *Los Angeles Times*. Years later, he would look back at Bryant's performance against Indiana and recall it as the first time Kobe was really Kobe. Bryant had flashed what he could do by his lonesome in bits and spurts before, but he always had O'Neal or another veteran teammate on the court to contend with. Against those Pacers in Game 4, the game was firmly his to win or lose. For Heisler, the moment also marked a definitive shift in how players arrived in the NBA. Heisler himself had been part of a revolutionary period of sports journalism. He was in Philadelphia in 1969 at the age of 25, fresh out of journalism school and ready to take on the city's sports scene. He was part of the Chipmunks, a new breed of sportswriters given the name by the legendary journalist Jimmy Cannon when he one day spotted a group of young sports journalists hurriedly chatting. They were different from the older generation of writers who revered sports figures and wove myths about their heroic deeds on the field. These writers now sought out hard news stories and treated games with the same seriousness a city hall reporter covered council meetings. Instead of friends, they had sources. Instead of idolizing sports figures, they often made enemies, and a wall quickly developed between the sides. Heisler was assigned to the Philadelphia 76ers when the organization drafted Darryl Dawkins in 1975. The decision did not particularly strike Heisler as groundbreaking. The 76ers had been the NBA's worst team only a couple of seasons earlier and needed drastic improving. In that same draft, the 76ers took Lloyd Free, soon to be known as World B., and traded for Joe "Jellybean" Bryant. The trio, Heisler found, was inseparable and indistinguishable. Listening to their conversations, Heisler thought, one could not discern who had gone to college and who had not. It was Dawkins who first came to Heisler, telling him that he wanted a story written about the lack of playing time awarded to him by their coach, Gene Shue. Free soon followed with a similar request. When Joe Bryant asked Heisler to write the same story about his own need to play more, Heisler asked him to hold on, that he still had to get Free's complaint published. Shue wanted a defensive center who rebounded, like the one he already had in Caldwell Jones. It was natural that Dawkins often rode the pine. He was a fan favorite, though, because of his tremendous dunking ability, but never advanced much beyond that level. *He got so much so soon, it was enough for him,* Heisler thought. No matter what tactic he tried, Shue could not mold the high school prodigy. His scout Jack McMahon returned from a high school All-Star Game the following year and touted a player named Darrell Griffith as the most talented draftable player, no matter what the class. Shue brushed him off. "We're not going to go through this again," he said.

Due to the troubles encountered by Dawkins and Bill Willoughby, Heisler was not surprised that the pipeline of high schoolers going to the NBA had closed for so long. But then, by the time Heisler had arrived in Los Angeles, Garnett came onto the scene. *Anyone with half a brain could see his talent,* Heisler thought. Kobe Bryant followed. Heisler saw that he had his father's small face and big ears and a great deal of his basketball talent. But Heisler knew the family well enough to realize that Bryant had received his desire to fight through adversity from his mother, Pamela. One day in Chicago, Heisler ran into Kobe Bryant at the predraft camp and introduced himself, informing Bryant that he had covered his father. To Heisler, Bryant was young and earnest. *Not unlike talking to my paper boy,* he thought. Bryant told Heisler that he was soon headed to Los Angeles to work out for the Lakers. Heisler did not think much about it at the time, but realized later that this was the fateful session where Jerry West would decide to do his best to draft Bryant. Heisler was there to chronicle those early days when people first wondered whether a player of Bryant's size out of high school could survive the NBA and then if Bryant could learn to play as a member of a team. Heisler knew it was the first time Bryant had ever played with players of considerable talent. He had never had to back off before and Heisler wondered whether it would have even mattered if he had played with better players before. He compared Bryant to a lone wolf. He was wild on the court, but fearless. He watched those air balls against Utah during Bryant's rookie season and never saw Bryant again overmatched on the court. It seemed that every fall, Bryant arrived with something else perfected—his jumper, his jab step, his crossover—after a summer of endless work. Slowly, the talent outshone the flaws. In the All-Star Game against Michael Jordan a year before the championship, Heisler charted Kobe Bryant's shot attempts. "He's taken eleven shots the thirteen times he's touched the ball," Heisler whispered to Raymond Ridder, who worked in the Lakers' public relations department. "That's two less than he took in the rookie All-Star Game last year," Ridder responded. After that game, when it seemed that Bryant had matched Jordan, Heisler ran into Joe Bryant at Madison Square Garden. "That was a pretty good game he had," Heisler said of Kobe Bryant's performance. All Joe Bryant responded with was "See?" To Heisler, there were only a couple of people who first predicted Bryant's complete stardom: Kobe Bryant and his family. Joe Bryant's prediction had once seemed far off to John Nash, who, even though he had desperately wanted to draft Kobe Bryant, did not envision him becoming an NBA star so quickly. Joe Bryant's original forecast of his son's instant stardom may have been off. But it was not off by much.

14.

The energy in the gym suddenly shifted. Tyson Chandler felt it, his back to the door as he went through a workout at the Boys & Girls Club of Santa Monica. Chandler knew *he* had entered without having to swivel his head. A voice followed that Chandler immediately recognized. Any kid with even a fleeting interest in basketball would have. It was deep and modulated. "Tyson," the voice said, "when you're doing this drill, you need to pay attention to how you're planting your foot." Chandler still hesitated to turn around. He was already nervous and feared being made even more timid. Finally, he decided it would be disrespectful not to acknowledge the advice. "OK, Mr., uh, Jordan," Chandler bashfully said. "I'm not sure what to call you."

"Just call me Mike," Michael Jordan responded.

Chandler mumbled and tried returning to his workout as though the greatest player in history were not sitting in judgment of him. It was the spring of 2001 and Jordan had recently and unexpectedly returned to the NBA as a part owner of the Washington Wizards with authority over their basketball decisions. The arrangement had been fashioned quickly. Jordan had spent the lockout-shortened season decompressing from the game's glare and spotlight. Rumors of a comeback occasionally surfaced, but never from Jordan himself. Still, a competitor needed his fix. Ted Leonsis, a senior executive with America Online and one of Washington's minority owners, bet correctly that Jordan sought a new challenge to whet his competitive appetite. A dinner between Jordan and Abe and Irene Pollin helped consummate the deal. Abe Pollin had purchased the Baltimore Bullets all the way back in 1964, eventually moving them to Washington, D.C., and changing the team's name. Pollin was a link to the game's earlier days. He had been made more wealthy by its popularity spike, but he also now paid millions to players whose salaries had once been much more manageable. That they dined in the first place was a surprise to those who knew both. Pollin and Jordan had shared a heated exchange during the lockout when Pollin complained about escalating player contracts. "If you can't make a profit, you should sell your team," Jordan said. At the time, the comment infuriated Pollin. But at dinner, he found Jordan affable and with direction on how to turn the franchise around. He started envisioning a successful partnership.

The Wizards, after all, were traditionally one of the NBA's doormats. The organization had not won a playoff series since before Jordan had entered the NBA, in 1984. For Jordan, running a team would present a fresh, different test. He was 36 at the time of the dinner, ancient if he were still viewed as an athlete, yet a young age to chart one's next stage in life. They announced the agreement in time for Jordan to watch the Wizards play out the string on another disappointing run. Washington finished the 2000–2001 season with a franchise-worst 19 wins as Kobe Bryant and the Lakers celebrated another championship. Only the Golden State Warriors (17 wins) and the remnants of Jordan's former team, the Bulls (15), were more lackluster. Rod Higgins, Jordan's assistant, represented the organization at the draft's lottery that May. The process established the order in which the teams would select in the draft and was weighted to allow the worst teams higher probabilities at landing the best selection. On the way to catch his flight to New Jersey, Higgins stopped and pocketed a penny he found. He had been looking for a good luck charm. "I didn't know the penny had a hole in it," Higgins would painfully joke years later. As Jordan played golf to avoid the selection's tension, Higgins squirmed as the process unfolded. Jordan and Higgins envisioned a long rebuilding process. They had already began shedding the large contracts of Rod Strickland, Mitch Richmond, and Juwan Howard, the team's aging core, in order to create financial flexibility for the roster. A top pick would instantly fast-track the overhaul. The Bulls entered the lottery with the best odds of landing the top pick, but fell to fourth once the results were announced. The Warriors, with the second-best odds, dropped to fifth. The Atlanta Hawks had moved up to the third selection and the Clippers gained the second choice, leaving Washington with the top pick. "Michael is still everywhere," quipped Alvin Gentry, the former Pistons coach who now headed the Clippers.

Jordan's fortune was undeniable that evening. Not only had he landed the top pick, but he also scuttled the plans of Jerry Krause, who had coveted the selection for Chicago. But the pool of draftable prospects did not include a clear-cut favorite top pick, like a Shaquille O'Neal or an Allen Iverson. Instead, the players in that year's draft came to signify a shift in the game's evolution. The two top prospects were Shane Battier, a tested, senior forward from Duke who had won every major college award, and Pau Gasol, a multidimensional forward from Spain. They were joined by a trio of high school big men judged as having unlimited potential: Tyson Chandler, Eddy Curry, and Kwame Brown. No high school player had ever been taken first overall in the draft. The expectations for the top player were weighty, even for a college player. A top selection is expected to enter the NBA, contribute immediately, and transform a franchise. Most scouts predicted that Battier had already reached his ceiling as a college player and benefited from Duke's team-oriented system. Gasol was an unknown commodity. Pollin had declined to scout Kevin Garnett just a few years earlier because he was only a high schooler. Now, his franchise's future hinged on this draft class of talented prep players.

Almost immediately, Jordan debated plucking one of the high school players and began to scout them earnestly.

He watched Chandler in Santa Monica. Predraft workouts had turned into something of a cat-and-mouse game between the organizations, agents, and players. The intimate sessions provided teams with a better, deeper portrait of the players they would shortly invest millions in. They became even more crucial once high school players trickled into the league. A scout could sit through a high school game, but how much insight could really be gained by watching a future NBA player tear through weaker competition? By hosting the player, the franchise could put him through its own set of drills, scrimmages, and personality tests. By this time, though, players sometimes refused requests for workouts. Kobe Bryant had privately dazzled executives and coaches from Phoenix to Boston before the Lakers homed in on him. Bryant's agent, Arn Tellem, began denying requests from subsequent teams for individual sessions once Jerry West coveted Bryant. Eric Fleisher did not allow Garnett to work out for teams after Garnett's impressive group performance and out of fear that his injury would be revealed. Some players declined workouts from organizations they did not want to play for. Some refused them because the team drafted past where they wanted to be taken. Some abstained because they did not want to be worked out and judged against their competition. For the players, the workouts were job interviews. Because their draft position coincided with the salary of their first contract, they had much at stake in each session.

Players faced unrelenting pressure to perform and impress. Few high schoolers were as uniquely prepped for the scrutiny as Tyson Chandler, an elastic and scrawny post player from California. Chandler had decided early on that he would not duck any of the workouts. He was aware that he was already projected as a high pick and had more to lose than to gain. But he did not want anyone drafted before him. Chandler left his high school in Compton after leading them to a state championship in March. He took independent classes to graduate with his class, but high school was already clearly in his rearview mirror.

Chandler moved in with Tom Lewis, a former basketball player at Pepperdine University. The pair trained constantly. Chandler was so skinny that people joked he had to watch for cracks in the ground, lest he fall into one when walking. He was 7 feet 1 inch and weighed only 205 pounds. He hoped to add about 20 pounds by the time of the workouts to withstand the physical toll the sessions would take on his body. Chandler would eat breakfast and ingest a protein shake in the morning and train and eat again before napping. He repeated the cycle throughout the day, slowly adding just enough weight to his frail frame in time for the workouts. He tried unsuccessfully to strip the emotions from them. *Millions are not to be won or lost here,* he tried convincing himself. He was not trying to woo the Clippers, the Wizards, or the Bulls. This was just like any workout he would be doing in the summertime. But the NBA dignities who watched him made it impossible not to be conscious of the stakes. Jerry West once walked into one of Chandler's workouts, just as Jordan had. Chandler knew less about West as the great NBA player and more about him as the great NBA general manager with enough conviction to draft Kobe Bryant. West left Chandler's workout shortly after he had entered. *Man, I blew it,* Chandler thought. He was comforted when West later told his trainer that Chandler had been like Bryant and he had only needed a fleeting glimpse of his play to know that Chandler had a bright NBA future.

Such predictions for Chandler's future had been made for some time. He had spent the first few years of his life growing up on his grandfather's farm in Hanford, California. Cleo Threadgill built the farmhouse himself. Chandler milked cows, fed chickens, and plowed fields. He listened and learned when his grandfather preached that success resulted from hard work and self-discipline. Chandler's own father was not in his life. He was aware that Frank Chandler stood 6 feet 8 inches tall and had played basketball at San Jose State. In 1992, Chandler's mother, Vernie Threadgill, accepted a job in San Bernardino and the pair moved. The contrast from the calm of the farm to the noise of the city was striking. They lived in a crime-ridden area when Chandler hit adolescence. He grew so fast that none of his clothes or shoes fit for long. He was gangly and scrawny, an easy target who was teased mercilessly. Basketball proved to be about the only thing his size was good for. One day, when he was 14, Chandler's undermanned AAU team manhandled the Orange County All-Stars. Those opponents had been handpicked by Pat Barrett, a coach who was one of the most prominent figures on southern California's AAU scene and on Nike's payroll. He poached Chandler, lavishing him with Nike shoes and gear. The television news program *60 Minutes* featured Chandler on a segment that highlighted the influence athletic shoe companies sought over young, impressionable basketball players. At an early age, perhaps at an age that even he is now uncomfortable with, Chandler recognized that others would try to take advantage of him, his future, and his potential earnings. He realized it was a two-way street and a means to establish his dream of playing in the NBA. "It was no longer innocent and it was no longer wholesome," Chandler said years later. "I had to understand it was a dog-eat-dog world." Soon after joining Barrett's team, Chandler changed high schools and traveled the 120-mile round-trip of California freeway from San Bernardino to Dominguez High School in Compton, where he could gain more exposure and a national following. Tayshaun Prince and Kenny Brunner, two of Barrett's other players, also prepped at the school.

Unlike most of the players who had arrived in the NBA from high school before Chandler, he never treated college as a serious option. Most of the big-time schools did not even bother recruiting Chandler and he likewise never bothered taking any of the college entrance exams. He visited only one college, the University of Michigan, on an unofficial trip. Chandler borrowed against the credit from his future earnings with lenders. As a high school senior, he drove a Cadillac Escalade and wore a Rolex watch.

His Dominguez High team played across the country during Chandler's senior season. In December 2000, Chandler played in St. Louis against Eddy Curry in the Shop 'n Save/KMOX Shootout. Curry was the only player rated as high as Chandler. He was projected as the second coming of Shaquille O'Neal. He had a mammoth frame, soft hands, and nimble feet. Curry had grown up wanting to be a gymnast and, while his body outgrew acrobatics, he retained uncanny agility for a 300-pound man-boy with size-17 sneakers. Curry prospered at Thornwood High School, a small school in the Chicago suburbs. He committed to play college ball at nearby DePaul. Bill Bradshaw, the school's athletic director, once hosted Curry's family. It struck him as curious when Gayle Curry wondered whether her son would play if Steven Hunter, then the school's center, remained at the school for another year, instead of opting for the NBA.

Here is a kid who is going to be a lottery pick in the NBA if he wanted to be, one of the best freshmen in the country if he decided to go to DePaul, and his mom is legitimately concerned about how much playing time he is going to get if Steven Hunter is here, Bradshaw thought. "He will get as much playing time as he wants," Bradshaw responded to her queries. Curry remained easygoing and jovial, despite his giant stature, which drew stares. The hoopla had taken Curry's parents by surprise. Eddy Sr. was a truck driver who drove a rig cross-country. Gayle worked for a day-care center. The offers came all of a sudden out of nowhere from everywhere. Colleges offered them new jobs and to pay their bills if their son chose to play for them.

But as the game against Chandler approached, college looked to be less of an option for Curry. It seemed as though all of the NBA had packed into the Savvis Center. A glance around the arena revealed Pete Babcock of Atlanta; Rick Sund, who had moved on from the Pistons to Seattle; and Glen Grunwald of Toronto among the 13,000 attendees. Jerry Krause, forever clandestine, attended with his deputies, Gar Forman and B. J. Armstrong, and sat far away from his peers. Only two of the NBA's 29 teams had failed to send representatives to the matchup. Babcock, for one, felt awkward as he found his seat. He was still hesitant about scouting high school players, yet could not fully explain why. It just did not feel right and it was not where he wanted to be. But the matchup provided a rare glimpse of equal talents at that stage of their game. Curry and Chandler had failed to meet in the AAU circuit and, while both had been attendees at Nike Camp for two years, they never matched up against each other. The executives wanted to see whether Chandler could handle Curry's size and if Curry could contend with Chandler's athleticism. Chandler had greatly looked forward to the game. He knew that a few games would play a role in determining his future and this matchup was one of them. Chandler had heard that Curry was large. Upon initially seeing him, he realized Curry was not just large, but huge, and already had a body made for the NBA. Chandler also thought Curry was out of shape. He planned to take advantage of that by sprinting as fast as he could up and down the court. The game would provide a relief for Chandler. Only a week earlier, Dominguez's coach, Russell Otis, had been suspended after being arraigned on charges that he had molested a student who had formerly played on the team.

Few high school basketball games had been more anticipated. The game failed to live up to the buildup, however. Curry had been sick that week and missed a practice. He had to adhere to the long-standing policy of his coach, Kevin Hayhurst. A player who missed a practice for any reason could not start the next game. The crowd booed the announcement that Jeff Briney would begin the game in Curry's place. Curry subbed in at the first dead ball, 44 seconds into the game. Curry and Chandler refused to exchange any pleasantries or offer any acknowledgment. Curry promptly missed his first seven shots. Chandler was faster than Curry, but having to wrestle with someone who outweighed him by 100 pounds quickly tired him out. He grabbed only one rebound. Both of the top prospects finished with 16 points. Neither wowed anyone. Curry missed 13 of his 18 shots and drifted away from the paint far too often on offense before fouling out with 24 seconds remaining in the game. Chandler converted 7 of his 10 first-half shots, but faltered in the second half when he managed only four points. Chandler's Dominguez team squeaked by with a 54–50 victory. "It was anticlimactic," Sonny Vaccaro recalled years later. Curry, afterward, told reporters he was suffering from the flu and had trouble breathing. "Only he knew if he was sick or not," an

18-year-old Chandler said after the game. "I was always taught not to make excuses. If he was on the court, he was playing."

Chandler correctly figured that it would not be the last time he would be matched against Eddy Curry. As expected, both would declare for the NBA draft within months of the game. Chandler anticipated that the top selection would be whittled down to a choice between himself and Curry. He did not take into account Kwame Brown's sudden, meteoric rise. "Kwame burst on the scene at the last moment," Chandler recalled. "Myself and Eddy, throughout our high school careers, had put in that work to establish where we were and I felt like Kwame kind of came out of nowhere and jumped us all of a sudden."

• • •

B illy Donovan sensed the hesitation in the voice of his prized recruit. Donovan had once been an NBA player, although briefly, and appreciated the forces that the elite amateur players now faced. Donovan coached at the University of Florida and had quickly lifted the program to great heights. The NBA's lure began chipping away at his talent and now Kwame Brown, in the spring of 2001, had just informed Donovan that he would forsake his commitment to the Gators to become a professional. To Donovan, Brown sounded as though he were trying to convince himself of the decision and not Donovan.

"I understand," Donovan said.

Donovan had watched Brown the previous couple of years. The two shared a close relationship, ever since an acquaintance informed Donovan about this 6-foot-11-inch sophomore out in Brunswick, Georgia. Most leads like that proved to be false. Donovan, more curious than anything, went to see Brown and left impressed. He offered him a scholarship soon after and, in November 2000, Brown signed his letter of intent with Florida. He possessed an innocence about him that Donovan enjoyed. *He was a sweet kid*, Donovan thought, a positive trait just about anywhere else, other than in a high-level athlete. In that capacity, a mean streak was often required for success.

To Donovan, Brown was a high schooler with high school problems. Brown concerned himself with the prom and his grades—not about fast-tracking his way to fame and fortune. Donovan took notice when more and more NBA personnel began popping up at Brown's games at Glynn Academy. In the crowd, the logos of various NBA teams could not be missed. Brown's stock among NBA personnel slowly began to rise and then skyrocketed. He was projected as a late first-round pick, then a middle rounder. Donovan had scouted Brown for so long that he was keenly aware of his many positive attributes. He was also aware of his flaws and how he could overcome his weaknesses. His body seemed designed for the NBA. His game was all power and athleticism. Donovan felt that he could not argue with Brown's decision. He had a future to secure and a family to uplift. What kid in his situation could walk away from a guaranteed fortune?

"Coach, I don't want to do this," Brown confided in Donovan shortly after informing him of his choice. When Donovan asked why, Brown responded: "If I'm the number one player taken, I know the expectations. I'm so far away from being the number one pick. I'm not ready for this." In recalling the conversation, Donovan said he felt sorry that Brown shouldered such a burden. "In his heart of hearts, he really wanted to come to college," Donovan recalled. "I think he knew he was not ready. He had to go. He was really doing it for his family. But he was really concerned about the little stuff." He asked Donovan whether he had to live by himself if he went to the NBA and how he should have his dry cleaning done. "That's one extreme to the next," said Donovan, who more than a decade later would leave the college ranks to coach in the NBA for the Oklahoma City Thunder.

Joyce Brown wanted her son to attend college. But her family needed positivity in their lives almost as much as the financial boost her son's declaration would provide. Kwame Brown was born in Charleston, South Carolina, as the seventh of eight children to Willie James and Joyce Brown. For years, Joyce Brown tried leaving the damaging relationship she had with her husband. He abused drugs and physically and emotionally abused her. No one was spared whenever his sudden, violent mood swings occurred. The cycle was destructive. Yet, he was always able to lure her back until, one day, Joyce Brown left for good and returned to her hometown of Brunswick. She finalized the divorce in 1989. A year later, Willie James Brown was confined to life in prison without parole after being convicted of the murder of his girlfriend with an ax handle. Brunswick, a port city of about 15,000, is located between Jacksonville and Savannah. The family lived in an area called Dixville and nicknamed "The Bottom." They had nowhere to go but up. The neighborhood teemed with churches and bars. Most months of the year, the humidity made it impossible to step outside and remain sweat-free for more than a couple of minutes. Brunswick housed many of the service providers to the nearby Golden Isles, a group of four barrier islands where the rich sometimes vacationed and lived. Joyce Brown cleaned hotel rooms at the Brunswick Days Inn before going on disability in 1993 with a degenerative disk in her back. She supplemented her disability checks with babysitting gigs. A bicycle served as the family's main means of transportation. Brown's older brothers compensated for the family's poverty by turning to crime. Willie James Brown Jr. drew a 12-and-a-half-year sentence for selling crack cocaine. Tolbert Lee Brown was convicted of a shooting for which he was sentenced to a 15-year stint in state prison.

The family tried insulating Brown from the despair. His older brothers would tell him to walk away. He was bused to an elementary school outside of Dixville. When Dan Moore contemplated accepting Glynn Academy's coaching job, he watched some of the middle schoolers run up and down the court one day. Upon seeing Kwame, who was already about 6 feet 5 inches tall, Moore agreed to the job. Brown's brother, Tabari, already starred for the team and Moore envisioned a pipeline of talented Brown players for years to come. Kwame Brown, Moore found, could occasionally get upset quickly. As a freshman, he grew frustrated at one practice, punched a wall, and broke his hand. He also had problems being on time. Brown was occasionally late to practices or to the bus for away games. On those occasions, Moore would signal the driver to leave without his star player. Overall, though, Kwame was a joy for Moore to coach. He was articulate and smart. He was willing to learn. Moore sometimes even asked Brown to babysit his boys. Looking back, Moore could not recall one time they had engaged in an argument. Plus, Brown was so athletic that Moore had to design new drills to challenge him. One involved Brown jumping from outside the key on one block to the opposite block, while contesting shots. Still, nobody could successfully score over Brown. He was growing into a well-rounded player and a stable individual, aided by the mentorship provided by John Williams. Williams served as the associate director of a nearby youth ministry and his involvement with the basketball program predated Moore's arrival. He occasionally gave the kids motivational talks and helped find them part-time jobs. For Brown, Williams filled a gaping void. He was one of the first male influences Brown came across without an ulterior motive. While Tyson Chandler drove around in his flashy SUV, Brown steered Williams's Buick Century. Williams made a promise to Brown that he would lend him the car if he maintained high marks in school. Brown averaged 20.1 points, 13.3 rebounds, and 5.8 blocks as a senior, guiding Glynn Academy to the state's Final Four tournament. He had 17 points, 7 rebounds, and 5 blocked shots at the McDonald's All-American Game. Brown had previously performed at some of the sneaker camps and played decently. On that national stage at Cameron Indoor Stadium in Durham, North Carolina, he starred and for the first time began seriously contemplating jumping straight to the NBA.

Moore did not weigh in on Brown's decision. He did not believe it was his place to be involved. Brown was a teenager and Moore preferred him to remain one as long as he could. As NBA personnel filtered into his gym throughout the season, Moore kept Brown insulated from them all. "Use basketball," he would tell Brown. "Don't let basketball use you." Moore believed that Brown would attend Florida until the day Brown informed Billy Donovan of his decision. Moore later accepted and rationalized the decision. "When he would be twenty-one years old, he would already be making nineteen million dollars," Moore said. "When I was twenty-one, I was looking for a job." Brown allowed Williams to act as his facilitator. Brown himself ducked most of the interview requests and questions about his future. Brown announced his NBA intentions with a statement. "There are those who would say that the transition from high school to the NBA will be a difficult one," it read. "To those people, I say that difficult transitions are not new to my family and me. In fact, adversities have made my family stronger." Clad in a black suit and vest, Brown attended his high school's prom with his girlfriend, Joy, hours after issuing the press release.

He purchased a home in Gainesville near Billy Donovan and asked to prepare for the draft at the University of Florida. Donovan took one look at Brown and knew he was not in the best of shape. In Donovan's opinion, Brown loved to play basketball, but he did not seem to enjoy working out. "Kwame, you're going to have to get in a lot better shape," Donovan advised him. "You're going to have to push yourself more." Donovan no longer had any stake in Brown's future. He still wanted to help, yet he predicted that Brown was headed into a make-or-break situation unprepared.

The training helped. Brown performed for all the teams with the top picks and impressed at each stop. Curry was bigger. Chandler was longer. Brown was the best combination of the two and possibly the best athlete of the three. Michael Jordan worked out Brown, Chandler, and Curry on separate occasions. Jordan sometimes shared the workouts, personally testing their skills and fueling interest that he harbored an ulterior motive in wanting to work himself into shape for a comeback attempt. As the draft approached, the Wizards requested one last workout that would feature Brown against Chandler. The request initially irked Brown. He felt he had already proved himself worthy of the top selection.

Brown was relentless against Chandler in the showdown. He powered through Chandler in some of the drills. He was faster than him in others. He could and did do it all—outmuscling Chandler in the post and skillfully maneuvering by him on the perimeter. Brown, Rod Higgins thought, could play inside and outside and possibly develop into another Kevin Garnett. Too often, Chandler floated out to the perimeter in the workout. He told Higgins that he wanted to play like Rasheed Wallace, a tall inside-outside forward with a pure stroke. But Higgins doubted that Chandler's NBA future would be in that capacity. Higgins thought of his own NBA career. He had entered the NBA in 1982 after graduating from Fresno State. He knew that he would have never been prepared for the NBA fresh out of high school, but this was a new wave of players. It was tough, Higgins thought. The executives had to project where players would be five years into the future with a teenager now often harboring inflated expectations of his NBA career. To Higgins, that represented a guessing game that was part of the game's beauty and curse. Chandler did not know it, but the Wizards had scheduled the workout to confirm their conviction to draft Brown. Chandler possessed a sinking feeling once it ended. He had a brief conversation with Jordan and realized he was no longer in the running to be the top selection. Brown also talked to Jordan before departing, making a bold proclamation that piqued the competitor in Jordan. It was one a younger Jordan might have made had he been granted a similar stage. "I promise you if you draft me," Brown said confidentially, "you will never regret it."

15.

The first phone call Butch Carter received after being appointed coach of the Toronto Raptors in 1998 came from Alvis Smith and Joel Hopkins. The call surprised Carter, but Smith and Hopkins had much invested in the organization and in one player in particular. They had groomed and cultivated Tracy McGrady into a phenom, only to watch him gain rust and lose confidence during Darrell Walker's coaching tenure in Toronto. Smith and Hopkins fretted that McGrady would likewise seldom play under Carter, who had teamed with Isiah Thomas at Indiana before embarking on an NBA playing career. "Give me a little time," Carter told them. The NBA, he immediately realized, was a much different league than the one he had played in several years before. Coaching was a juggling act of different agendas that extended beyond his players. "When the high school guys came in, they brought all these high school coaches and AAU coaches with them and they wanted the quickest pot of gold they could put their hands on," Carter recalled.

Carter came to judge McGrady through a different prism than Walker had. Carter had coached at his alma mater, Ohio's Middletown

High School, upon retiring from professional basketball in 1986. Those players were fragile, with their bodies and minds both still in development. Carter doubted McGrady, no matter his talent, was much different. He decided that he would not judge McGrady based on his progress in practice against men. *You can't throw Tracy McGrady against teammates like Charles Oakley or Doug Christie and expect to get a positive result,* he reasoned. McGrady, Carter figured, had all the attributes to be a star. He was as athletic as any player he had ever seen. But he was still a kid. He could fall asleep anywhere at any time, a trait that his teammate Damon Stoudamire did not attribute to laziness but to the fact that he was still growing. Carter decided he would evaluate McGrady based on the work he did around practice, like the time he put in on the treadmill and watching videos. "They don't run two-year-olds in the Kentucky Derby and that's for a reason," Carter said. On the court, he asked McGrady for one solid hour of work a day. He wanted to transition McGrady's body into the NBA, getting him through 30 injury-free games his rookie year, comparable, somewhat, to a college season, and 60 games the following year. McGrady also started attending sessions with DeNita Turner, a personal management consultant, charged with helping McGrady learn to budget his time and establish professional goals. Carter considered the meetings with Turner vital. He wanted Turner to teach McGrady the need to be selfish. "Most coaches who don't understand young players view selfish as something bad," Carter said in recalling his reasoning. "My thing as a coach is, I can't get a player to be at the level he needs to be at unless he is selfish. He's got to be selfish to invest in himself sometimes."

McGrady improved, only to stumble on roadblocks. McGrady still did not know what it meant to be a professional. Carter fed him a steady diet of playing time, telling him that no matter what the score, he was to check into the game with six minutes remaining in the first quarter. Carter would routinely call a play for McGrady after he subbed in, designing it to quickly allow McGrady to take a shot and to ease into the flow of the game. A player, Carter believed, only gained confidence through playing and not if he was fearful that a coach would yank him out at the first mistake. But after one All-Star break, McGrady had returned to practice sluggish and was merely going through the motions. *His body is here,* Carter thought, *but his mind is still somewhere in Florida.* Carter instructed McGrady to miss all of his rotations in their next game. McGrady again found his back stuck to the bench. After the game, Carter told McGrady that this would be the result whenever he put so little effort into practicing. "Right then, he and I came to an agreement," Carter said. Smith and Hopkins soon came to appreciate Carter's push-and-pull approach in maturing McGrady. "I wanted Tracy to play," Smith recalled. "But ultimately, Butch was right. I was wrong. He wasn't playing, but with a young talent like that, you've got to bring him along."

Butch Carter's tactics yielded results sooner than Smith could have hoped, as McGrady quickly morphed into a star, seemingly overnight. In 1998, McGrady united with Vince Carter, his distant cousin, and the two become a potent combination. McGrady flashed all the signs of becoming a franchise player: he could shoot, handle the ball, and play defense. He was long and still young. McGrady's belief in himself had been built under Butch Carter's stewardship. "He cared more about the person than the player," McGrady said. "He made sure my mind was right. He knew that if my mind was right, then everything else would take care of itself and it helped me a lot." McGrady started being touted as a Sixth Man of the Year award candidate midway through his third season. He played magnificently in a first-round playoff loss to the Knicks, sometimes outshining Vince Carter, who had taken the league by storm with his otherworldly athleticism. "On that team, Tracy was the best defender, he could guard three positions," Butch Carter recalled. "He knew all the plays. He knew all the counters. He just wasn't strong enough to make a play in the fourth quarter the way Vince was."

McGrady's future was bright, but not in Toronto. He had just started showing signs of his future stardom by the time rumors surfaced that he wanted to be the team's main option, a role he could never fill while being Vince Carter's wingman, and that he craved the additional exposure he would receive by playing for a team in the

United States. He reached stardom at a juncture that worried every team nurturing high school players. Their understanding of the game and their fledgling contributions to a team would coincide with when they arrived at free agency, and the team had groomed them only for them to sign and peak elsewhere.

Jerry Krause waited to pounce. He came to believe that he had made a mistake in not obtaining McGrady outright as a rookie when he had the opportunity and now planned to lure him during free agency. His Bulls desperately needed McGrady. The collapse of their championship team was striking and swift. The Bulls slogged through the lockout-truncated season, winning 13 games, the worst in the Eastern Conference. They were rewarded with the draft's top pick in 1999 and took Elton Brand, a talented forward who became one of the first players to leave Duke University with remaining college eligibility. Brand played capably, but Chicago again faltered, finishing the season with a dismal 17–65 record. It was painful, but the struggle played into Krause's plan. A championship team could not be built overnight. He was biding his time, stockpiling high draft picks, preserving salary cap space, and awaiting the summer of 2000. He would recruit McGrady and other talented free agents like Tim Duncan and Grant Hill. McGrady had not been a starter throughout the bulk of his Toronto tenure. He wanted to be wooed and made to feel wanted. He had options. Toronto desperately wanted McGrady to stay put and even fired Butch Carter once dissension between the coach and his veteran players fractured the team. The Orlando Magic, like Chicago, had stockpiled salary space in hopes of landing a marquee player and reestablishing the team as the dominant franchise it had been before Shaquille O'Neal departed for the Lakers.

In July 2000, Tracy McGrady and Alvis Smith exited their plane from Orlando and walked out of Gate C-20 at Chicago's O'Hare International Airport. The city, not just the Bulls, gave them a hero's welcome. Two cheerleaders and the team's mascot, Benny the Bull, waved a banner, reading "T-Mac, Chicago's No. 1." A band performed "Sweet Home, Chicago," as fans shouted, "T-Mac! T-Mac!"

Jerry Krause and B. J. Armstrong, Jordan's former backcourt mate who had become Krause's assistant, awaited the pair and embraced. Krause regarded the meeting as more of a reunion than anything else. For McGrady, the scene was surreal. He imagined stepping outside of Vince Carter's shadow, taking Michael Jordan's torch, and leading the Bulls again into relevance. The trip spanned two days. McGrady listened to Krause's pitch, followed by one from Elton Brand; attended a Cubs–White Sox game; and cruised around Lake Michigan.

They dined him and piqued McGrady's interest. Krause did not know it, but McGrady had already made up his mind. He chose Orlando, making a deal for $67.5 million over six years at the age of 21. "Tracy never should have left Toronto, but there were two reasons: his guys couldn't get the deal he got with [McGrady's agent] Arn [Tellem] with the owners in Toronto because the owners in Toronto don't know jack about basketball," Butch Carter said. "They don't know anything about how these young guys are making their decisions and that it's the people around them. We brought Alvis Smith up there to see if he could sit down and cut a deal with [minority owner Larry] Tanenbaum, and Tanenbaum didn't have a clue. Everybody forgets that the league puts in these salary caps, so everybody says, 'OK, how do you manipulate the salary cap?' You get into the league sooner and you move your guys where you can get the greatest endorsement dollars."

The Magic possessed better role players, a dynamic young coach in Doc Rivers, and had also added Grant Hill. McGrady envisioned the duo as the next Jordan and Pippen. Most importantly, Orlando was home. "I worked for two years on Tracy," Krause recalled. "Through people around him, through him. But at the last moment, if I remember right, Tracy's mother killed the deal because she wanted him in Florida." McGrady recalled making the decision for himself. "Nothing was really going to take me away from signing back home," McGrady said. "Hindsight looking back? Of course, it would have been a perfect situation to stay right there [in Toronto]." The move was against the wishes of Alvis Smith, the first significant crack in their relationship. Smith told McGrady that he did not think the Magic would win and his body would be punished by absorbing a heavy workload. "I didn't want Tracy to go to the Orlando Magic," Smith recalled. "We had the choice to come here to Orlando or go to Chicago. I wanted him to go to Chicago, because I felt like their strengthening program was so much better than everybody else's." In Orlando, McGrady developed into one of the game's most dynamic scorers. But his penchant for not practicing hard had also trailed him home. "He was getting by just on ability, not ability and work ethic," said Johnny Davis, an assistant coach under Rivers in Orlando. "He didn't have the combination. It wasn't natural for him. Had he had a work ethic, maybe the standard of excellence for him would've been higher, both individually and in his ability to raise a team with his play." Hill suffered injuries that undermined his promising career. He was never again the premier player he had been in his early career in Detroit. True to Smith's prediction, McGrady was tasked with shouldering Orlando's workload and the team, with him, never made it out of the first round of the playoffs.

• • •

All along, Jerry Krause believed that skillful organizations obtained championships, not individual players. He had watched as the Celtics sat idly by as Larry Bird and the rest of Boston's core aged and the organization slipped into mediocrity. It was better, Krause thought, to rebuild on the fly and anticipate the inevitable need to overhaul. Twice now, Tracy McGrady had evaded him. But smart franchises possessed alternative blueprints for success. The Bulls suffered through another miserable season in 2000–2001 and finished with just 15 wins. Michael Jordan's Wizards had won the 2001 draft lottery. Krause's Bulls landed the fourth pick. He still judged that draft as one that could change his organization's fortunes. He had spent much of the season evaluating and scouting a quartet of talented high school seniors: Kwame Brown, Tyson Chandler, Eddy Curry, and DeSagana Diop, an unpolished teenager from Senegal with potential.

NBA executives anticipated that as many as six prep players could be taken at the 2001 draft, in New York's Madison Square Garden. The teenagers had spent so much time together that they had come to respect one another. This was a journey that they would start together. On the day before the draft, they talked among themselves, wondering who among them would be Michael Jordan's chosen heir. For weeks, Jordan entertained the notion of trading the pick and landing an established player or additional draft picks. Most of the teams picking immediately after Washington, including Jerry Krause's Bulls, made trade offers to Jordan for the top selection. In the end, he kept the pick, homing in on one player. Jordan made NBA history in taking Kwame Brown, who became the first player out of high school drafted first overall. Kevin Garnett, Kobe Bryant, Tracy McGrady, and other future All-Stars had to wait to be picked on their draft days. Brown stood up slowly from his seat after hearing his name and hugged his mother before smiling and shaking David Stern's hand. He had expected the announcement. Still, the moment moved him. "I've never been so overwhelmed and nervous in my life," Brown told reporters. "I'm now the representative of all high school seniors, and I have to show it wasn't a mistake."

"My big dream is to beat [Michael Jordan] one day," Brown would say at his introductory press conference in Washington, D.C. "That is a dream," Jordan concurred. He added in the conference: "We feel like we have a quality kid and his potential is unbelievable. We don't know what this kid is capable of doing—that's the beauty of why we drafted him. We don't know. In a couple of years, he may be a star."

The Clippers picked second. A year earlier, they had selected Darius Miles from East Saint Louis third overall, previously the highest a prep player had been chosen. It had been a learning experience for both him and the organization. The Clippers were awful. Miles did not have to earn his minutes. He was handed them. Miles became the first high schooler to be named to the NBA All-Rookie first team. He was amazingly athletic, but also immature. Miles declined to invest in his game over the summer through training. He told his coach, Alvin Gentry, that he wanted to act in a movie. The gig, Miles claimed, would net him $900,000. "Darius, do you understand that if you work on your game, you could get eighty-five million one day?" Gentry asked. The discrepancy did not seem to sink in. In 2001, the Clippers took an elated Tyson Chandler after the Wizards drafted Brown. Chandler was happy to stay near home, even if the Clippers had historically struggled. But the Clippers were hesitant about introducing consecutive high schoolers into the NBA and turning a young team younger. Unbeknownst to Chandler, they had a deal in place to send him to the Bulls if the draft unraveled the way Krause had hoped. It all depended on what the Hawks did with the third pick. Word had filtered back to him that the Hawks were interested in the big kid from Spain, Pau Gasol. Neither the Bulls nor the Wizards had spent much effort evaluating Gasol, but they would realize their mistake later. Herb Rudoy, who had represented Darryl Dawkins, became Gasol's agent. He asked Washington's Rod Higgins to take another look at Gasol in the days leading up to the draft. But Washington was set on Brown. "That was before the [international] scouting aspect really blew up," Higgins said. "We weren't prepared for it, I'll say it like that. He snuck under the radar big-time." Krause said he had been advised by others in his organization that Gasol was not worth scouting. Gasol later developed into a multidimensional interior player, and finally joined the Bulls in 2014 after winning two championships with the Lakers. "This is not to demean anybody, but we were told not to see Gasol," Krause said. "Whoever was in charge of that thing kept saying, 'Don't see him.' We said 'OK.' Was that a mistake? Probably, yes. We should have seen him. We didn't." The Hawks indeed selected Gasol with the third pick and traded his draft rights to the Memphis Grizzlies.

Jerry Krause felt a surge of adrenaline. Gasol's selection had facilitated his plan. Krause played the greatest all-in hand with high schoolers the NBA would ever witness. He took Eddy Curry with the fourth pick and agreed to trade Elton Brand to the Clippers for the rights to Chandler. He had decided earlier that he would only make the trade if Curry was still on the board for Chicago's pick. Krause specifically wanted to pair the two in his frontcourt. Brand had been one of Chicago's few bright spots after Jordan's departure. He had earned co–Rookie of the Year honors with Steve Francis and appeared destined to average 20 points and 10 rebounds throughout his career. He was established and dependable. But he was short and the organization reached the conclusion that Brand had already maximized his talent at a young age. Curry and Chandler were new, the promise of their potential limitless. Krause believed that Chandler and Curry could co-dominate the NBA. Even Brand did not argue with the logic. "You've got these two young guys, one's a seven-foot pogo stick and the other's a six-foot-ten-inch three-hundred-pounder that can do back flips," Brand said. The Bulls had judged the big men in college and high school who would likely matriculate into the league over the next few years. None of the prospects on the horizon matched up to Chandler and Curry. Krause felt as if he had cornered the future market of interior players. He had not felt such elation since landing Scottie Pippen and Horace Grant in the same draft 14 years earlier. "There were a lot of people who said we were nuts, and we took those kids in the same year," Krause recalled. Chandler, Krause thought, was the better defender. Curry, he decided, needed the shortest time to develop an NBA offensive game. Krause filled out the rest of the roster with veteran players like Charles Oakley and Greg Anthony. "We knew taking two of them was a risk," Krause said. "But we also felt they were the two best players available at that point. Obviously, we didn't think it was enough of a risk to stop us."

Jamal Crawford had hosted Chandler on his unofficial visit to the University of Michigan a few months earlier. The pair laughed when Crawford informed Chandler that he had been the subject of one of Crawford's class discussions about the ethics of showering a high school basketball player with attention and adulation. Crawford had also become fast friends with Curry when Curry visited the Bulls before a game during his senior year of high school. Now the trio were teammates, known as the "Baby Bulls." Crawford already wore number 1 on his jersey. Chandler asked to wear number 2, but John Ligmanowski, the equipment manager, cautioned against it. Every recent player who had worn that number had been traded, cut, or injured. Chandler opted to wear number 3. An undaunted Curry requested number 2. "Gonna break the curse," he declared.

Just a few months later, tiny bolts of electricity coursed through Eddy Curry's body during the pregame layup line. This was it. He was here, in the NBA, with the Bulls, about to open a season of renewed expectations at the United Center against the Indiana Pacers. Curry gazed into the crowd. His family and friends sat in the stands. He had bought an extra 26 tickets to accommodate them all. He wanted to do so much. He did not know how much he would play. When he did, he hoped to quickly find the game's rhythm and settle down. Bulls coach Tim Floyd summoned Curry into the game's first half in place of Brad Miller. When Krause had hired Floyd to replace Phil Jackson, the former Iowa State coach held on to the fading hope that Jordan would still return to play for the Bulls. Now, Floyd was entering the fourth year of a rebuilding plan with no expiration date in sight. His team's fortunes hinged on the development of two teenagers. Floyd doubted that he had ever depended on two freshman as heavily when he was a college coach.

Unfortunately for Curry, the game did not slow down. If anything, the pace quickened faster than he had ever imagined basketball could be played. Curry air-balled his first shot as Chandler sat idling on the bench. The teams played closely in the first half and the Bulls pulled to within 65–64 with a little over a minute remaining in the fourth quarter. The Bulls switched to a zone defense. Jermaine O'Neal, long and wiry, found the gaps inside it. O'Neal, who had entered the NBA five years earlier, had finally found a home and a fit in Indiana. He had been good enough to play in Portland, but was buried within a talented, veteran roster. While in Portland, the birth of his daughter, Asjia, accelerated his maturation. He had first met Mesha Roper at the Adidas headquarters when she was still a student at Portland State University. The two began dating, and it wasn't long before O'Neal told Roper the same thing he had once told his mother: he wanted to be a father as a young man. As with his early entry to the NBA, he knew he was not prepared, but he was ready to throw everything he had into parenthood. "I knew I was going to be the best father that I could possibly be," O'Neal recalled. "I just felt like that was one way for me to get out all the hurt, anger, and pain that I had toward my father—because he wasn't around, because he didn't care enough to support me and treat me like a kid's supposed to be treated." Because he was unhappy with his lack of playing time in Portland, the Trail Blazers had traded O'Neal and Joe Kleine to Indiana for Dale Davis, an All-Star. Indiana executive Donnie Walsh and Isiah Thomas, who had become Indiana's coach after a power struggle in Toronto, agreed to take a gamble on the little-used O'Neal. They traded Davis—an Indiana staple who had led the Pacers in rebounding for seven straight seasons—for O'Neal, an unknown quantity. For the first time in his career, O'Neal was far from the team's youngest player. Indiana had drafted high schoolers Al Harrington and Jonathan Bender in successive years to pair with veterans like Reggie Miller, Rik Smits, and Travis Best. Thomas had followed O'Neal since his high school career in Indiana. He compared granting O'Neal an opportunity to a teacher spotting potential in a troubled student. They lived near each other in Indiana and O'Neal spent many hours at Thomas's home. O'Neal's minutes skyrocketed in Indiana, from 12.3 per game in his final season in Portland to 32.6 per game in his first year with the Pacers.

Against Chicago, O'Neal scored 20 of his 25 points in the second half, giving Indiana a healthy lead. He also dunked over Curry, who missed five of his six shots, securing a layup in the meaningless final minute of Indiana's 98–73 victory. Chandler did not fare much better and hardly played, ending with one free throw and two missed shots in six minutes.

The season quickly worsened for the Bulls. They never stood much of a chance. The team's makeup was ill conceived with a coach who had tired of projects. Instead of developing Chandler and Curry through playing time, Floyd elected to play the team's elder veterans. The rookies played erratically, sporadically. The Bulls lost 12 of their first 13 games. After one early-season defeat, a loss by nearly 30 points in Orlando, a dejected Chandler cried in the locker room. He had been used to winning throughout his life and the constant losing started weighing on him. Fans, Chandler believed, did not judge him as being a finished product, but he was still expected to be a contributor, one worthy of his high draft slot. At that time, he was neither. "What's your problem?" Floyd asked Chandler.

"What do you mean what's my problem?" Chandler asked. Floyd repeated his question.

"Losing's my problem," Chandler responded.

"If you can't handle losing in the NBA, you won't have a long career," Floyd said.

"I don't want to be able to handle it," Chandler responded through his tears.

Floyd resigned 25 games into the season. He was replaced by Bill Cartwright, who had once been considered to have enough talent to jump to the NBA from high school in the days of Bill Willoughby and Darryl Dawkins. Cartwright had been one of the league's most respected and feared big men. He sought to teach Curry and Chandler the fundamentals of the game. He soon realized that the commitment extended beyond the basketball court. Krause had hired a cook for the organization, essentially charged with preparing the two teenagers breakfast and lunch. Curry had two Rottweiler puppies and wondered who would take care of them when the team traveled for road games. When a police officer informed Curry that he could not drive his new all-terrain vehicle in the city, he simply parked it at the Bulls' training center, abandoning it there for weeks. "Even though they are two separate people, each of them has their own challenges," Cartwright said. "They were the same challenges of being away from home. Even though Eddy lived here, he was still on his own. And they were both dealing with family and friends, getting around, everything that a kid would go through their freshman year of college, except now they're dealing with it in real life." Krause scheduled regular meetings to gauge the progress of the pair on and off the court. He decided, soon after, to meet with them one-on-one instead. Chandler, he found, was much more mature. "They were two different kinds of kids," Krause recalled.

"They were both real good kids. That's why we took them. We had faith in the fact they would both mature." On advice from those in the Bulls organization, both bypassed living downtown and rented condominiums near the team's suburban practice facility. Tom Lewis moved in with Chandler, and the two kept busy during downtime by playing video games and pool. Lewis came to feel pity for Curry, who seemed to have everyone around him with their hand out but nobody to pat his back or offer guidance. Donnie Kirksey, a former mentor to Curry, routinely witnessed that behavior from those close to NBA players. "You're fighting things from parents who want to get things, you have friends who have their agendas, you have girls and baby mamas," Kirksey said. "It was just so much. It was just so much distraction for him, and if he looks back over it, he would do it different."

To Chandler, it was as if the organization had drafted the pair, hitching its future with theirs, without a strategy to develop them. "The toughest thing for me was there wasn't much of a plan, now looking back at it, for myself and Eddy," Chandler said. That the fate of the franchise was on his shoulders eluded Curry. "I didn't really realize it until later on," Curry said. "We were young. We were having fun, working hard. We didn't realize we were the ones supposed to turn the whole thing around." In 2003, Jerry Krause retired from the Bulls, citing health issues. He still believed that he had left a core in place that would reel the Bulls back into competitiveness. Chicago had just missed the playoffs for the fifth straight season. Jay Williams, a point guard who had joined the team by then, had quickly noticed the difference between Chandler and Curry. "When Tyson would make a big-time play, he would come off the court and he would be so pumped up that you could see the emotion on his face," Williams recalled. "He had that kind of passion about the game. When Eddy would make a big play, he wouldn't have any emotion. It was kind of like a stone-cold killer. He had that look, but maybe not that mentality of a killer."

16.

A familiar stage and setting awaited Michael Jordan. He only needed a flick of his wrist and a wag of his tongue to seal the accustomed ending. The game had tightened at Madison Square Garden and the time had dwindled. The ball found Jordan's capable hands. He was 38, his frame bulkier now than the lithe one that had once flown around arenas across the country. His jersey was altogether foreign, that of the Wizards and no longer the Bulls. He had again returned as an NBA player after three years in retirement. The announcement surprised few and seemed inevitable after weeks of leaked whispers concerning his clandestine workouts. Some fans had left the NBA when Jordan did, a departure reflected in slipping television ratings, and hoped he could recapture his previous feats or, even better, add to them. Others worried that he would tarnish the last impression he'd left as a player, an image time-capsuled with his picturesque jumper over Bryon Russell and the Jazz in the 1998 finals. Washington had been a failing franchise for years. Suddenly, Jordan breathed life and dollars into the organization. Nike, likewise, could count on a spike in sales through Jordan's personal shoe and clothing line, Air Jordan.

The brand alone represented about $300 million of the company's annual sales.

The Wizards trailed the Knicks by three points in his first game back in late 2001, with about 16 seconds remaining. Jordan rose, releasing a three-point shot from the right wing. He had tendinitis in his shooting hand. His knees were already bothering him from his hurried attempt to rush back into playing shape. The ball fell short, kissed iron, and gently careened into the hands of the Knicks' Kurt Thomas. Jordan was mostly un-Jordan-like. He managed 19 points, but missed 14 of his 21 shots. "The biggest difference is I'm a little bit older than the last time I shot the ball," Jordan said in a news conference after the game. "My game's a little bit different, my teammates are a little bit different."

Kwame Brown was one of those new teammates. Originally, Brown had enjoyed being drafted by Jordan and handpicked by the best man to ever play the game. On one of those hot and humid Georgia days, Brunswick held Kwame Brown Day the July after he had been drafted. Brown traveled by motorcade to a parade at the city's old city hall. Brad Brown, Brunswick's mayor, had never felt short in his life until he handed Brown the city's key and a proclamation. Slowly, Brown felt confident about this new step in his life. He had left behind the doubt he had expressed with Billy Donovan. In Brunswick, he could not escape his newfound celebrity. He wanted a place where he could be himself and not constantly be pestered for autographs, to pose for pictures, or to dispense advice. He thought he could evade some of the spotlight in Gainesville. But one night he engaged in a scuffle at a bar and injured his shooting hand.

Doug Collins found Brown distracted. That Jordan had hired Collins to coach the franchise represented something of a surprise. Years ago, a young Jordan had played under Collins in Chicago. Collins was once an excellent player himself and a teammate of Darryl Dawkins's in Philadelphia. As a coach, he drove his players hard, alienating some, and possessed a drive to work and obsess over the game that few shared. A younger Jordan perhaps did not appreciate Collins's compulsions. He did not interfere when the organization fired Collins in 1989 after leading the Bulls to their first conference finals in 15 years. In time, Jordan had come to appreciate Collins's approach and wanted a passionate, knowledgeable coach for his Wizards. By then, Collins had come to accept that the young generation of players was hard to coach. He had enjoyed his time as a basketball analyst; he was regarded as one of the game's best commentators. Yet he accepted the challenge in 2001 when Jordan beckoned. Brown's cell phone went off incessantly during one of his first meetings with Collins. Collins asked Brown to turn it off. But Brown's mind was already split between helping his family financially and accepting his newfound celebrity. Collins worried about the external factors tugging at Brown. He wanted Brown to concentrate fully on basketball and basketball alone. "You saw this young player who was six feet eleven inches, two hundred forty pounds, quick, could run, and you start thinking about all the potential for this young guy," Collins remembered. "What happens is you get burdened with being that number one pick and all the pressure that goes with that."

That season, the NBA experimented with a pilot program to mentor younger players. A few teams hired recently retired players to help the organization's younger players assimilate into the NBA lifestyle. Duane Ferrell was appointed to Washington. Ferrell had starred for Georgia Tech in college and retired in 1999 after playing several seasons in the NBA. To Ferrell, it seemed that a team's veteran players were all about 32 or 33 when he had played. Suddenly, in the new NBA, a player could be regarded as a veteran yet only be a couple years older than a rookie. The Wizards boasted a cadre of young players, like Brendan Haywood, Bobby Simmons, and Richard Hamilton. They had all experienced college life. Ferrell ended up devoting the bulk of his time and effort to Brown. "All eyes were on him, the expectations were on him, the future of the franchise was on his shoulders," Ferrell said. "There was a lot of responsibility and I don't even think he could perceive of how people would view him being the number one pick." The expectations of Brown had heightened beyond his control. With Jordan's return, he could no longer be brought along and developed slowly. The reclamation of the Wizards was no longer a years-long project. Jordan's window to win was short. In order for Jordan's return to be a success and the Wizards to be competitive, Brown had to contribute immediately. "Michael didn't have much time left in the tank to really make the Wizards respectable and profitable as an owner and as a player," Ferrell recalled. "His window was very small, and Kwame needed to make a huge leap in a matter of months and he was just not ready for that."

Ferrell felt that Brown had grown up too fast. Brown was quiet by nature. It took time for them to develop a relationship. The team's younger players, Brown included, occasionally tested Ferrell by committing minor indiscretions to see if word of them would trickle back to Collins, Jordan, or Rod Higgins. Ferrell, likewise, treated every misstep as a teaching opportunity, one where he could hopefully guide and influence his young charges. Ferrell came to learn of Brown's splintered family and lack of male role models, that he had been looked on and talked to as an adult from an early age. Brown was mature in some aspects of life, but painfully naive in others. Things routine to Ferrell were utterly foreign to Brown. Brown once phoned Ferrell during the team's training camp in Jordan's hometown of Wilmington, North Carolina. "Duane, I'm hungry," Brown said.

"What do you mean you're hungry?" Ferrell said. "You got your per diem."

"I'm hungry but I don't feel like going anywhere," Brown said.

"Why don't you just order room service?" Ferrell asked.

"What's room service?" Brown inquired.

"Really?" Ferrell said. "You see that book in your room on the coffee table? Grab that and go through that and you can order something to eat. They'll bring it to your room."

Joyce Brown had planned to relocate with her son. But Kwame Brown wanted to live alone and enjoy his independence for the first time. He moved into an apartment in Alexandria, Virginia, with John Richards, a law-student friend from Brunswick. Richards left shortly into the arrangement. At the urging of Arn Tellem, one of his associates, Richard Lopez, moved in with Brown. Lopez, like Ferrell, found that he devoted most of his time to helping Brown learn life's practicalities, like washing clothes and how to shop for groceries. Still, Brown enjoyed his new life. He quickly traded the beat-up, borrowed car from his mentor, John Williams, for a Mercedes S500, even if he had little idea how to navigate Washington, D.C.'s confusing streets.

During a scrimmage at his first training camp, Brown argued for a foul, feeling he had been unnecessarily hacked by veterans Jahidi White and Christian Laettner. The *Washington Post*'s Michael Leahy reported that Jordan approached Brown. "You fucking flaming faggot," he said to Brown, according to Leahy. "You don't get a foul call on a goddamn little touch foul, you fucking faggot. You don't bring that faggoty shit here. Get your goddamn ass back on the floor and play. I don't want to hear that fucking shit out of you again. Get your ass back and play, you faggot." Jordan could be nurturing one moment and unrelenting the next. He would build people up only to strip them of their confidence, either through verbal jabs or by making them feel hopeless on defense. Jordan had acted that way throughout his entire career. It was his method of finding who could play through pressure. Brown, part of a younger generation unaccustomed to those types of verbal attacks, wilted. "Michael would push his buttons to try to get him going, but Mike did that with everyone," Ferrell said. "He wanted to see who he could trust at the end of the game, so he would challenge you mentally, physically to see if you would break down. He would find out exactly who you are. Kwame didn't have that kind of pride and venom that Mike had as a player. There was no one in the gym that had it. Kwame wasn't the only one, but it was the simple fact that Michael wanted to test him, to see what he had in him."

In that training camp, Brown often looked lost. He was out of shape and sulked. He wore an expression of bewilderment and regret that Ferrell would remember for years. *He looks like he doesn't know if he made the right decision to come straight to the pros*, Ferrell thought. Ferrell opted not to talk to Brown about the look afterward. Brown, he knew, could not retrace his steps. He was a professional now, whether he regretted the decision or not, whether he was ready or not. The learning curve would only get steeper, not easier.

"Kwame, why can't you get this concept?" an exasperated Collins asked during one practice.

Brown always talked back whenever Collins tried tutoring him. The retorts only further frustrated Collins. Ferrell did not view Brown's acts as disrespectful. It was just another sign that Brown had grown up fast and two-way conversations between adults had been normal all his life. "Why won't you just let me play?" Brown asked.

"Because you don't know how to play," Collins responded.

Collins did not realize what a blank slate Brown was. He often instructed Ferrell to pull Brown to the side and talk with him as Collins continued instructing the rest of the team. "What's wrong?" Ferrell asked Brown.

"I've never played man-to-man defense before," Brown said. The response shocked Ferrell. Man-to-man defense, the ability of one player to guard another, was one of the game's staples and should be one of the first learning points for any player at any level. "Are you serious?" Ferrell asked.

"Yeah, they would just tell me to stand in the middle and put my hands up and play zone," Brown said.

Brown had concentrated on lifting weights and gaining mass after being drafted. He felt that he had to add muscle in order to battle his older competition. In doing so, he had sacrificed his quickness and agility, traits that had endeared him to the organization. The taxing training sessions took a toll on his maturing body. He hurt his back and his hamstring. Combined with his hand injury from Gainesville, Brown was behind before he had even started. Brown was a physical presence without any offensive go-to move. He was likable and wanted to be liked by his teammates. He shunned being the guy, but wanted to be one of the guys. But the constant criticism from Collins and Jordan caused his confidence to plummet. He felt that he had given them all the respect he could, yet got none in return. He was a statue when he did play, afraid to do anything out of fear he would be doing it wrong. "Kwame had great troubles in having great practices," said Johnny Bach, an assistant coach under Collins. "He just didn't have them. He had some people around him that came up from his home-town and tried to help him. Everyone tried to help him, but frankly, looking back, that added to everyone's expectations."

Brown sprained his ankle in the loss to the Knicks during Jordan's first game back and sat out Washington's next four games. His goal during the games was not to dominate or even contribute. He just concentrated on doing his best not to look bad. The Wizards lost 9 of their first 11 games. Jordan would show flashes of his previous self, but it was obvious he was not the same player he'd been. His own struggles to confront athletic mortality and the overall haplessness of the Wizards bothered him incessantly. Jordan began ostracizing himself from his teammates and Brown, who had once looked to him as a mentor. Brown felt as though he was being blamed for all of the organization's misfortunes. By midseason, stress caused Brown's face to erupt in acne. He had trouble breathing on the court. Collins, who has said he would have approached Brown's NBA introduction differently if handed a do-over, finally noticed the pressure on Brown and placed him on the injured list. As Brown's early career trudged on, Ferrell continued to check in on him. Ferrell would notice beer cans scattered throughout Brown's home when he visited. "C'mon Kwame," Ferrell would say. "You can't have cans of beers all around and be partying like this. That's not going to do it." Ferrell attributed it all to a spiraling downward cycle. Brown's confidence wavered. His play tightened on the court. He played worse, causing him to play less. He lost more confidence.

"You're trying to get out there and play and live up to the demand of excellence," Collins said. "But in the back of your mind, you're telling yourself, *I knew I wasn't ready for this.*" Brown's relationship with Jordan continued to deteriorate. Charles Oakley, one of Jordan's close friends and de facto body guards, came to the Wizards in 2002. Oakley had experience not just in the NBA, but in introducing young players to the league. He was in Toronto when Tracy McGrady first showed his promise and he played with Tyson Chandler and Eddy Curry in Chicago during their rookie year. In Toronto, he told McGrady and Vince Carter that he would support them. In Chicago, he was outspoken when he felt that Tim Floyd had attributed the bulk of the team's struggles to Chandler and Curry. He wanted to ease the way for younger players, but no one messed with Jordan in Oakley's presence. Oakley watched as Brown one day swiped a cup of Gatorade from Jordan's hands. Brown sat down, ready to drink from the cup. Oakley took it from Brown's hands and proceeded to dump it over Brown's head. "We were just dying laughing, because nobody was going to mess with Oakley," Ferrell recalled. "Kwame just sat there and they all just laughed."

• • •

B y the time Washington finally turned a corner as a franchise, both Michael Jordan and Kwame Brown had unceremoniously left the organization. Jordan could only replicate his past feats occasionally in the two seasons that spanned his return. The thought of his old self returning drove more fear into opponents than his actual abilities. He was crafty and had a jab step, the threat of him driving to the rim to make a defender backpedal, allowing him space to pull up for a jumper, became his primary offensive weapon. The Wizards suffered an all-too-familiar blowout in mid-April 2003, this time against the Philadelphia 76ers. Jordan had returned to the bench midway through the fourth quarter with just 13 points. Philadelphia fans, sensing it would be Jordan's final appearance as a player, began chanting his name. Collins prodded Jordan to reenter for one final cameo. He needed that needling, but finally obliged. Philadelphia's Eric Snow intentionally fouled Jordan, who stroked two free throws for the last of his 32,292 career points and checked back out to a deafening three-minute standing ovation. He waved with his right hand and grinned widely, embarrassed at the prolonged farewell. The moment provided his final worthwhile memory in Washington. Jordan had hoped to revert to his prior role with the franchise as president of basketball operations. To return as a player, Jordan had had to sell his stake in the team and relinquish his power. Abe Pollin declined to allow Jordan back in his former role. Jordan felt betrayed. He had drummed up remarkable interest in the organization and the team, only to have Pollin turn his back on him. In a final insult, Pollin offered to pay Jordan $10 million as a sign of appreciation. Their meeting devolved into a spate of name calling. After a brief respite, the relationship had come full circle to when Jordan and Pollin had clashed during the lockout.

Brown did not last much longer as a Wizard. Washington finally qualified for the playoffs in 2005 under Doug Collins's replacement, Eddie Jordan (unrelated to Michael Jordan). Brown called in sick to a practice and morning shoot-around in Washington's first-round playoff series against Chicago. He was more upset than anything, having played a season-low four minutes in the previous game. That represented the final straw for Eddie Jordan and Ernie Grunfeld, the executive who replaced Michael Jordan. They suspended Brown. Renewed optimism had existed for Brown when the pair first inherited the team. Everything had clicked for players like Kobe Bryant and Tracy McGrady in their third NBA seasons. Instead, Brown suffered through an injury-riddled season. When healthy, he played unreliably and unremarkably. The outsized expectations, to his detriment, remained. When Brown checked into a game against Seattle in January 2005, Washington's home audience uniformly booed. A beaten Brown told Michael Lee, who covered the team for the *Washington Post,* that he could not fault the reaction from the fans. "They knew I was injured," he said. "They knew my foot was hurt. From a fan perspective, they see this big guy coming in, they're like, 'What is he going to do?' If I was out there, I would've second-guessed the coach. I would've booed, too. I would've said the same thing." Washington traded Brown to the Lakers in the summer of 2005. "It was a tough adjustment for him mentally," recalled Brendan Haywood, drafted to the Wizards the same summer as Brown. "Coming in with Michael Jordan on the team, there was an immense pressure and [it] didn't really work out well for him in D.C. If he would have went somewhere else, he probably would have ended up being a way better basketball player. He was super talented, one of the strongest yet quickest bigs I've played against."

If Brown's career was judged by his lofty draft status, it collapsed far short of expectations. Even Tyson Chandler came to the conclusion that he himself had been better off not being drafted first. "Some of the stories that I heard Kwame had to endure and go through, I felt like it took a toll on him and ultimately his career, his confidence," Chandler said. "It probably worked out best for me to be drafted second." In the end, few players actually match the outsize projections of their younger days. Judged by a different standard, one of stability and longevity, Brown's career evolved into a success. He rededicated himself as a strong, sturdy defensive player. He was not a star by any means and bounced around the NBA. Yet, he found a contract and somewhere to play into his 30s in a league tailored for younger men with constant turnover. "He relaxed because the heat wasn't on him as much as he moved on," Ferrell said. "I'm happy for him because I didn't think he was going to last that long, to be honest."

Oddly enough, both Michael Jordan and Doug Collins later acquired Brown on their next teams. Jordan landed Brown in Charlotte, where he had become the franchise's majority owner. "With Kwame, I thought as he got older and particularly when he was with the Lakers, he was a hell of a defender on those low-post scorers," said Rod Higgins, who also joined Charlotte as its general manager. "When you come in as a high school player, you don't know who you are. If his mind-set was to come into the league and say, 'I want to be the next Ben Wallace,' he probably could have been the next Ben Wallace. But when you come out of high school, you have all of these thoughts of what you think you should be. You might not ever be what you think you should be." In 2012, Collins signed Brown in Philadelphia, where he had become coach of the 76ers. "As time went on, Kwame found his niche," Collins said. "He had gotten to a point in his career where he had hung his hat on defending the post, rebounding, doing the things to help your team win."

Tyson Chandler, of the three lauded big men taken at the top of the 2001 draft, was the only one who came close to reaching his potential. He only reached that destination after struggling for years.

Through it all, he came to believe that his efforts would eventually pay dividends. He left fantasies of becoming another Rasheed Wallace by the wayside. He concentrated on his defense, listening to Bill Cartwright's instructions that the best offensive players were susceptible to bad games, but a defensive stalwart could successfully impact his team day in and day out.

The Bulls hired Scott Skiles as coach in 2003. Skiles had little use for nonsense and became the type of driver Eddy Curry needed as motivation. Skiles had been a hard-nosed point guard as a player. He questioned Curry's passion to play the game. A reporter once asked Skiles what Curry needed to do in order to improve his rebounding. Skiles famously and simply replied, "Jump." For much of 2004–2005, Chandler and Curry became the dynamic duo that Krause once envisioned: Curry, the scorer, and Chandler, the defender and antagonist. "He's always been a great defender," Curry said of Chandler. "He was always a real hard-nosed player. Back then, I think we really fed off each other. What I lacked in defense, he picked it up and then some." The Bulls improved by 24 games that season and qualified for the playoffs for the first time since Jordan left. Curry paced the team in scoring. An irregular heartbeat sidelined him before the playoffs. Doctors cleared him to practice, but the organization pushed for him to undergo DNA testing to assess whether he had a congenital heart condition. Curry declined on privacy grounds, even though the Bulls offered to pay him a $400,000 annuity for 50 years if the test revealed a defect that prevented him from playing. Before either side could resolve the issue, the Knicks traded for Curry. The dream of a devastating Curry-and-Chandler combination had ended before either turned 23 years old. Chandler lasted one more year in Chicago. His confidence had swooned. He often did not even look for his shot on offense. His scoring and rebounding both dropped precipitously. The home crowd occasionally booed him. The Bulls traded Chandler to the Hornets in the summer of 2006 for J. R. Smith and P. J. Brown. Chandler represented the last Krause pick on Chicago's roster.

Curry initially found success in New York. He played under Isiah

Thomas, who centered his offense around Curry. Curry averaged a career-best 19.5 points and 7 rebounds and scored 43 points in an overtime victory against Milwaukee. "He was like most young players," Thomas remembered. "He loved to play and hadn't necessarily gathered the NBA know-how. There is a certain four-, five-, six-year stage that you go through of growth in the NBA where you're still kind of learning the ropes and having a good time and traveling, meeting people, playing basketball, and having fun. Then, the second stage of that is, 'OK. I've had enough fun. Now I want to win championships and be a part of a championship team and a championship organization.'" But Curry soon lost whatever confidence he had gained. The Knicks acquired Zach Randolph in the 2007 off-season and Thomas envisioned merging the two prodigious interior talents into an unstoppable offensive frontcourt. Randolph and Curry, he imagined, would score from either side of the block, and no one offensive player would be able to penetrate the interior with the two big men standing guard in the paint. Instead, Curry and Randolph got in each other's way on offense. They rarely guarded on defense. Randolph, the slightly better defensive player of the two, claimed most of the minutes. Curry's minutes became infrequent. "I could never tell with Eddy," said Donnie Walsh, who became the Knicks' president after leaving Indiana. "I wanted to think he knew what kind of career he could have and that he was trying to do it. But I can't give you the answer." Curry's on-court struggles soon paled in comparison to his off-the-court financial issues and personal tragedies. Armed burglars tied up Curry and his family and robbed them at their Chicago-area home in 2007. His ex-girlfriend and infant daughter were murdered a year and a half later. "He had a lot of real life-altering things going on, and it was like one after the other," said Quentin Richardson, his teammate in New York for four seasons. "You could take any of those things and it would be a huge deal, and he had several of them one after another." A bank began foreclosure proceedings on his Chicago-area home, and Curry was sued multiple times over nonpayment for jewelry and clothing. "Mr. Curry appears to be a very, very generous man," Donald David, a lawyer for Allstar Capital, who lent money to Curry, told the *New York Daily News*. "He appears to have taken it upon himself to support every person named Curry on the East Coast." Curry asked the Knicks for a substantial advance of millions of his salary, despite contributing little on the court midway through a contract that paid him $60 million over six years.

Ironically, Chandler eventually became the interior defensive player the Knicks badly coveted. He had arrived in New Orleans into the care of Hornets coach Byron Scott after his trade from Chicago. Scott had studied Chandler when Chandler had played in high school. He hardly recognized the player who showed up to practice in New Orleans. "Most people when they first looked at Tyson wanted him to be the next Kevin Garnett, because when he was in high school he was a seven-footer who could make the jump shot," Scott said. "But when you get to the pros, you have to adjust your game for the betterment of the team, and he was able to do that. He had lost a lot of confidence on the offensive end, but could still get some things done if put in the right situation." Scott told Chandler that he could and should average a double-double. He called plays for him in the post. Chris Paul, New Orleans's All-Star point guard, often put Chandler in the right situation by delivering him passes near the basket. Chandler grabbed a career-high 12.4 rebounds and averaged 9.5 points in 2006–2007. He had carved out his niche in the league. He advanced to anchor the Mavericks championship team in 2011, earn a gold medal in London at the 2012 Olympic Games, and was named the NBA Defensive Player of the Year with the Knicks. He found stability in the NBA and in his life, a state that eluded Curry. "I knew Eddy's career would go one of two ways because of his personality," Chandler said. "I'm not saying that as a shot by any means because I love Eddy. I still think to this day, Eddy could have been the best big man of our generation. He had all the tools. It was just the circumstances that led him to not pan out to what myself and others had expected of him. But I always thought he had the ability. It was always about work ethic."

17.

A basketball player's success relies on unflinching confidence. A player who believes he will miss a shot usually misses it. If he hesitates after making one errant shot, that mind-set will infect his next attempts. The best players are confident to the point of cockiness. Basketball players from New York City exemplify that mentality. They don't just want to win. They have to, as though their masculinity is on the line each time they step onto a court. The city is touted as the mecca of basketball, where outsiders make pilgrimages to see if they can play with the best at famed parks like Rucker and West Fourth Street. The city once clutched that title and reputation rightfully. In its day, it produced some of the finest players ever to play the game, those like Kareem Abdul-Jabbar, Bob Cousy, and Tiny Archibald. In later years, the standing turned ceremonial and reverential. The Knicks last celebrated an NBA championship in 1973. The number of New York schoolyard prodigies who rose from the playground to the NBA likewise dwindled. False prophets came along often. The lights shone brightly and early on any player who developed young in New York. Nearly all stumbled, slipped, and collapsed on their path to greatness.

Brooklyn's Stephon Marbury was the most recent to veer from that path. He flashed signs of dominance as a quick, powerful point guard who could hoist a long jumper with the same ease with which he shot a layup. But that same mentality and conviction that had aided him in his rise to the NBA afflicted him as a professional. He became a malcontent, part of the new class of players seeking to be catered to by organizations and awarded huge contracts before proving worthy of them. Marbury became an All-Star, but also a sizable headache for teams as he ping-ponged around the league. A few years later, Sebastian Telfair, Marbury's cousin, earned similar acclaim. Telfair was a ballyhooed Brooklyn point guard who signed a large contract with Adidas and became the focal point of a front page *New York Times* article before ever stepping onto an NBA court. He declared for the 2004 draft out of high school, passing on a commitment to the University of Louisville. The Portland Trail Blazers selected Telfair with the 13th overall selection. But Telfair's career fell well short of the predicted stardom and he became little more than a journeyman throughout his NBA career. When Portland GM John Nash drafted Telfair, he recalled telling him that because of his diminutive size, he would have to pressure the other point guards on defense and push the ball on offense in order to be successful. Instead, Nash said, Telfair preferred playing in a stationary offense. "He learned pretty quickly he was getting his shot blocked a lot because of his size," Nash said. "He just wasn't big enough to go to the basket and deal with big guys. His confidence took a hit after a while."

Lenny Cooke was sandwiched between Marbury and Telfair as New York's next hyped and talented phenom. In the summer of 2000, Cooke arrived at the ABCD camp ranked among high school's best players. He wanted to depart as the best. "I'm leaving with MVP," he boasted to Debbie Bortner as he climbed out of her truck at Fairleigh Dickinson University. Players made reputations in New York. They became legends at ABCD. A strong couple of days at the camp could propel a high school player to the same echelon among NBA scouts as two or three solid years playing at a major university, like Duke or North Carolina. The successes among camp graduates, like Kobe Bryant and Tracy McGrady, increased the camp's mass appeal. If you wanted to be the best, you played against the best and the best came to the ABCD camp. Through the years, the roster did not drastically overshadow the talent Nike lured to its camp. Yet, Nike no longer featured Sonny Vaccaro, who was a siren to the young players as he built relationships and established bonds. "Sonny had a braggadocio about him like he was a prizefighter," Chris Rivers recalled fondly. "Sonny had no problem telling you what was about to happen. He was a promoter." Rivers aligned himself with Vaccaro in 1997 after coaching the Oakland Soldiers, one of the premier AAU teams on the West Coast. His job evolved into forging relationships with players and their families and staying in contact with them throughout the course of the year. Of course, the relationship would be mutual, and the beginning of a link with Adidas would form. Every year, it seemed, the camp featured an epic showdown between prospects who would be in the NBA within a year or two. Shortly after Cooke had made his declaration to Bortner, the camp buzzed about the on-court confrontation between Kwame Brown and Eddy Curry. Only, Rivers could not find Curry the day of the matchup. He banged on hotel door after hotel door, amazed that somehow a teenager as large as Curry could disappear. He finally found Curry, who had overslept in the room of a friend. Curry shrugged off his drowsiness and he and Brown put on the advertised show. "It was the game of the week," Rivers remembered. "He and Kwame went at it and everybody knew they were going to be some of the top picks in the draft." Still, Rivers provided a disclaimer to those who came to the camp. "If you've got a guy and you think he's *that guy,* I will give him the stage to prove it. But the bright lights are too bright for a lot of people."

Not for Lenny Cooke. He walked on the courts as though he owned them. At 18, he was older than most of his classmates because of years lost to academic trouble. He was a svelte, 6-foot-6-inch player, stronger, more athletic, and brasher than his opponents. He could attack a defender any way he chose, dropping back to shoot, blowing past him, or simply going through him. He was from New York and played like it at the camp under the watchful eyes of many NBA scouts. The NBA, by then, had dipped a toe into the camp. Not only did the league allow its employees to attend, some assistants and personnel coached at the camp as well. It almost served as a white flag, the league saying, *If these high schoolers are going to be in our league soon, we may as well get to know them as early as we can.*

Bill Willoughby knew of Cooke. He was Cooke in a different era, when the expectations to produce, placed on prodigy ballplayers, were not as immediate. His career over, Willoughby still lived nearby in 2000. He enjoyed talking to kids and wanted to provide them with more guidance than he himself had received. He worried that trouble loomed beneath Cooke's hard exterior. One day at the camp, Willoughby pulled Cooke aside. Already, rumors were circulating that Cooke would jump to the NBA, even though he had a year of high school remaining—two if he attended prep school for a year. "Look, go to St. John's for a year or two," Willoughby advised. "Do it like Ron Artest and then come out like that because you're giving the wrong impression." Cooke nodded his head. They exchanged phone numbers. Neither remained in frequent contact with the other. Cooke set the camp ablaze, finishing near the top of the 200-plus players, which, for a New York native, meant he was somewhere on his way to being the next Jordan or Dr. J. He was the top player for the first couple of days before striking his right hand on the backboard, an injury that limited him the rest of the way. Cooke even had time to test Kobe Bryant's restraint. Bryant talked to the kids and, during the session, Cooke confidentially challenged him to a one-on-one game. "When you get to the league, I'll beat you in various ways," Bryant answered. "What can you say to a champion and MVP at the time?" Cooke remembered. "There is nothing you can say. After the lecture was over, he knew my name. That made me even more bigheaded, like *Kobe knows me. How you know me?*" Willoughby called Cooke after still hearing that Cooke wanted to jump straight to the NBA. A man answered and said he was Cooke's brother and Cooke was not available. Willoughby knew he had the right number. "It was him," Willoughby said. "He didn't want to talk to me. He didn't want to listen."

He did not have to. Cooke was the best, and he was ticketed for stardom. He dominated future NBA All-Stars like Amar'e Stoudemire, Carmelo Anthony, and Joakim Noah, his onetime AAU teammate. They emulated Cooke, wanting to be him.

Cooke would never play a second in the NBA.

• • •

The first time Debbie Bortner met Lenny Cooke, he wore a flimsy spring jacket in the middle of winter's cold. The wind ruffled the jacket, causing the already short sleeves to ride even higher on his arms. Bortner would soon find the rest of Cooke's background harrowing. He had grown up in Atlantic City and relocated with his family to a neglected corner of Brooklyn. There, in Bushwick, the family lived near a cemetery on Decatur Street on the second floor of a wooden building frequented by rats and warmed by an oven. The building would be condemned within the next couple of years. Gunshots occasionally stirred Cooke from his sleep at night. He dodged the prostitutes and drug dealers on his way to school or—more often than not—en route to the park to hang out with friends. Bortner still found Cooke likable and always quick with a smile. Initial impressions meant a lot to her. She was bold and opinionated. No one had to guess what was on her mind. She let everyone know. Her husband, Ken, ran a successful newspaper-insert printing business, eventually selling it to Rupert Murdoch. With time and money, Bortner launched herself into her children's activities. She managed and helped coach her son, Brian Raimondi, in AAU for the Panthers of Long Island. Bortner was an unusual sight in amateur basketball, a white woman whose blond ponytail followed her up and down the sidelines. Someone had spotted Cooke one day shooting baskets in the playground and asked him to try out for the team. That day, Tyrone Green, one of the team's coaches, bluntly told the players that the chances of anyone making the roster were slim. *You don't even know me, you've never seen me play basketball before, how do you know I'm not good enough to make your team?* Cooke thought. It was a slight and, for a New York player, a slight fueled motivation. Cooke impressed everyone at the tryouts—while wearing Hush Puppies—and soon dominated the team. Cooke came to appreciate Brian Raimondi as a little brother. They became inseparable and Cooke transferred from a high school he hardly attended to join Raimondi at La Salle Academy, a private school in Manhattan. Others soon started noticing Cooke's game. "That's when I really took advantage of it, knowing I was talented enough to play against some of the top players in the country," Cooke remembered.

He took advantage of everything he could. The hour did not matter. New York never slept and seldom did Cooke. He could always find a party or club that would lift its rope, open its doors, and allow him inside a world of temptation. He hung out with athletes and rappers, as though they were peers with matching bank accounts. "The things men were doing, I was doing at sixteen, seventeen, eighteen years old," Cooke recalled. "I was in the club at four and five in the morning while y'all was getting ready for school the next day. I never thought it was going to end." The more he partied, the less school became a priority and his faltering grades plummeted further. Cooke often plopped his head on a desk and tried for a couple hours of sleep on the rare occasions he did attend class. "Everybody was in line to give him shit," Bortner recalled. "Sneakers, clothes. Everybody did." Cooke, she believed, was a well-meaning kid who could go places if he kept his head on straight. New York could blind anyone, especially an impressionable teenager who had come from nothing overnight. Cooke, sensing the same, asked Bortner if he could move into their house in New Jersey's Old Tappan. Cooke's parents, Alfreda and Vernon Hendrix, planned to move to Virginia with his three younger siblings. Cooke worried about being out of sight, out of mind and that his ranking would drop if he left New York.

He also desperately needed an education. Cooke had been promoted annually up until high school. His previous schools had passed him on and he became someone else's to neglect for that school year. The automatic promotions stopped in high school. Cooke's woeful grades forced him to be held back twice in four years. He thought he had been learning, despite his frequent absences, only to now realize that he would not come close to qualifying for college. He thought of becoming a millionaire every day, of being like Magic Johnson, a basketball legend and entrepreneur, and building a movie theater where his former home, now boarded up, stood in Brooklyn. Yet, he could barely read. Bortner agreed to the move. She had done it before, allowing her son's teammates extended stays at her home. She promised Cooke's mother that she would watch over Cooke as though he were one of her own children. The plan would be for Cooke to fully extricate himself from the city. Cooke and Raimondi transferred to Northern Valley Regional High School at Old Tappan. Cooke drew so many college scouts whenever he played that Bortner hoped some of their eyes would also land on her son.

Tom Kaechele, the school's athletic director, refused to believe the transfer until the moment Cooke and Bortner showed up in his office. The transfer proved similarly striking for Cooke. He had been around a few white people before, but never this many. He was one of only six African-Americans in the school. He had been in school, but not often, and only now, surrounded by college-bound students, did he realize how hopelessly far behind he had fallen. But his future was in basketball. "A publicity stunt" was how Cooke described his transfer to the high school in later years. Old Tappan was a pit stop, even if Cooke had to sit out for about a month to gain academic eligibility to play. One day an administrator suggested that Kaechele peek into the gym. Cooke was putting on a show before the student body. Kaechele walked the short distance from his office across the hall to the gym. School had only recently let out, yet it seemed as if half the student body packed the gym, where steel rods hung from the ceiling to support the basket. Cooke performed dunk after dunk to the applause of the students. Kaechele looked to the ceiling. The steel bars trembled. Dust danced to the ground. Kaechele worried that

Cooke's weight would bring down the basket and the steel bars. "You can't jam in practice anymore," he declared. "Those baskets are going to get ripped right out of the ceiling." That day, Kaechele felt like the most unpopular administrator in the school.

The plan of teaming Cooke and Brian Raimondi never materialized. Raimondi broke his wrist just a few days before Cooke became eligible. Cooke finally made his anticipated debut in late January 2001. He finished off an alley-oop within the first five seconds of the game against Northern Valley at Demarest and converted 17 of his 22 shots, outscoring the opposition by himself, 37–35. Kaechele watched the performance closely. He had once coached baseball at Rutgers University in New Brunswick, New Jersey, and could spot an athlete when he saw one. Cooke was an athlete. He was so superbly gifted that it seemed defenders sometimes accidentally got in Cooke's way. But Kaechele felt his advice to Cooke was not being heard and he was surprised at the first game to learn that Cooke was already a father. "Keep your head level," Kaechele told him. "Stay with us. Ask us questions. Please keep us close to the situation. Please keep clean. Don't take any of these offers. Let us know everything that's going on." Kaechele felt as though Cooke listened, but none of the words registered. "You can only offer so much and if they don't sit down and take your advice, it's pointless," he said. "He was being pulled in nine thousand different directions when he was here. It was a lot of fun when it was happening, but there was a lot of stuff that made you think, *Oh man, he's going down the wrong path.*" Kaechele believed that Cooke would make a living out of the sport. He was familiar with the trajectory of Bill Willoughby's journeyman career and thought Cooke would be successful, even if he just emulated what many considered to be Willoughby's disappointing time in the NBA. *If that's the path he's going to take, then God bless him. He might be successful in that path,* Kaechele rationalized. "Did I feel bad for him?" he said. "I just felt I had doubts. Trepidation, that's the proper word. You knew it wasn't going to be peaches and cream." Still, he, like many others at the school, enjoyed the boost in interest that Cooke provided. A school that used to sell about 400 tickets a game now resorted to preselling some 900 seats. Fans packed the stands for the freshman game and stayed through the junior varsity game, all to ensure a seat to watch Cooke perform in the last matchup of the evening. Two security guards became about 10, some directing traffic and some making sure no fans snuck in through the back.

The joyride lasted all of eight games. Kevin Brentnall, the young coach of Old Tappan, could not locate Cooke as the team prepared to play Sparta in a postseason tournament game. The bus was prepared to leave. Brentnall asked Kaechele what he should do.

"What you should do is sit his rear end for at least the quarter, maybe the half," Kaechele said. "I don't care if it's the state tournament or not. You've been down this road already with him this year. You know how irresponsible and immature he's been. You can't sacrifice the rest of your team. You've got to stick with your principles."

Cooke arrived at the game late. Brentnall sat him for the first quarter in a game lost, 69–63, in overtime. With that, Cooke had exhausted his high school eligibility. He was 19, yet still classified as a high school junior because of his transient high school beginnings. Cooke stayed for another year at the school as Brian Raimondi went off to college. He began returning to Brooklyn nearly every day, visiting old haunts and friends. Cooke came to resent being known, in his mind, as Lenny from Old Tappan. He wanted to be known as Lenny from Brooklyn. His friends teased him, saying that Bortner sought to make him white. Cooke listened. No one had really stood up for him in his life. Everyone had ulterior motives. He came to rationalize that Bortner only housed him to land a future payday off him. "Lenny, the only thing I care about is the color green," Bortner would tell him. "It's not black. It's not white. It's money. You want the money. God put you here to play basketball and that's what you do. That's what you do well. That's your gift. Everybody gets something and that's your gift." She had all the money she needed. She had come to genuinely care for Cooke, although she still insisted he follow her rules. Those rules included attending school and not traveling into the city so often. Cooke, stubborn, left for a week and crashed from couch to couch before returning.

Bortner had just returned from vacationing in Thailand when she tried stirring Cooke for school one morning. Cooke informed Bortner that he would not be attending school that day. Instead, he said, he would be moving to Michigan with his friend Damany Eastman to focus on basketball and finish school. Bortner knew that an agent had to be involved and Cooke could not make such a drastic decision alone. "I need to do this," Cooke said, refusing to reveal who had facilitated the move. Bortner cried. "You're selling yourself to the lowest bidder," she argued. She knew Cooke had been given money. She thought of her own life trajectory, marrying at 18. *I look back and wish my parents would have put handcuffs on me.* If they had, Bortner knew she would have fought even more vigorously. That choice was hers and this one would be Cooke's. On the cusp of adulthood, Cooke had to make mature choices, Bortner believed, and also live with the consequences.

They hugged and both said, "I love you." A driver arrived to take Cooke to the airport. Bortner's tears continued as the black Town Car left her driveway.

"It was not a moral thing to do, not at all," Bortner said years later. "It was an immoral thing to take a child like Lenny from a home where he was being well taken care of. It's not as if he needed that money. But when you come to a kid who came from somewhere with nothing and you wave that kind of cash in front of him—I don't know. I don't even know what to say. I just wish it had been different . . . So many people portrayed it as *Lenny walked out on her. Lenny did this to her.* Lenny did not do anything to me. Lenny did these things to himself. He didn't hurt me. The only reason I was hurt is because I knew he was hurting himself."

At the time, Cooke believed he was helping his family. He knew that not playing and being out of the spotlight had affected his draft stock. Cooke said he met a runner for an agent from Immortal Sports & Entertainment named Terence Greene during one of his many late nights out in New York City. "I met him in a club one night, and he asked me if I wanted to be represented," Cooke said. "And he was like, 'Well, if you come to the hotel the next day and sign this contract with us, we got a lump sum of money for you.' And that's how it went down. I ended up going to the hotel, all of us went up there, I signed the contract, and he gave me the lump sum of money."

"How do you say no?" Cooke asked years later. "At the time, I wasn't at Debbie's. I wasn't in Michigan yet. I was just here and there. I should have spoken to Debbie. Why I didn't, I don't know. I still don't know."

Cooke said he received $350,000. "It lasted me probably a good year and a half, if that," he said. But Greene, a former University of Michigan coach, said that Cooke did not receive a lump sum of money. "Hell, no," Greene said. "When Lenny said he was going pro, Lenny got a $30,000 credit line. He wanted more than that, but I wouldn't let it happen." Cooke felt conflicted over leaving Bortner's home. "It was emotional at times when I first left . . . to go get represented by an agent that I knew nothing about," Cooke said. "I just have been used a lot throughout my career. He was just one of the dudes that I was with in Michigan. He was one of the first people that showed me it's a business. You can get fucked over, because they damn sure did it."

Cooke tried enrolling at Mott Adult High School in Flint, Michigan, in an attempt to gain a high school diploma. Greene had once coached at the school. Cooke said he was denied entry because the school year had already started. "I've never let somebody stay in my home," Greene said. "Never. I don't care what it is. But Lenny looked like he wanted to get his life together and get in school and work out and he wasn't able to play basketball anymore. And that's what we were focusing on, focusing on basketball and books, getting his diploma first and not trying to get to the NBA because Lenny, his mind was already made up that he was going pro." Greene said he hoped that being away from home would help Cooke concentrate. He found him more distracted than ever during their training sessions. "He wasn't playing well," Greene said. "He went back to New York and what really happened with Lenny, in my opinion, was the NBA lifestyle and everybody pulling on him and really making him feel like he had got there before he got there . . . It was fighting, pulling teeth getting him back, because he was hanging in clubs all the time."

In May 2002, Cooke returned to New York for a press conference at Junior's in Brooklyn. Six years earlier, Brooklyn's own Stephon Marbury had picked that venue for his own declaration. Cooke wore black and he adorned his neck, wrist, and neck with shiny jewelry. "It was a hard decision for me," he said, "but I've decided to put my name in the NBA draft." Applause rang out from his friends. Bortner did not attend the event. Cooke said he had been assured of being selected in the first round by his agent, Mike Harrison, but he injured his right toe at the predraft camp and could not perform for teams. He hoped that organizations had already seen enough of his play. But teams were wary of his long layoff, concerned that he had left Bortner's care, and worried about his overall commitment to the game. The night of the draft, Cooke felt like an expectant kid at Christmas, full of hopes and dreams, only to awaken to find nothing beneath the tree. He went undrafted, and a frustrated Cooke left Harrison, Greene, and their agency. "I wrote a note, got it notarized, I had my paperwork from the contract we had, had it notarized," Cooke said. "I don't owe you shit. I'm not committed to you anymore. I'm finished with you."

• • •

Emporia is a tiny Virginia city, a dot for most people on their way to larger hubs, not all that far from where Moses Malone once made a fateful decision to enter professional basketball out of high school. Local residents here take back roads past endless fields of green grass to avoid the highway patrolled by cops who strictly enforce the speed limit.

It's a humid summer day in June 2013. Anita Solomon, Cooke's fiancée, opens the front door for a visitor. She excuses herself to attend to their young daughter and says Cooke will be out in a little while. Remnants of a dream dashed are abundant in the tiny home.

News of Cooke popped up only intermittently since he had gone undrafted. He played for summer league entrants from the Boston Celtics and Seattle SuperSonics. He filtered through basketball's domestic minor leagues and played in the Philippines and China. In late 2004, Cooke found himself in Los Angeles with the Jam of the American Basketball Association. He was not wearing a seat belt as a passenger in the car of teammate Nick Sheppard, while the pair made their way along rain-slicked Beverly Hills roads. Sheppard crashed the car into a light post. Sheppard, wearing a seat belt, sustained no major injuries. The accident left Cooke comatose with a broken left shin and femur. Doctors feared that he would lose the leg to amputation. They preserved it through two marathon surgeries, but cautioned him that his basketball career was likely over. Cooke was in a wheelchair for four months. His weight ballooned to about 275 pounds. Yet, the words of the doctors remained with him. Cooke began waking up every morning to jog on a treadmill and perform leg presses. He worked himself into decent enough shape to return to the Philippines and play. But he was not the same athlete as he had been. Cooke could no longer blow past defenders and instead plodded through them, backing them down. His body was not used to playing with the added weight. He ruptured one Achilles tendon, only to return to play again—this time with the Rockford Lightning of the Continental Basketball Association—before blowing out his other Achilles. His competitive playing career was over.

He had had everything before he could appreciate it. He appreciated everything when he had nothing. For a while, Cooke was better known in New York City than any Knick or Net. With the exception of Kobe Bryant, perhaps no other high school player achieved the same level of superstardom at such an early age as Cooke had. His failing represented everything that goes wrong when a system is corrupted—from parents who provided little direction to an educational system that blindly promoted him and a basketball system eager to accept him as long as he produced. In recent months, he had made a resurgence. When his star power looked so bright, Adam Shopkorn, a young filmmaker, wanted to film a prep basketball star and document how he handled his growing fame. It took a while for Shopkorn to gain Cooke's trust—everyone wanted something from him in those days—before Cooke finally allowed Shopkorn into his world, camera and all. The two lost touch as

Cooke veered off the path to stardom. Shopkorn eventually picked the project back up and finished it with independent filmmaking brothers Joshua and Ben Safdie. Cooke had recently traveled to New York for a screening. He hoped the film would be a second beginning.

Coming from around a corner, Cooke greets his visitor and asks for the visitor's impressions of Emporia. "There ain't nothing here, man," he says. "Nothing here." His once-powerful, athletic frame is gone, a casualty to time, injury, and inactivity. He looks more like an NFL offensive lineman than a basketball shooting guard. He offers a short tour. A framed photo of a younger, slimmer Cooke with Magic Johnson hangs on a mantel. "Those trophies came from the King tournament while I was at La Salle," he says, motioning to massive trophies. "High Scorer Award and MVP of the Tournament—those came from Five-Star Camp. Those three in the middle, the plaque, and that. Those two right there, the one right behind the Five-Star, is the MVP of Rucker. The seven-footer is the Rucker Park Championship."

They live with their young daughter, Nyvaeh. Cooke came up with the name, a play on heaven spelled backward. Cooke's son now lives in Brooklyn. Cooke is reflective and thoughtful.

"I'm a mature man," he says. "I ain't in the best situation right now. I've been doing a lot of bullshit, but it ain't about me no more. It ain't about basketball or nothing like that for me no more. My family needs me more than anything now. At times, it bothered me. Especially when night comes around and it's like, *Damn, you know you are supposed to be there.* The fellas sitting there like, 'You see his bum ass on TV?' Other than that, it don't bother me."

When asked what he does for work, Cooke answers that he hopes to start a nonprofit and mentor young athletes. Other than that? "Being a father, looking for work," he says. "I maintain." He is at whatever peace one can find in being selected for greatness, close enough to see it, only to have it vanish. He is still conflicted, at times holding himself accountable and at other moments voicing anger at those who misled him. He occasionally disappears from home to visit Atlantic City and Brooklyn. "They made this person," Cooke says. "I didn't do it. I wasn't the one who gave me the money, or allowed me to get bigheaded. Ranking me in the country, ranking me number one in the country or number one in the city. Allowing me in clubs I had no business in. They did this to me. They did that."

Cooke said he played for the amateur team that paid the most money. He considered himself a basketball mercenary. Payment of amateur players was prohibited, but organizations always offered, according to Cooke. "Whoever came with the most money, that's who I played with," Cooke would say years later. "Whether it was with Riverside, the Panthers, Gauchos, it didn't matter. Whoever was going to give me the most money at the time, that's who I was saving. All of them paid me. I know those are mistakes, but they made those mistakes, too. Because they aren't supposed to pay no high school students to play or give me whatever they gave me."

"These guys, LeBron, Carmelo, Amar'e, they had their guidance," he continues. "They had someone that was their coach from six years old or they had their father, who knows sports or played basketball. I didn't have that. So all the decisions I made, it was either between me or Debbie, and nine times out of ten, I didn't listen to her, either. It's all bad luck. Sometimes, I think if I ever had good luck, I wouldn't know what to do with it."

That is part of the answer, but Cooke's plight is more layered and nuanced. The start of his decline can be pinpointed to the ABCD camp in 2001, the year after he had trounced his competition. That summer, Cooke's fall intersected with the rise of another player forecasted for NBA stardom.

· · ·

For days, Gary Charles had been warned by Maverick Carter that his friend from Akron, Ohio, would take the ABCD camp by storm. "Yeah, yeah," Charles said in brushing him off. By then, Charles had heard and seen it all. He coached the Long Island Panthers, one of the country's powerhouse AAU team. Like Chris Rivers, Charles had been with Vaccaro for years, linking up with him in 1991. Each year's crop of campers brought a fresh wave of excitement. Charles was in the stands when Stephon Marbury took off near the foul line and dunked over a helpless, hapless defender. Bedlam broke out all at once. A once-sedate crowd awoke, leaping in unison, with some of the people streaming onto the court. Marbury nonchalantly walked out of the gym. Charles noticed that someone had caught the dunk on video. A line formed behind the cameraman. Every few seconds, Charles heard yells and gasps from whoever had just watched the replay. That was the atmosphere that the camp created. It was a party, a coronation, and a window into the future and the NBA's next star. Kobe Bryant played at the camp the year after Marbury. Charles remembers Bryant lifting off from the corner, "like he started out in Atlanta, Georgia, made a turn around Maryland and came down in Jersey and dunked the ball so hard on someone that the place went crazy," Charles said.

"Is that better than Stephon?" Bryant asked Charles after finishing the slam.

"Kobe, that's pretty good, but it's not better than Steph."

"Damn," Bryant said, turning to jog back on defense.

Charles forged a relationship with Bryant and his family, serving as a liaison while working with Vaccaro to land Bryant his first shoe contract. Charles sat in the stands surveying the camp's game in 2000, the year that Cooke made his one-on-one challenge to Bryant. One could watch four games simultaneously from the stands, the courts next to one another. Charles was watching games when Bryant walked in and approached him. Bryant greeted Charles and remained quiet for the next couple of minutes as he watched the action. "Where's Lenny?" Bryant asked.

"He's playing over there," Charles said, motioning to a court on the far end.

Charles's gaze returned to another court. A few minutes passed. Charles forgot that Bryant was next to him. Charles received a tap on his shoulder from Bryant after about 15 minutes. "Oh shit," he said. "Kobe, what's up?"

"Lenny Cooke's not ready for me," Bryant said, rising to leave. "I'll see you later." Charles finally realized Bryant's purpose. *Oh shit, he came just to measure Lenny Cooke*, Charles thought. *That shows you how good the camp is and how serious Kobe is. Kobe wanted to see what was up, who was coming along.* Charles could have saved Bryant the time. He knew Cooke would not stand a chance against Bryant. At the time, Cooke was probably the nation's best high school player, but Bryant was one of the best NBA players. Charles had coached Cooke one time with the Panthers. But as he rose within the team's ranks and his stature grew, Charles predicted future problems. Sometimes, Cooke would wonder why he could not shoot every possession. "Dude, you're one of five guys on the court," Charles would say. "Pass the ball. Get these guys involved." Charles knew the emotions of teenagers spanned a wide range. When kids yelled at him, Charles just yelled louder. Still, he felt he could see the direction Cooke would travel. He decided he wanted to spare himself the grief and allowed Cooke to walk away from the team. Debbie Bortner and her son left the program as well. Tyrone Green, another of the team's coaches, argued against the decision. "You don't let the number one player in the country go," Green said. "Why Lenny?"

"The other kids will follow our lead," Charles said. "Lenny won't. At some point, he's going to want to do his own thing and I don't want to deal with it. We've got to make a change now."

Charles believed Cooke possessed enough raw talent to make it in the NBA. To Charles, Cooke was like a young Mike Tyson, full of swagger and able to intimidate an opponent before even stepping onto the court. Charles looked at how Cooke walked onto Court 2 in the Rothman Center at Fairleigh Dickinson before his game against the kid from Akron. "Lenny was all show," Charles said. "He was New York with a lot of flair to his game. There was this calmness about LeBron. He was just taking everything in stride."

A mix of college and pro scouts sat in the stands, along with a crowd prepared to root for the hometown hero, Cooke. Cooke would play for the Warriors against James's Suns. Cooke did not think much of the matchup. He had already dismissed the team of Carmelo Anthony earlier in the day. James was a year younger than Anthony and had yet to build the same reputation.

Cooke was not ready for LeBron James. James opened the game with a three-pointer. Cooke fouled James the next two possessions and James collected on five free throws, putting his Suns up 8–0. The New York–leaning crowd had just settled into their seats and was already worried. Lenny Cooke called for the ball as James dropped into a defensive stance and Cooke whipped the ball through his legs as though it were tied to a yo-yo. James blocked his path to the rim. A surprised Cooke gathered himself again. In most instances, his crossover was enough to provide a path for an easy layup. Cooke tried the move again. Again James was not fooled. The crowd realized the importance of the sequence and started clapping. Cooke attempted the same move yet again. James did not bite. Cooke, almost resignedly, heaved up a long jumper. The ball cut through the net and the crowd erupted. At first glance, it looked as if Cooke had won the possession, but anyone who had watched more closely knew better. James had been a roadblock to Cooke three times in a single possession. After the shot, Charles glanced at James. "He looked like it was no big thing," Charles remembered. "The game is going on and you can see it in LeBron's eyes, he was in it for his team to win, whereas Lenny wanted to put on a show. The more that the game carried on, the more I became fascinated with this kid."

James controlled the game's pace though his passing, defense, and timely shots. Cooke's teammates picked him up, providing a one-point edge as time wound down. James received the ball with a running start and streaked up the court's right side. He beat Cooke off the dribble. Cooke, scrambling to catch up, tried fouling James by grabbing the back of his arm. James released the ball just shy of the three-point line in an awkward running shot. The ball swooshed through the net.

"That shit had to be luckiest shit ever," Cooke said years later. "Ever. He [hasn't] hit one of those since he has been in the league. Not like that, no sir. That had to be the luckiest shit. If he would have missed that shot I would have won by one, by two. How would the tables turn then?"

Instead, Cooke was dethroned, a loser on his own court to an unknown kid from the Midwest.

"How the fuck you make that shot?" Cooke asked.

"I just threw it up," James said.

Charles finally saw James show emotion, celebrating the win with his team. "He had decided all along that he was keeping it inside and now that he made that shot, he knew he had arrived and the whole world knew he had arrived," Charles said. "I don't think Lenny was the same after that shot."

"It's probably the most important shot a high school kid has ever made if you allow history to play out," Sonny Vaccaro said. "Lenny Cooke was the guy. He was New York. What you saw in those ten seconds was the transferring of the baton and LeBron never let it down. If Lenny wins the game, LeBron is still great and all that, but maybe Lenny Cooke's life changes."

James finished with 24 points. Cooke managed only 9 points.

"I had no idea," James said of the importance of the shot. "Only thing I cared about was winning the game, and I was excited about that. I had no idea about what type of impact it had, still don't."

18.

D ick Vitale was once among the throng of college coaches haplessly recruiting Moses Malone. Vitale thought he had an honest shot at landing him—as did a couple of hundred other universities. He coached at the University of Detroit in the mid-1970s and agreed to talk at an awards ceremony in Virginia honoring Malone. He hoped to land some face time with Malone during the event, except Malone never showed. Vitale began to worry about how he would justify the trip and went to Malone's house to see if he could meet with him there. The hours slipped by. Night crept in. Vitale continued to wait. Finally, as he prepared to leave, he heard dogs barking. It was Malone, who arrived at his door to find an elated Vitale. Vitale's happiness was short-lived. Malone informed Vitale that he would sign with Maryland, but was still contemplating forgoing college altogether for professional basketball. Vitale dejectedly returned home. Both found themselves in the NBA a couple years later. Vitale had advanced to coach the Pistons, which played one evening against Malone's Rockets. "Hey," Malone called out to Vitale before the game. "Remember that old house you visited me in?" Vitale responded that he did. "Well, we don't live in there anymore," Malone said cheekily.

Vitale's NBA coaching career was brief. He stepped timidly into broadcasting after a little over a year coaching the Pistons and surprised himself by being a natural. Vitale announced ESPN's first college basketball game in December 1979 and became the sport's voice, blending energy and enthusiasm with his catchphrases ("prime-time player," "diaper dandy," "trifecta") that have become part of the college game's vocabulary. Vitale's prominence coincided with the rise of ESPN, a sports cable network that originated with a $9,000 investment from Getty Oil and evolved into a multibillion-dollar enterprise that dominated the 24-hour sports cycle by broadcasting, analyzing, and evaluating games and athletes across the world.

Vitale was grateful and loyal. He considered himself a company man, but still felt he should speak up against a decision ESPN made in December 2002. The network had decided to air a regular-season high school game on ESPN2 that would pit St. Vincent–St. Mary of Akron, Ohio, against Virginia's Oak Hill Academy at Cleveland State's Convocation Center. Vitale knew the hype that surrounded Akron's LeBron James. The James legend had grown exponentially after his victorious showdown with Lenny Cooke. James provided a type of litmus test for the media and his school's administration about whether a certain imaginary line should be crossed. By now, the entrance of high school players into the NBA was an annual occurrence. But none had been as widely followed as James. The debate over the NBA drafting athletes right out of high school grew as James's exploits quickly catapulted him to superstardom. There had been rumors at one time that James would not only skip college, but also his senior year of high school to join the NBA. *Was his youth being stolen? Should the media be highlighting him so much? Should his school profit off the talents of this phenom? Should the kid be able to profit from his own talents while in high school?* James was named Ohio's Mr. Basketball for consecutive years and was featured as a junior on the cover of *Sports Illustrated*, anointed as the Chosen One. Most of St. Vincent–St. Mary's games had been moved from the high school to the University of Akron's James A. Rhodes Arena—where they outdrew the college's team. A handful of the games could be watched throughout northeast Ohio for $7 on pay-per-view. The school argued that it was just trying to meet the demands of its alumni and its growing fan base.

ESPN would broadcast the game nationally. The pressure would be extreme on anyone, let alone a kid from a small city. The network also wanted Vitale to partner with Bill Walton, a talented basketball player in his own day who was now an analyst. The duo had never worked together before and Vitale figured the temporary partnership was intended to expand interest if the on-court product faltered. Vitale worried about the precedent being established and favored an NBA age minimum of 20. He voiced his hesitation, but then relented. "Fine, if you want us to go, I'll do the game," he said. "But, remember, this is a high school kid. We don't even do college games together," he said, referring to being teamed with Walton for the broadcast. Criticism mounted as the December 12 game approached. "If CBS had asked me, I wouldn't do the game," Billy Packer, a college basketball color analyst, declared to *USA Today*. "This is what sports have become—hyping someone before he's accomplished something. James didn't even carry his high school team to the state championship last year and now the NBA's Stu Jackson wants to consider having him on the U.S. Olympic team. Come on."

The idea of showcasing James on ESPN and national television had come from outside the company. Rashid Ghazi worked as a partner for Paragon Marketing Group, an agency that focused on corporate consulting, athlete sponsorships, and endorsements. Ghazi was a basketball junkie and grew up an avid DePaul fan who paid close attention to college recruiting. His background included creating high school athletic events, like a showdown between the top players in Chicago and New York, seeking out sponsorships, and selling the packages to local television distributors. Ghazi had also produced a documentary series for Fox Sports in Chicago that centered on high school basketball stars in the city—one being Eddy Curry. One day a friend approached him with the possibility of broadcasting one of

James's games, noting that James was a big deal in Cleveland. Ghazi had been interested in taking high school sports national for some time and thought there would be an interest in Oak Hill, the number-one-ranked team in the nation. "I'd seen a lot of success in our high school games in Chicago," Ghazi said. "I'd seen a lot of success on the documentary series that we did on the inner-city basketball kids in Chicago. I thought, *Why not call up ESPN?*"

"Hey, I've got an idea for you," Ghazi told Burke Magnus, ESPN's director of brand management. "Would you guys be interested in televising a high school game with LeBron James? Everyone has heard of him, but no one has seen him play. Best-case scenario, you've got the next Michael Jordan or Magic Johnson to showcase when he was in high school. Worst case is you've got phenomenal footage for your NBA draft, because all indications are he's going to go directly to the NBA. What a great way to promote that you've got the NBA draft coming up. If he decides to go to college, you guys are in the business of college sports. What a great way to promote a kid that will definitely change the landscape of college sports if he chooses to go that way. There's a huge interest in watching him and this is something completely unique that hasn't been done before. You guys are the network to try this."

Ghazi found little downside to broadcasting high school games. The exploits of high school players, he figured, had already been publicized for years. "The moment you quit [covering] high school sports, and you just record the box scores in the papers, is the moment I'll stop publicizing games," he would tell newspaper reporters who argued he had tainted the purity of amateur players. Besides, he rationalized, other sports had shown players at a young age. "I don't see one person complaining about an 18-year-old tennis player being on TV, or a 16-year-old vying for a gold medal," Ghazi said. "But all of a sudden, when it comes to basketball players, everyone starts to rush to judgment. They do that when it comes to television, to their careers, and whether they should go pro or not. Everyone seems to feel like they've got an ownership over basketball for some reason versus the other sports."

At the time, Magnus was primarily responsible for the network's men's college basketball program and scheduling. The network, Magnus figured, had already broadcast the Little League World Series for years. Those kids were much younger than James, who had been exposed on a national level already. It struck him as an odd ethical debate. *It's not like we discovered him out of the blue,* Magnus reasoned. *He had already been on the cover of* Sports Illustrated. *He was well known in basketball circles and he was really taking his notoriety and the phenomenon that he was to the broader, general sports audience.* "The concerns were twofold," Magnus remembered. "One was you have the real conservative thinkers that thought that we were somehow ruining the purity of high school athletics, or maybe shining a spotlight on a kid too early. They weren't the loudest voices, though. There was another faction that thought that there wasn't a national audience for it. We are in the viewership business and there's a lot of people who said, 'I don't care how good the kid is, this is not going to get traction nationally.' We just decided that it was worth the risk, and the risk was very low." To Magnus, the thought that the kids would suffer from overexposure was ridiculous. The best kids had already been recognized at the local and statewide level for years.

The network decided to go all-in on James. It would have Vitale and Walton broadcast the game with Dan Shulman and Jay Bilas. "I don't know what the solution is," Vitale would say years later. "You can't hide talent. That's the one thing I want to make very clear. A lot of people say, 'Too much publicity. Too much notoriety.' But you can't hide talent. When a guy's that gifted and that talented, you're going to get exposure, and handling that exposure includes the responsibilities of the coaches, the administrators, everybody around them to give them an education of the process. You can't just let it go on without having a person that educates them about that because it's a valuable part of it, just learning how to communicate, how to handle a microphone, how to handle interviews. That should all be part of the process and that's part of growing as a student-athlete."

• • •

G loria James gave birth to LeBron James when she was just 16. She never had a lasting relationship with James's biological father, instead raising her son with the help of her mother and grandmother. The two died a year apart, and the North Akron house they resided in on Hickory Street was too big for Gloria to maintain and was condemned. The family faced hardships and moved from one friend's house to another and from couch to couch, the reality of a black unwed teenage mother who had not found her own place in the world before being tasked with raising a son. LeBron James missed days and weeks of elementary school at a time. The man his mom dated, and who became his surrogate father and helped look after him, often ran afoul of the law.

LeBron James lived with Frankie Walker, his youth coach, for about two years as a child, while his mother tried to straighten out her life. It was Walker who first put a ball into the young boy's hands and taught him how to play the game. Soon after, James teamed with Dru Joyce II and his son, Dru Joyce III, in a recreation league and, later, on the AAU circuit. The boys looked for any means to enhance their skills, and word filtered through the neighborhood about an ex-college coach who hosted an open gym on Sunday nights. Keith Dambrot had once coached at Central Michigan University before changing careers and becoming a stockbroker. He still conducted clinics at the Jewish Community Center on Akron's west side when Joyce II brought his players one weekend evening. Dambrot immediately noticed James, who was gangly and just entering adolescence as a seventh grader. "He was fabulous physically, but he was just way better at understanding the game with his IQ," Dambrot recalled. "That's what really separated him."

The clinics prompted Dambrot to try coaching again. The game had never really left him. He agreed to coach St. Vincent–St. Mary in 1998 and James and his core of friends—including Joyce III, Sian Cotton, and Romeo Travis—opted for the school instead of Buchtel High, the nearby almost all-black school. Dambrot told people after James's freshman year that his protégé would evolve into an NBA player. "Three games into his sophomore year," Dambrot said, "I knew he would never go to college." The team once played in the small town of Salem, Ohio. James led them to another resounding victory and had gone to take a shower. He walked out of the school to find the customary line of people eagerly waiting to get his autograph. Dambrot noticed that some of the opposition, those who had just played against James, had skipped taking a shower to get in line. "It seemed kind of strange. You had just played the game, the kid is in the shower, and they're still in their uniforms," Dambrot said. "It was like traveling around with Elton John."

Things that would seem unusual anywhere else became routine around James. Everyone wanted something from him. "Trying to shield him, I felt an unbelievable pressure," Dambrot said. "I knew the only way he wasn't going to be a pro was if he kind of lost his way, whether it was drugs, alcohol, women, or babies. So I really tried to do a good job of shielding him [from] that and [tried] to teach him to do the right things as a player and person . . . basically, I didn't kiss his ass like most of the stars are treated now. I held him to a higher standard because I knew he could make a lot of money." The NBA had its eyes on James from early on. John Lucas, the coach of the Cavaliers who had once watched a young Kobe Bryant and had roomed with Moses Malone, asked James to work out with his team. The league fined the Cavaliers $150,000 and suspended Lucas for two games after he had hosted the amateur. "It was a tough situation because the better we got, the worse they ran our team," Lucas recalled. "So they would have a better shot to get him," by landing a top selection in the draft.

• • •

Satellite trucks preparing to beam the game across the nation were parked long before James arrived for his first nationally broadcast game. A blimp hovered overhead. More than 100 journalists—some from New York and Los Angeles—were credentialed to either anoint James as the best player since Michael Jordan or denounce the attention and adulation that he had received. They packed in elbow-to-elbow along the mezzanine level of the arena. Parking lots that normally sold spaces for a couple of bucks charged $20 that evening. ESPN opened its telecast by comparing James with some of the NBA's greats—Jordan, Magic, and others—and wondering if James's path would one day match their storied careers.

Steven Culp, an assistant coach for St. Vincent–St. Mary, had the same feeling approaching the game as he did watching James against Lenny Cooke at the ABCD camp. Culp had sat in the stands among NBA personnel for that showdown. When Cooke scored first and the crowd roared, Culp whispered to the scout next to him, "It's about to get ugly." James had shown few nerves then and he showed none now as tipoff approached against Oak Hill. The teams met before the game and Culp recalled the Oak Hill players displaying apprehension. "When they saw him, you could see the look in their faces," Culp said. "They wouldn't even look him in the face. They put their heads down. You got a feeling that they knew it wasn't going to go well."

James looked a decade older than his competition as his 23rd-ranked Fighting Irish prepared to take on Oak Hill, the top-ranked team in the country. He was 6 feet 8 inches and 240 pounds. James wore a green headband and patches to cover up his tattoos—a policy the Catholic school enforced—and green and gold Adidas shoes, a Tracy McGrady model, fashioned specifically for him by the company. James had encountered Oak Hill twice before, losing both games. But Oak Hill was a changed team, with only one returning rotation player. Carmelo Anthony, a smooth-shooting forward who would lead Syracuse to a national championship as a freshman, was the team's most noticeable loss.

Courtside seats fetched more than $100. Vegas ran a betting line for the game.

Dru Joyce II, who had replaced Dambrot as the St. Vincent–St. Mary head coach, cautioned his team to play its game. Oak Hill took an early seven-point lead. James started the game slowly, missing on his first three shots. On television, Walton cautioned James to become more assertive. Culp, on the sidelines, did not worry. He had seen James in other contests wait to gain a feel for the game before playing more aggressively. James often liked to allow his teammates to score early and often before racking up his points. James scored his first points on a follow-up dunk off Corey Jones's missed jumper with 3:05 left in the first quarter. The night belonged to James from there on. He raised his hands, asking the audience to do the same, after one thunderous dunk. He pounded his chest after hitting a three-pointer.

Vitale turned to Walton within the first few minutes of the game. "Redhead, let me tell you something, my man," he said. "This kid is better than advertised. He's better than what people even said and that's tough to believe."

James ended the game with 31 points and a number of rim-rattling dunks and behind-the-back assists. "He seems to have overcome a sluggish start," Walton joked midway through the game. James converted 12 of his 25 shots, while adding 13 rebounds and 6 assists in 32 minutes. St. Vincent–St. Mary trumped Oak Hill by 20 points. It was less a basketball game and more an affirmation of James's talents and potential for the 11,523 fans in attendance and the millions who watched ESPN broadcast the game into their living rooms.

"When I sat back and really thought about St. Vincent–St. Mary being on national television, it's crazy," James told reporters afterward. "But I don't think it's too much pressure."

After the game, James admitted to Vitale that he had gone to bed nervous the previous night. "Man, you're everything plus," Vitale said to him. "Remember now what I'm going to tell you. You're going to be hit upon by everyone, leeches like you can't believe. Be intelligent. Make good decisions. Surround yourself with good people."

Walton stopped James as he walked off the court.

"Congratulations," Walton said, according to the *Associated Press*.

"Thanks for coming," James replied.

"No," Walton said. "Thanks for having me."

• • •

T he game got a rating of 1.97, translating to a reach of 1.67 million homes across the country. It represented ESPN's third-highest-rated basketball game ever. "It was everything we'd hope for," Magnus said. "It [had] a huge audience."

Ghazi had worked furiously to secure sponsors before the game. He called more than 150 companies, telling them about a phenom, a future NBA star they could be tied in with from the beginning. Only Progressive Insurance, Spalding, and Gatorade paid to sponsor the game. Progressive was based in Cleveland and still knew little about James. "I know who James LeBron is," said one of the people Ghazi worked with early on at the company. Ghazi guaranteed them all a rating of at least 0.5, knowing that if it underdelivered, he would have to return some of the sponsorship payment to the companies. He was likewise thrilled over the ratings.

"Before the game took place, Adidas, Nike, and Reebok all knew who LeBron was," Ghazi said. "College basketball, recruiting fans, and diehard NBA fans all knew who LeBron was. After that day, because of the game, the ratings, the highlights, the publicity, and the media coverage, the average fan knew who LeBron was. More importantly for LeBron and his future, the marketer who does not have a brand directly tied to the sports business—they may sell a car or bubblegum, a drink or beverage—they all know who LeBron was. From a branding standpoint, he really put his name out there." ESPN hurriedly planned to broadcast another of James's games the following month, one in California against Santa Ana's Mater Dei.

James supported a burgeoning economy that his talent and work had created. Yet, under the amateur rules, only others could profit off him at the time. *USA Today* estimated that James generated $1.5 million his senior year of high school for his school, promoters, arena owners, cable television, online auctions, and others. "The young man is being exploited by people all around the country," Clair Muscaro, commissioner of the Ohio High School Athletic Association, said to the newspaper. "Fifty dollars a ticket is ridiculous. But we have no control over ticket prices for regular-season games, only the playoffs." The school sold season tickets for James's senior season at $125 for adults. Students tickets could be had for $3 a game. The local newspaper, the *Cleveland Plain Dealer*, figured that James's presence made the school an extra $275,000. James stopped signing copies of his *Sports Illustrated* article after he saw them being auctioned online for more than $200. James's game tapes sold online for nearly $50. His bobbleheads fetched more than $100. Counterfeit basketball cards of James also sold quickly online. Scalpers sold tickets for three and four times the face value outside most of his home games.

"Think about the parents, okay?" said Frank Jessie, the school's athletic director during James's junior year. "Let's say you're charging ten to twelve dollars a ticket and you're gonna play eight to ten games at home. You're talking about a school where there's tuition money, books, expenses, and now you have [to pay] ten or twelve dollars to see your own kid play. It didn't seem equitable to me."

Jessie had played basketball at St. Vincent–St. Mary and rose to become an assistant on Bob Huggins's staff at the University of Cincinnati before returning to the high school. "My experience with him was nothing but positive," Jessie said of his interactions with James. But the publicity James received wreaked havoc at the small school. "We had four telephone lines going to St. Vincent–St. Mary at that time," Jessie recalled. "Many times, all four lines [were] tied up. The athletic department basically put a burden on the rest of the school. If somebody wanted to call in and see if the baseball game was rained out or something, or to check on somebody's grades, it was pretty tough . . . the whole situation kind of bothered me a little bit, to be honest. But that's the way it was. It was there when I got there and I tried to deal with it the best I could."

Jessie said he was offered a bribe of $5,000 for James to play in certain games, with his presence ensuring a packed crowd. "I said, 'Hey, I'm not a saint, but if somebody is going to try to bribe me, it's gotta be [for] more than that,'" Jessie said. "There's a good amount of money to be made. So what some people do, and I didn't mention names, but some of these promoters would try to buy off the person or persons on where the team was going to play. You could easily give somebody five grand and have a big payday." Jessie decided to leave his job after James's junior season. "I coached there and I loved the school," he said. "I have the utmost admiration for LeBron. But it was philosophical differences and I went my own way."

Everyone, it seemed, but James was allowed to profit. He even floated the possibility of petitioning the NBA to enable him to declare for the draft after his junior year of high school. The idea never gained much traction, although it brought James even more attention, in that a high schooler from Ohio would even bring up the notion. "I really never thought much about him leaving after his junior year because I just thought he was too close to the guys on the team, really," Keith Dambrot said. "Those are his childhood friends. That's one of the reasons he stayed at St. V all those years. He knew he could be a pro no matter where he was and he wasn't going to leave his friends and the guys he grew up with."

James still had all eyes on him. The Ohio High School Athletic Association conducted a two-week investigation after James was spotted driving a Hummer H2 vehicle worth over $80,000 before deciding that no amateur rules had been broken. Gloria James had taken out a loan based on James's future earnings to secure the luxury car. But the association ruled James ineligible after the *Cleveland Plain Dealer* reported that James had been given throwback jerseys of Wes Unseld and Gale Sayers, valued together at $845, in exchange for posing for photos that would be hung at Cleveland's Next Urban Gear and Music. The case was taken to court, where a judge ruled the association could not declare James ineligible.

• • •

James surprised no one by forgoing college and declaring for the 2003 NBA draft. The night before the draft's lottery, Aaron Goodwin, James's agent, worked hurriedly to finalize James's shoe deal. He did not want the market James played in to factor into the contract's worth.

Before James, Tracy McGrady had served as the high point for how much a shoe company would pay for a prep star. James stretched those limits and then some. Nike, Adidas, and Reebok had all been after James for years. James coyly played them all—wearing Adidas shoes at Nike's big camps and Nike shoes at ABCD camp. Sonny Vaccaro and Adidas had furnished St. Vincent–St. Mary with shoes for the whole team. The other shoe companies wangled their way in, too. Nike hired Maverick Carter, one of James's close friends, to work for the company. Reebok offered the most upfront money. Goodwin put James up in an Akron hotel. Reebok executives stayed in the same place, expecting to make a deal with James.

Vaccaro and Adidas dropped out of the running when the company opted not to offer the $10-million-a-year contract Vaccaro had promised to James. In truth, Vaccaro did not even believe that this would have been enough to lure James. "I never thought Phil Knight would lose him, even if we would have given him a hundred million dollars that day," Vaccaro said. "What [Adidas] made me do is mislead the kid. That's why I quit. That's a fact . . . it was always Adidas and then Nike. There's no question in my mind. Adidas screwed up bigger than any shoe company ever screwed up in their life. They never recovered from LeBron."

James chose Nike, signing a deal that would pay him more than $90 million over seven years.

He could finally profit from his own talents, years after others had made money off him. Vaccaro credited it all to James's beginnings against Cooke at his camp. "The camp basically made ninety million dollars for LeBron if you want to take it to the nth degree," Vaccaro said.

ABC decided to broadcast the NBA draft lottery's results in prime time for the first time—a result of the high interest in James and his future destination. James's hometown Cavaliers and the Denver Nuggets shared equal odds of winning the lottery at 22.5 percent. Meanwhile, the Memphis Grizzlies had only a 6.4 percent chance at the top pick. The struggling franchise had traded their pick to the Detroit Pistons a while ago and could only maintain the selection if they wound up winning the lottery. Improbably, as the draft order was revealed, only Memphis and Cleveland remained. Jerry West, the Lakers' great who had drafted Kobe Bryant, was now Memphis's general manager. He appeared devastated when the lottery revealed that not only had the Cavaliers won the top pick and would take James, but Memphis would also have to relinquish its second overall pick to Detroit. "It didn't take a genius to look at LeBron James and know what he was going to be," West said years later.

The Cavaliers did little to hide their glee at a future with James. The franchise had struggled for years and now had a homegrown kid with the talent to lead them into the playoffs. Cleveland hired Paul Silas to coach the team. Silas was a respected NBA veteran who had won three championships as a player. James astounded Silas when he talked knowingly about Silas's days of playing in the NBA with the Celtics on the first day the pair met. No player had gained the level of attention James had in high school. No player would also be as equipped as James was to enter the NBA from high school. But he did experience one early speed bump.

"We had a lot of players there that did not like him that much because the media and everybody, they would talk about him, how great he was going to be," Silas remembered. One practice, Silas noticed James was down. Silas would ask his team to shoot 100 free throws before every practice and James idled by himself in a corner. Silas summoned him to his office. From his own playing days, Silas knew that leadership had to be given and not demanded. He wanted James to earn his leadership role, even if it hurt the egos of some of the other players on the team.

"You've got to change," Silas told him. "What they're saying means nothing to you. You're going to be one of the best players ever."

Soon after that conversation, the Cavaliers traded away Ricky

Davis, a swingman who had been the team's leading scorer and who had bristled at the prospect of taking a backseat and fewer shots to accommodate a teenager. James flourished after the trade and was named the league's Rookie of the Year. He had been the most touted high school player in history and somehow the hype still fell short of the final product. "He could do anything," said Silas, who ended up coaching James during his first two NBA seasons. "He could run. He could shoot. He could jump. He could defend. He could block shots and he understood the game. To me, that was the key. He understood how to play and he was so young, but understood everything."

James arrived at superstardom during his sophomore season, when he averaged 27.2 points and became the youngest player selected to the All-NBA Team. In 2007, James led his severely outmanned Cavaliers (the team was composed of him and a bunch of role players) to the finals against the San Antonio Spurs, where they fell in four games. His play impressed. Just as surprising, his off-court image continued to sparkle. James mostly avoided controversy, despite constant scrutiny, and claimed the first of his four MVPs in 2009. His reputation took a substantial hit when he very publicly left the Cavaliers in 2010 during free agency for the Miami Heat. But after two title wins and four consecutive championship appearances, James reversed course, returning to the Cavaliers and delivering them to the 2015 NBA Finals, where Cleveland lost to the Golden State Warriors. The journey all began with that dream. "This is the cream of the crop at this point," James said. "It gets no higher than this and, for a basketball player, it was a dream of mine to be able to have the impact I've had in this league. It has been surprising at times. It's been overwhelming. It's been gratifying. At the same time, it's something I don't take for granted."

19.

There is no single trait shared by the high schoolers who reached their preordained stardom and those who fell short. There are certain commonalties, of course, among those who succeeded. They were generally mentally and physically mature beyond their years, had received strong guidance from family members or coaches they respected, and possessed an inner desire to improve their skills. Paul Silas was not the only one who accurately predicted a bright future for LeBron James in the NBA. The passage of time is the only accurate forecaster. A good part of an NBA executive's job—when all the analysis and tape study is done—is guesswork and crossing of fingers. "We all think we're geniuses," said Masai Ujiri, Toronto's well-respected general manager. "It's luck, in my opinion, a lot of times."

How else do you explain the enormous gulf between the careers of LeBron James and Ndudi Ebi? Kevin McHale and the Minnesota Timberwolves took Ebi with the 26th overall selection out of a Houston high school in 2003—the same year James was drafted. Ebi was long and athletic, viewed as the second coming of Kevin Garnett. McHale made the decision largely after watching Ebi aggressively defend James at a practice before the McDonald's All-American Game. "I thought we'd take a runner on him and just see what he could do," McHale recalled. "He was just one of those guys that wasn't ready." Ebi seldom played during his first two years and scoffed at a demotion to the NBA Development League. "You can quote me on this: I'm not a developmental player," he told the *St. Paul Pioneer Press* in 2005. "I've been playing against NBA guys since I was fifteen years old. I'm not a developmental player. Period."

He never played in another NBA game. Minnesota waived Ebi after he had spent just over two years with the organization and absorbed the remainder of his guaranteed contract.

McHale had originally hoped to bring Ebi along slowly and mentor him, as he had done with a teenage Garnett. McHale believed he had selected a gym rat, but those who had been close to Ebi noticed a difference in him once he entered the NBA. Greg Glenn coached Ebi at Westbury Christian School. Ebi was born in London and raised in Nigeria before relocating to the United States as a teenager. Back then, Glenn remembers Ebi always trying to improve himself. Ebi would lift weights after practice, even when Glenn pleaded with him to allow his body time to recover. Ebi carried a notebook full of self-scribbled motivational passages that he read for inspiration. Ebi matured quickly as a basketball player. He accepted a scholarship to the University of Arizona before changing course and setting his sights on the NBA. After Ebi announced his professional intentions, a reporter asked Glenn his thoughts. Glenn answered honestly and said he did not think Ebi was ready for the jump. The response bothered Ebi and frayed their relationship. "My agent told me there would be haters like you," Glenn recalled Ebi telling him.

"That's not what I'm saying," Glenn said. "I was asked for my opinion and I gave it. I apologize if it hurts your feelings. I just answered the question the best I could at the time with what I thought at the time. It doesn't mean I don't want the best for you." Glenn went from being a confidant of Ebi's to being ostracized by him. "For someone who invested as much time and energy and even love for the kid, I was now the bad guy," Glenn said. "I hate that. I thought we had more to our relationship than that."

Ebi never advanced beyond his status of being a project. He appeared lost on offense and displayed little interest in playing defense. He sulked at riding the bench. After his truncated NBA career, Ebi played internationally in countries like Italy, Israel, and China. He had little he wanted to say about his NBA career when reached by phone. In a conversation during the summer of 2013, Ebi seemed defensive. He alternated between saying he did not have a story to tell and expressing a desire to write his own book. Finally, he summed up his thoughts. "What did I learn in all my years in the NBA?" he asked. "You know what I'll tell you? The Staples Center has the best nachos."

He became regarded as an example of how a player can tumble when drafted on potential and assured millions. Flip Saunders coached both Garnett and Ebi in Minnesota. "That's the difference between a Kevin Garnett and a Ndudi Ebi," Saunders said. "That's what you learn. Kevin Garnett used to keep notes on players when he was younger, keep stats on what a guy did for their next meeting. Ndudi Ebi, he didn't have that. Part of it was that Kevin never felt that what he got, that he was owed that. He felt that he had to earn everything, where Ndudi Ebi, like a lot of those guys, felt that they were owed something. When you feel that you're owed something, you're never going to respect the game the way it needs to be respected."

Ebi was one of five high school players drafted by NBA teams in 2003. James became a star. The rest had no shoe companies bidding for their endorsements or commercials trumpeting their NBA arrival. They fought for their NBA survival and collectively stumbled during their rookie seasons, combining to play for just 82 minutes in 2003–2004. James topped that by himself by his third professional game. They were not viewed as immediate franchise cornerstones, but projects stashed away with the hope that one day they would develop into dependable NBA players. Kendrick Perkins, a prepster from Texas, was tapped as the next Shaquille O'Neal when Memphis took him and dealt him to Boston. "We felt like he was a project," said Danny Ainge,

Boston's president of basketball operations. "He needed to develop his body. I really liked him as a kid and his work ethic. But he was sort of a heavy, lumbering kid." Travis Outlaw was a sky reacher with an explosive game when Portland landed the Mississippi native with the 23rd overall pick. "When I first saw Travis Outlaw, I had serious concerns that he would ever make it as an NBA player," said John Nash, who by then worked in Portland's front office. "His stamina wasn't very good. He did not shoot very well." The pair never came close to reaching those lofty expectations, but bounced back from rocky NBA introductions to carve out sustainable NBA careers as role players.

James Lang was the final high school player selected in the 2003 NBA draft. He was a gentle giant with a quick smile and a dream of one day playing in the NBA. He is now partially paralyzed, the victim of a massive stroke the day after Thanksgiving in 2009 that left him mostly incapable of talking.

"It's tough for him because he loves sports," said Wanda Harris, Lang's mother. "LeBron and everybody that he went to [the] McDonald's [All-American Game] with, he sees them and that's all he watches. They bonded and he's always watching them. Can't get their names out, but he said, 'I know them.' I know he knows them."

• • •

Dr. Levan Parker first noticed about half of James Lang as Lang approached the double doors, while Parker conducted Bible study with students at Birmingham's Central Park Christian School. *They are going to have to open both doors for this giant,* Parker thought. Instead, Lang opened one and maneuvered his massive frame inside the room.

Lang was not big. He was mammoth—probably the largest kid his age that Parker had ever seen. Lang stood 6 feet 10 inches and weighed nearly 400 pounds. He had already made a mark in basketball in two years at a high school in Mobile, but struggled academically. Wanda Harris wanted Lang to succeed in both school and basketball. She knew her son likely had a professional future in basketball. She also recognized that a sports career does not last forever. She had been recommended to Parker's program by a friend. Parker was the school's headmaster and basketball coach, both judge and jury, and a person Harris figured would be as concerned about Lang in the classroom as much as on the court.

She allowed Lang to transfer schools and live with a host family. Harris offered Parker a warning before departing. "Sir, what I want you to know is that you have to monitor him all the time," Harris warned Parker. "You have to check his shoes because he'll hide candy in his shoes." The request caught Parker off guard. He enjoyed pushing the game's tempo to its limits by having his team guard the entire floor. He wondered if Lang could adapt to his style. He also was not going to inspect Lang's shoes. "You can call me Big Baby," Lang informed Parker.

"You don't think I'm going to call you that, do you?" Parker asked.

"Yes, I do," Lang replied. "I got that name in kindergarten and I'm proud of it every day. I go home and my mom says I am a big baby and I am."

Parker decided that he would not cater to Lang. Lang would have to meet the team's conditioning requirements, just like every other player. "I'll give you a little time to get in shape and work on it," Parker said. "But you're going to do it. You can do it if you want to. You can drink all the Cokes that you want to, but you are going to make these times if you want to play." Parker found Lang to be one of the nicest kids he had ever coached. Lang was innocent and quiet. His large frame hid a kid who seemed younger than his teenage years. Wanting to please his mother, Lang shed nearly 70 pounds the summer before his senior year of high school. He was still heavy and sometimes labored up the court, but he showed energy in sustainable spurts. He had soft hands and could maneuver in traffic. The results proved disastrous for opponents. College coaches started attending Lang's games. Tubby Smith of Kentucky showed up. So did Rick Pitino, the Louisville coach. They were soon joined by NBA personnel. Lang heard he could make the jump straight to the NBA and started seriously contemplating the decision.

He decided that it had been a lifetime goal. If he could reach it, why delay it?

Lang knew he had much work left in improving his conditioning, diet, and play. Had Lang been drafted in the first round, he would have been the recipient of a three-year guaranteed contract and enough time to incubate properly. Instead, Lang landed at the Hornets in the second round with no guarantee of making the team. Tim Floyd had wound up coaching in New Orleans by then and could be excused if he had already had his fill of the high school experience following the disaster of introducing Tyson Chandler and Eddy Curry into the NBA and the Bulls organization. Bob Bass, the executive who drafted and traded Kobe Bryant in Charlotte, initially saw promise in Lang. But Bass came to the conclusion that Lang would not work himself onto the active roster anytime soon. Lang spent the first part of the season on the injured list before being released near Christmas. He played some minor league basketball and bounced around leagues in Spain, Canada, and elsewhere. The Atlanta Hawks and Toronto Raptors signed Lang to 10-day contracts, although he never made an appearance with either team. Fatigue and conditioning always held him back. Players talk about hitting a wall and pushing through it when they're tired. Lang stopped when the wall hit him.

In November 2006—more than three years after being drafted—Lang made his NBA debut for the Washington Wizards. He had been inactive for the team's previous 13 games. He had only been in the team's official uniform for the annual team picture. That November night, Lang did not expect to play against the Hawks. He was eating in the arena's media room when a team staff member broke the news. Lang finished and put on his uniform. He did not play much—less than a minute. But his dream, even fleetingly, had been achieved. Lang played nearly 20 minutes in his next game, a mark that would serve as the high for his NBA career. The Wizards waived Lang in January. He later conceded that he ate himself out of the league by regularly consuming fast food before and after games.

Lang kept dim hopes of a return flickering into 2009 when he signed with the Utah Flash of the NBA Development League. The Flash released him for what the organization described as "medical reasons." He was not heavy—weighing about 280 pounds—but was constantly fatigued. A couple of trips up and down the court tired him out. Brad Jones, the Flash's coach, told the *Washington Times* that Lang's heart had tested abnormally and he had high blood pressure.

Lang suffered a massive stroke in November while celebrating Thanksgiving at his grandmother's home in Alabama. Doctors did not know whether he would survive the night. Blood was coagulating throughout his body.

• • •

W anda Harris remained practical in a stressful situation. Her family called her tough and that may be an understatement. Harris said that, following the stroke, Lang had "one [clot] on his brain the size of a softball. He had one on his heart. He had them all the way down his side."

The doctor, Harris said, cried when he learned Lang was only 26 years old. He had a son the same age. "Look, you need to get yourself together," Harris recalled telling him. She asked for another doctor. Joseph, her husband, stepped outside the room at the Mobile Infirmary Medical Center to compose himself. Wanda Harris told him to be strong. She went window-shopping, possessing that much faith that her son would survive. "Our job is when we get home," she told her family. "Y'all go ahead on. The nurses got him. They'll call me."

Lang survived and is still recovering. A colon cleanse, designed to accelerate weight loss, and Lang's failure to take his blood pressure medicine, likely contributed to the stroke.

The NBA riches that Lang had hoped for never materialized. Life had to go on for Wanda Harris as it had all along. She still had other children to raise. Lang enjoys watching basketball and has a girlfriend who spends hours with him. The family harbored few regrets about Lang's basketball experience. They felt as though they did not take any shortcuts and Lang did everything he could for his career. They could have taken shortcuts when the colleges came to recruit Lang, Wanda Harris said.

"At that time my husband was ill, they had certain doctors that they could get him recommended to. Our vehicle wasn't working . . ." Harris said about the offers from some college coaches. She declined to specify from which schools.

"That's just not who we are. My husband and I, stuff don't make us, we make stuff," Harris said. "That didn't impress us . . . I guess they feel like if you're poor and you're black you're just going to jump for the win. No." The agent the family hired, Tony Dutt, treated Lang like a member of his own family, Harris said. It was up to Lang to produce. "It's common sense," Harris said. "If McDonald's hired you to be a manager, you're going to have to do what the franchise said to do. If you don't do that, they're going to get rid of you. It doesn't matter how many times they call your name and call you Big Baby and showboat you around. It's business at the end of the day."

Harris did acknowledge one change she would have made. "I would've told him, though, that he couldn't go to the NBA, that he had to do two years in college," she said. "I would've declined [to let any NBA coaches come] to see him. That's what I would've done, but he had to make some decisions by himself."

. . .

That reflection is one arrived at through the passage of time.

Earl Smith Jr. offered a contrasting stance when his son contemplated the same decision.

Smith's son, J. R. Smith, entered the 2004 McDonald's All-American Game known more as a local talent in New Jersey than a national phenom. At the All-Star Game, J. R. Smith buried several long shots to score 25 points and claim co-MVP honors with Dwight Howard at the Ford Center in Oklahoma City. Smith decided soon after to pass on his college commitment to North Carolina and enter the NBA draft. Smith Jr. had played college basketball in New Jersey. The way he saw it, the longer a prospect remained in college, the more his draft stock sank. "Come out of high school and [you're] in the top thirty of the NBA draft," he said. "You go to college, you get exposed. Now, you're out of the draft. You've got to get to the money when you can go and make a few million dollars without doing that manual labor. You can get an education later. I know how hard it is. I worked a long time to even try and make a million dollars. It don't come easy."

J. R. Smith was part of a landmark class of high school–to–pro players. The New Orleans Hornets took him 18th overall as one of 8 high school players drafted within the first 19 selections. Howard, a tall prospect from Georgia, headlined the class, becoming the third high school player taken first overall in four years when the Orlando Magic tapped him over Emeka Okafor, a proven college player. Howard immediately showed his promise as a rookie. The rest of the class stumbled early on—some never recovered to sustain their NBA careers. In New Orleans, Jim Cleamons served as an assistant coach on Byron Scott's staff. As a player, Cleamons helped propel the 1972 Lakers to a championship as a reliable defender, following a collegiate career spent at Ohio State. He advanced to coaching, sitting on Phil Jackson's benches in Chicago and Los Angeles. Cleamons said it was nearly impossible for a high school player to properly understand the NBA's ebb and flow, both on and off the court. He watched, and often tried to step between, J. R. Smith and Scott as they bickered over playing time and work habits.

"There's so much about the game that they do not understand, that you cannot tell them that they don't understand because it's basketball and they've been playing basketball since they were in elementary school," Cleamons said. "But they haven't played it at this level against grown men who they haven't heard about and don't have any respect for, but are actually pretty good, even though they are not All-Star, marquee players. You've got a young kid straight out of high school trying to run around and negotiate screens, fight around picks. They've never been attacked that way on the defensive end. They've always been the guy who's been getting the screens set for them.

"It's not J.R. It's the system," Cleamons continued. "We're talking out of both sides of our mouths and they're caught in the middle because they are impressionable because they want to play and they want approval. We want to talk about them doing things and then when it doesn't happen, we want to throw them under the bus and say, 'They haven't done this. They haven't done that.' Well, is it their fault? Or is it the way we teach them? Is it our expectation of what we want from them? When I say we, I'm talking about the coaches. And then, you've got to go back to the agents. What are the agents telling them? What are the general managers saying in contract negotiations? What are the people they trusted growing up telling them? What are Mom and Dad telling them behind the scenes? What are girlfriends and wives talking about when they show their rings and coats and what they're driving? It's the whole kit and kaboodle. It's pure, unadulterated American capitalism on one hand versus coaches trying to win ball games and championships, and the kids are caught in the middle."

Players had motivation for wanting to begin their professional careers as soon as possible. The NBA was prospering and had financially bounced back since the struggles after Michael Jordan's retirement as a Bull. The league signed six-year broadcasting deals with ESPN, ABC, and TNT worth $4.6 billion in 2002. The mark was a significant jump from the television deals signed in 1998. That year, NBC had paid $1.6 billion for four years of televising rights and TBS/TNT forked over $840 million for the same period. The value of franchises had also skyrocketed. In 2002, Robert L. Johnson purchased an expansion team in Charlotte for $300 million. Only 15 years earlier, George Shinn paid $32.5 million to land Charlotte its original NBA franchise. Most interest in the league stemmed from the popularity of individual players and, by 2004, the majority of the league's brightest stars had entered the league out of high school. Kevin Garnett claimed the league's Most Valuable Player award in 2004, while Jermaine O'Neal finished third in the balloting. Kobe Bryant had won three straight championships. Tracy McGrady had captured two league scoring titles. And LeBron James won the league's Rookie of the Year in 2004 out of high school, following in the footsteps of Amar'e Stoudemire, who had won it straight out of high school the previous year.

Trouble still loomed. The NBA found itself at a crossroads that would determine its long-term future. It was financially profitable, but attendance and ratings were sagging. The league still had not found an heir to Michael Jordan. It constantly battled image issues amid concerns based on both reality and perception. Basketball is a rare sport. No equipment, helmets, or hats shielded the players' faces or bodies. They were out there for the fans to see, nearly as recognizable on the court as they were off it. Yet, more and more, it seemed as though players possessed a skewed perspective on reality and could not relate to the lives of everyday people. Latrell Sprewell, a gifted basketball player perhaps better known for choking his coach in a rage than for his four All-Star appearances, rejected a three-year, $21 million contract offer from Glen Taylor and the Timberwolves in 2004. In doing so, he told the *St. Paul Pioneer Press*: "I have a family to feed . . . If Taylor wants to see my family fed, he better cough up some money. Otherwise, you're going to see these kids in one of those Sally Struthers commercials soon." Kobe Bryant, once perceived as following in Jordan's footsteps, also had his own troubling issues. His championships arrived as he simultaneously bickered with Shaquille O'Neal in a public and bitter feud over who should be the team's primary leader. In 2003, authorities in Colorado charged Bryant with sexual assault, following an alleged incident with a 19-year-old hotel employee at the Lodge & Spa at Cordillera. Bryant was 24 years old, married, and had recently become a father. Bryant admitted to adultery, although he denied the allegations against him and insisted the encounter had been consensual. The case's hearings were played out publicly. Hearing dates occasionally resulted in Bryant having to attend court sessions, catch a plane, and play in a game, all in the same day. Prosecutors dropped the case when the alleged victim declined to provide testimony and Bryant later settled a civil suit stemming from the case out of court. Bryant apologized to the woman for the incident without admitting guilt. While his legal culpability had ended, Bryant's endorsing ability had eroded. Companies like Coca-Cola and McDonald's ended their affiliation with Bryant.

The league had come to be associated with hip-hop culture, a union that had always been an uneasy one for many. Within that culture, Allen Iverson, the Philadelphia 76ers' diminutive star, stood out. While Iverson had attended Georgetown University for two years, he was young and brash, sporting cornrows and tattoos. At one point, Iverson produced a rap single that contained homophobic and misogynistic lyrics. He represented a lightning rod for debate concerning the NBA's present and future. He was viewed as authentic by most young people, a player who overcame meager beginnings and his small stature—a generously listed 6 feet and 165 pounds—to dominate a game ruled by giants. He was one of their own, a star who could not be manufactured and remained true to himself. Another group, consisting of corporate sponsors and wealthy fans, saw Iverson as thuggish, the anti-Jordan, and a ball hog who complained about having to practice. Author David Halberstam once wrote that the perception of the league was that it was "far too black." It was still predominantly black and still trying to walk the tricky balance beam of catering to both urban and corporate fan bases. Only now, it went beyond mere perception; in reality, the NBA could be seen by some as filled with immature African-American millionaires.

But no single event threatened the NBA's viability like those on the night of November 19, 2004.

That evening, the Detroit Pistons hosted the Indiana Pacers in a game nationally televised by ESPN. A tense rivalry had developed between the teams. The matchup offered a rematch of an emotionally charged Eastern Conference Finals a season earlier. In Game 6 of that series, Indiana's Ron Artest delivered a forearm that resulted in a vicious flagrant foul to Detroit's Richard Hamilton. The Pistons won that series and advanced to claim the championship by topping the favored Lakers, a team that had disintegrated following the feud between Bryant and O'Neal. Bad blood and memories toward the other team flowed throughout the rosters. Detroit wanted to defend its ground. Indiana considered itself the better team.

It appeared to be Indiana's night as the Pacers pulled away in the fourth quarter. But the game turned increasingly testy—an elbow here and a push there. "Man, these fouls are getting harder and harder," Mark Montieth, who covered the Pacers for the *Indianapolis Star,* mentioned to a colleague from his courtside seat along press row. With 1:25 remaining and the game settled, Detroit's Ben Wallace knocked Artest into the basket support as he attempted a layup.

Indiana's Stephen Jackson attempted free throws a few seconds later. He remembers someone on the team telling Artest, "You can get one now"—meaning that Artest could deliver a hard foul to someone he had been battling throughout the game. Artest, who had already run afoul of the league through his constant eccentric and erratic behavior, fouled Wallace hard on a shot attempt. Wallace retaliated, delivering a two-arm shove to Artest's face. The push's force caused Artest to stumble backward and Wallace pursued him. Their momentum carried them close to the scorers' table, where both teams came together. The officiating crew of Tim Donaghy, Ron Garretson, and Tommy Nunez Jr. were timid in defusing the fracas. Mike Brown, a Pacers assistant coach, shared a relationship with Wallace. Brown pondered how he could calm the situation. "Debo, Debo," he said, using one of Wallace's nicknames. "It's not worth it. Go back. Come on." Wallace pulled back and stopped trying to reengage Artest. The players milled around, still jawing at one another. Stephen Jackson squared up with Detroit's Lindsey Hunter. They briefly sized each other up before both thought better of going further. Meanwhile, Artest decided to lie on the scorers' table. He had been told to try to disengage himself from situations when they became contentious and lying down was his response. It had the opposite effect. Several fans, now in close proximity to Artest, screamed obscenities at him. Wallace, who had calmed down, became agitated all over again during the lull and tossed his armband in Artest's direction.

Artest had just finished talking to Jim Gray, ESPN's sideline reporter. "Ron, don't leave," he said. "I want you after the game."

"OK," Artest responded.

Then, a fan named John Green hurled a plastic cup filled with Diet Coke into the air. The contents splattered on Artest. With all the tension in the air, the beverage acted like a grenade.

All hell broke loose.

Joe Dumars, by then Detroit's general manager, had retreated from the court to the inner belly of the arena. He walked alongside John Hammond, who had advanced to work with Dumars as his assistant general manager. Detroit's performance had frustrated the pair, who heard a sudden collective roar. "Joe, something either really good just happened or something really bad just happened," Hammond said, hoping that Detroit had somehow miraculously turned the game around in its waning moments.

Artest had raced into the stands. Instinctively, Mark Boyle, Indiana's play-by-play broadcaster, tried intervening and stood up. Artest trampled over him and Boyle sustained five fractured vertebrae. Mike Brown could not recall following Artest into the stands, but suddenly he found himself amid the havoc, having gone after him. Artest pushed over a fan, Michael Ryan, who had not thrown the cup. Green, the fan who had, tried putting Artest in a headlock. Another fan threw a beer at Artest and sprayed Jackson, who had chased after his teammate. Jackson punched wildly. Indiana's Fred Jones also went into the stands, where he was confronted with a missed haymaker from Ben Wallace's brother, David.

Artest remained in the stands for about 40 seconds before exiting and making his way back down to Indiana's bench. Two fans in Pistons jerseys wandered aimlessly onto the court and near Artest. The parties briefly looked at each other. Artest punched Alvin Shackleford, a blow that also made Charlie Haddad stumble. As Haddad started to rise,

Jermaine O'Neal gathered himself for a punch, cocking back his arm. But O'Neal stumbled, turning what would have been a devastating blow into a glancing one.

A confrontation between the Pacers and the Pistons had devolved into one between the Pacers and Detroit fans, who hurled more and more objects onto the court. The Pacers needed an exit strategy and the only option was a retreat through a tunnel and past many of the enraged fans. Chuck Person, an ex–NBA player working in Indiana's front office, had also left the game after the Pacers pulled away. He returned after hearing that Artest had vaulted into the stands, and he went after Artest. To Person, Artest had blacked out and was unaware of where he was. Person made eye contact with him in an attempt to calm him. Person felt as though the team were trapped in a gladiator-like scene, "where the fans were lions and we were just trying to escape with our lives," he said.

With Person's firm guidance, Artest finally left the court. Stephen Jackson followed through the tunnel, tearing at his own jersey and screaming at fans as they hurled drinks at him. His adrenaline surged. Jackson felt as though the Pacers had not only topped the Pistons, but had bested the entire city as well. O'Neal walked through the tunnel, incensed that coaches had pinned his hands down and he could not protect himself from the arsenal of debris flying at him. A chair came soaring through the air, narrowly missing players. Jamaal Tinsley, Indiana's point guard, returned after exiting the court, wielding a dustpan over his head before being pulled away.

The melee turned into the NBA's worst nightmare and largest challenge. It threatened to undermine the wholesome images that the league had worked decades to develop—ones of Magic Johnson's pearly smile and Michael Jordan's grace on and off the court. "You had some fans that thought that we were out-of-control thugs for whatever reason, not even knowing who we are, what we do for our communities," Jermaine O'Neal said years later. "And then you had the other half that really supported what was going on and who we were as players and as people." The replays aired on endless loops on television stations.

It provided fodder for thinly veiled racist diatribes. Rush Limbaugh, the conservative political commentator, described it as "the hip-hop culture on parade. This is gang behavior on parade minus the guns. That's the culture that the NBA has become." Commissioner David Stern released a statement the following day that read: "The events at last night's game were shocking, repulsive, and inexcusable—a humiliation for everyone associated with the NBA." He suspended nine players for a total of 146 games that resulted in nearly $10 million in lost salary. Oakland County prosecutors charged five players and five fans in the incident. The players pleaded no contest. Green received a 30-day jail sentence.

"I think it's fair to say that the NBA was the first sport that was widely viewed as a black sport," Stern told the *Washington Post*. "And whatever the numbers ultimately are for other sports, the NBA will always be treated a certain way because of that. Our players are so visible that if they have Afros or cornrows or tattoos—white or black—our consumers pick it up. So I think there are always some elements of race involved that affect judgments about the NBA."

Stern had been saddled with correcting the league's image after he had first been appointed as commissioner. He was now tasked with the same challenge—only with higher stakes.

20.

David Stern ended his term as NBA commissioner in February 2014, three decades to the day after he had started his tenure. The game's brightest current star, LeBron James, had not even been born when Stern became commissioner in 1984. Then, Stern maintained a bushy mustache, thick-rimmed glasses, and a slight paunch. Over the years, his hair aged to a stately snow white. The glasses became modern. The slight paunch grew slightly. He lost the mustache. Stern was 71 years old upon his exit, having presided over the NBA's great growth in profitability and popularity. Few could argue with the robust state Stern bequeathed the NBA upon his departure. The league grossed about $5.5 billion annually and, in the fall of 2014, signed a new television pact that would net it $2.66 billion a year. Player salaries averaged more than $5 million a year. The league and its players were widely beloved abroad, in countries like China and Spain, places that had only been vaguely familiar with the NBA when Stern first ascended to power. He shepherded the NBA through a number of controversies, putting out the fires, and drawing his own criticism based on everything from the relocation of franchises to the implementation of a player dress code, one of several contentious responses to the brawl between the Pacers and the Pistons.

Those advancements came for a reason. They were plotted, planned, and carried out. Stern was decisive and divisive. He was a negotiator who assumed his stance, dug in, and traditionally made the opposition come around and often agree with his viewpoint. That is why it was somewhat remarkable that Stern was sometimes not sure if he was on the right side of the issue of whether high school players should be allowed into the NBA. The league and the players association came to a compromise in June 2005 under Article X, Section 1, of the collective-bargaining agreement, which increased the league's age minimum from 18 to 19 years old and mandated that American players be at least a year removed from high school before becoming draft-eligible. The rule stated that international players would only be eligible to be drafted if they had turned at least 19 years old the calendar year of that draft. For the first time, NBA teams would also be allowed to assign their players to the NBA Development League during the first two years of their playing career, although the NBA lacked a true farm system, like that in baseball or hockey.

A door that had opened three decades earlier and a route that had introduced some of the greatest stars into the NBA, from Kevin Garnett to Kobe Bryant and LeBron James, was shuttered. "Lots of jobs have requirements that make for an older workforce," Stern told the *Boston Globe*. "This is a personal project of mine. A few points: One, we already have a minimum age, 18, dating back to 1976. Two, it is time to tell the communities that we serve that the sixth-grader, as Arthur Ashe used to say, is far more likely to be a rocket scientist, biology professor, etc., than a pro athlete. Three, I want to get NBA scouts out of high school gyms. It sends the wrong message for them to be there. Where does it stop? Four, older players can deal better with the stress and grind of the unique NBA season. Five, it is a business matter. A draft pick is a big investment. It is better to see a return in less than two years. But with all that said, it is a hard issue. Everyone can be right in this one."

Stern and Billy Hunter, the executive director of the players union, had postured for years on whether the NBA should prohibit high school players from joining its workforce. Hunter had been appointed the union's executive director in 1996. He had engaged in tough negotiations with Stern before. Neither budged for months in 1998, and the prolonged lockout ensued. In some cases, the pair flip-flopped stances on an age minimum. Stern had once said that it would be wrong denying high schoolers entrance into the NBA, while tennis and golf prodigies began their professional careers as adolescents. Meanwhile, whenever asked, Hunter stated his strong stance against the banning of high schoolers in the draft. "I'm not going to agree to an age [minimum], period," Hunter told the Bloomberg News Service in 2001. "Our players believe in the right of choice. Anybody who can perform should be permitted to come in. At eighteen, you can get married, go into the military, and be sentenced to death. You mean to tell me you shouldn't be allowed to play basketball?"

The league and its players had been negotiating a new labor agreement for months by the time of the brawl in Michigan. The fight provided an impetus for shoring up the league's image. Its players had come to be regarded as collectively immature and, whether or not that mentality was rooted in fact, the perception became the reality. The veteran bench player on the last legs of his career, who could provide mentoring and steadiness, had been mostly replaced by a teenager who had spent little or no time in college and still had much to learn about professionalism and navigating life. Players often turned up on police blotters. In Portland, the roster became derisively known as the "Jail Blazers," following a number of high-profile incidents involving members of the team. "We're not really going to worry about what the hell [the fans] think about us," Bonzi Wells, one of the team's offenders, said to *Sports Illustrated*. "They really don't matter to us. They can boo us every day, but they're still going to ask for our autographs if they see us on the street. That's why they're fans, and we're NBA players." In the aftermath of the brawl, Stern's dress code immediately drew the ire of some players who argued that it stripped them of their individuality.

The policy required that, among other rules, injured players wear a sports jacket and no visible necklaces or medallions while on the bench. "Just because you put a guy in a tuxedo, it doesn't mean he's a good guy," Allen Iverson told reporters in Philadelphia. Jermaine O'Neal was still dealing with the fallout of the brawl when the dress code was introduced. "I honestly believe that's why the dress code came into play," he said. "Because all of a sudden now the league is 'out of control.' I watched the so-called analysts, on national TV, say the NBA is too hip-hoppish. And it really blew me away that supposed analysts would even, first of all, say that. Your choice of music doesn't dictate who you are as a person. Right after the brawl, the dress code came into play." Players who had entered the NBA from high school, J. R. Smith and Shaun Livingston, wore long socks during a game in a quiet and mild protest. O'Neal thought that race factored into the new rules. Of all the American-born players drafted into the NBA from high school, only one—Robert Swift—was white. "As a black guy, you kind of think [race is] the reason why it's coming up," O'Neal said at the time. "You don't hear about it in baseball or hockey. To say you have to be twenty, twenty-one to get in the league, it's unconstitutional."

It was not. Instead, it was a rule agreed to by the union that represented NBA players. O'Neal was one of the few players who had taken the route from high school to the NBA to argue against an age minimum. "That's actually kind of the surprising thing," recalled Pat Garrity, a former NBA player and a member of the union's executive committee, a panel of players charged with acting in the interests of the players as a whole during the negotiations for a collective bargaining agreement. Garrity did not recall many active players arguing that high school players should be allowed to join their ranks. The players believed in the right of choice—and also in their right to make as much money as possible. The negotiations worked as a give-and-take bartering between the assemblage of lawyers maintained by the league and the players and Stern and Hunter. The importance of allowing high school players into the league fell somewhere below the fight to maintain the length of maximum player contracts and the sizes of annual raises. The league and the union found middle ground on several issues. The new deal lowered the maximum length of contracts from seven to six seasons and dropped the cap on annual raises. Stern accepted the 19-year-old age minimum, instead of his preferred 20-year-old minimum.

The choice was simple when everyone involved in the negotiations looked at the alternatives. At the time, Michael Curry was the president of the players union. He was a member of the Indiana Pacers and not a basketball prodigy, like most of the kids who had come straight into the NBA. Curry went undrafted after spending his college years at Georgia Southern and doing stints in basketball's minor league rungs and abroad in Italy and Spain. But he played hard-nosed defense and became a respectable veteran for several teams in an NBA career that spanned close to a decade. "It's a hard thing to do, try and satisfy 450 [players] because you have 450 guys who are CEOs of their own corporations," Curry said. "What if we didn't have guaranteed contracts and someone came out and got injured? You give yourself up when you're part of a group. But the guys that have not gotten to the NBA yet, they haven't become part of the group. I've heard all the sayings and people are absolutely right. If you go fight for your country at eighteen, can't you come into the NBA? They probably could if we didn't have guaranteed contracts. When you have a union and you make decisions, you give that up, but what we kept was more important."

After four days of intense negotiations, the sides announced the new deal in San Antonio before Game 6 of the NBA Finals between the Spurs and the Detroit Pistons, with the age minimum almost serving as an afterthought. The mandate was only briefly touched on when Hunter and Stern addressed the media in late June 2005. "Well, we have been negotiating rather intently for a period of time," Hunter said, gazing into the sea of reporters through his glasses. "I guess the two of us needed to ratchet up the rhetoric and we decided it was time to back away from the abyss and decide if we could really do a deal. What we did, we ended up spending about fourteen hours together last Friday, and we said, if we're going to be able to do it, now is the time. Otherwise, we know what the end result is going to be. So our president, Curry, came in, along with Antonio Davis and Pat Garrity from the players' side. We sat there along with David and forty owners and staff, and after about fourteen hours, we kind of moved closer and closer until we thought we had a framework for the deal." A reporter asked Stern if he believed the age minimum would legally prevail if challenged in court, in light of the recent suit filed by football's Maurice Clarett, challenging the NFL's early eligibility rules. The reporter's second question dealt with whether the rule change was aimed at removing NBA personnel from high school gymnasiums.

Sonny Vaccaro was one of the few who challenged the new rule immediately, telling the *New York Daily News*: "I thought Stern did what any head of a company does. He did everything he could for his owners and he basically had to give up nothing. It was one of the most one-sided negotiations I've ever seen in my life. The fact it lasted five seconds was a joke."

The questions veered toward other issues. In 2013, NBA players ousted Hunter from his executive role. Hunter had received complaints of nepotism because he employed several family members in the players union. His discharge was the result of a fractious fallout with Derek Fisher, a veteran player who had ascended to president of the union. Fisher initiated an outside review of the association's finances. The review found that Hunter had spent more than $100,000 on gifts for other executive committee members and had received $1.3 million for unused vacation time. Hunter recently said that he still believes the age minimum is financially motivated and inclusion into the NBA should be merit-based. "It's all about dollars," he said. "Because we knew that if a kid comes out early, then he's going to have an opportunity to make a lot more money than by the time he's put in his first two or three years [in college].

"The reality is that the rookies don't displace anybody because you're going to have thirty players coming and thirty players leaving no matter what," he continued in the spring of 2013. "So what they end up doing, they end up really displacing some college players who might've gotten drafted at a higher level or end up maybe not getting drafted at all because they've been displaced by a high school player coming in."

The Toronto Raptors prepared to play the Lakers in Los Angeles a few days later. Amir Johnson, then a member of the Raptors, laughed when recalling the moment he found out he had been drafted into the NBA. When the Pistons made Johnson the final high school player drafted with one of the second round's final picks just one week after the announcement of the age minimum, he could not rise off the couch to celebrate. Johnson, a pillar of a teen, had grown up in East Los Angeles and had pledged to play at the University of Louisville under Rick Pitino. He was so committed to Louisville that he had visited the dorm room where he planned to live, as Moses Malone had done at Maryland decades earlier. But a couple of impressive workouts changed his mind and he felt he could compete in the NBA. Eight other high school players had already been selected in that draft, beginning with Portland's pick of Seattle's Martell Webster with the sixth overall selection. Still, a current of electricity ran through Johnson's body when he heard his name called. But he could not move. "I was over at my auntie's house," Johnson explained. "We were all watching on the leather couch, no plastic. She had just taken the plastic off. When I got drafted I was stuck to the couch. I couldn't get up."

As a rookie, he had as much to learn off the court as on it. Johnson joined a deep and veteran-laden Pistons team, the same organization where Korleone Young had failed as a novice high schooler years earlier. Johnson played in just three games his rookie season, while bouncing back and forth between the Pistons and the NBA Development League. He was wise to have a support system around him. Johnson's mother, Deneen Griffin, moved in with him. A teammate, Antonio McDyess, bought Johnson his first suit. "Even though I really couldn't fit it at all because it was kind of big on me," Johnson said. And then there was the whole challenge of being able to afford a decent car, but not possessing a driver's license. "When I learned how to drive, it was tough, especially in Detroit because it was snowing out there," Johnson said. "I learned how to drive in the snow, the Michigan U-turn, how to pump your brakes, a bunch of stuff."

The qualities that separated Johnson from others who failed are clear. Johnson was not playing with the Pistons, so he asked to be demoted to the minors to gain some playing time. He tried staying away from the nightlife. He asked questions and listened to the answers. Having the distinction of being the last high school player drafted into the NBA holds little weight with Johnson. He said he was more content that he is still in the NBA now, having established himself in Toronto's frontcourt for years before signing with the Boston Celtics in the summer of 2015. "That's why I usually tell younger kids, if you really want to go to that next level, you have to work hard and put in that dedication, sacrifices, and the first thing is to get your schoolwork done," Johnson said. "You can't rely on basketball because it's not [usually] going to happen. You usually see players that just rely on it and not make it and go overseas."

· · ·

The NBA's prep-to-pro movement crested on the court in the 2009 NBA Finals between the Lakers and the Orlando Magic. By then, the league had banned high schoolers from entering the league years before. But players who had already made the jump piloted teams across the league. That finals pitted two stars in Kobe Bryant and Dwight Howard, players on opposite ends of the prep-to-pro spectrum. Bryant was part of the first wave of players who declared from high school and had already earned every NBA accolade imaginable. Howard, drafted first overall in 2004, was an athletic freak of a rim rattler who had ascended as one of the final NBA stars to have passed on college.

The Magic had seriously debated whether to use that first selection on Howard or Emeka Okafor, an All-American and a national championship winner from the University of Connecticut. Howard seemed grounded. His father worked as a Georgia state trooper. His mother taught at the tiny Christian school he had attended since the age of four. Only 13 members comprised Howard's graduating class. Howard seemed like a marketer's dream and routinely discussed bringing God into the NBA and placing a cross on the NBA's logo. "He was so raw, but had a good foundation," recalled Dave Twardzik, Orlando's director of player personnel at the time of the draft. "His father was a policeman and his mother was a tremendous influence in his life and he seemed to be really attached to his family. Not to say that Okafor was not, but with Dwight, we were very impressed with that, plus the upside to his game was tremendous in our eyes."

His upside included a frame that was nearly 7 feet tall and 250 pounds—a man's body. He started immediately as a power forward in Orlando. Johnny Davis, his first Magic coach, brought him along slowly and Howard had an immediate impact on games through his athleticism and defensive ability. Howard had fun on the court and developed into one of the league's premier inside forces. He led Orlando in blitzing through the 2009 playoffs and defeated LeBron James and Cleveland in the Eastern Conference Finals. But the Lakers topped Orlando in five games for Bryant's fourth championship and his first without Shaquille O'Neal as a teammate.

Soon after, Howard's polite image changed. News outlets reported that he had fathered several children out of wedlock, contrary to the Christian image he had cultivated. He forced his way out of Orlando through a trade to the Lakers in 2012 that involved Andrew Bynum, another prep-to-pro All-Star, being dealt from Los Angeles to Philadelphia. In Los Angeles, Howard's play was limited as he recovered from back surgery and he and Bryant never coalesced as teammates. Howard always played with a grin, while Bryant took the court with a constant scowl. "What surprises me the most about his career is I never thought, not in a million years, that he would ever be portrayed as a villain publicly," Johnny Davis said of Howard. "I hear things about him now and I say, 'That's not the same Dwight Howard that I know.'

I just can't believe the way that he's portrayed at times and I think it's unfair. I don't think the young man is as bad as people say."

In the summer of 2013, Howard left the Lakers and signed with the Houston Rockets. "The things that he excelled at in his rookie year are still the things that are on his calling card," Davis said. "That's rebounding, blocking shots, being tough around the basket. He really hasn't shown a tremendous amount of growth in terms of offensive skills, but he's still viable down there. It's not like you can just let him shoot. You have to contest the shot. That's the area [where] he really didn't make a whole lot of progress, from what I can see. I thought he would at this point be a much better free-throw shooter. I also thought that by this point in his career, a team would be able to throw him the ball and feel very comfortable. I don't know if that's the case."

• • •

The NBA's headquarters are located inside Manhattan's Olympic Tower. The offices span several high floors in Midtown East and sit atop people hustling from one destination to another deep down below. Stern shunned his suit's jacket as he sat down with a journalist and Mike Bass, the league's executive vice president of communications, at a large conference table. His retirement would be official in a few short months. In recent days, comments originating from the collegiate ranks had irked Stern. He made little effort to hide his disdain and mentioned them floating in the news before the interview with the reporter had really begun. "Did you see [NCAA president Mark] Emmert had some remarks this week?" he asked. The NBA's relationship with college basketball had once been symbiotic. The NCAA had served as a feeder system to the NBA. Players like Magic Johnson, Larry Bird, and many others first gained popularity and fame in college before carrying their names and reputations to the NBA. The age minimum changed all that. It created an influx of college players who otherwise would have entered the NBA out of high school. Instead, they spent a few months on a college campus before opting for professionalism afterward. College represented little more than a pit stop on the way to the NBA. They became known as "one-and-done players." Players like Kevin Durant were already NBA-caliber players and were instead instructed to make a short detour on the way to the NBA. "I guess they were trying to look at having a lot of kids coming into the league that really weren't ready or even mature," said Greg Oden, who played a season at Ohio State during the rule's first year of enforcement. "I definitely think it helped out that way. But there are some kids that are good enough to go. Kevin Durant would have been good enough to go." The better collegiate programs no longer carried stability or name recognition from one year to the next. The days of a Tim Duncan or a Shane Battier incubating for four years in college belonged to a different era. Emmert and Larry Scott, the commissioner of the Pac-12, had said that the NBA should allow players to come into its league out of high school or mandate that players stay in college for two or three years—establishing a system similar to the one that baseball employs. "It's a dynamic tension that we really need to work on because it's at the heart of part of what we're talking about here," Emmert said during a speech at Marquette University. "Why would we want to force someone to go to school when they really don't want to be there? But if you're going to come to us, you're going to be a student." Scott, speaking at the Pac-12 football media day in 2013, said, "Anyone that's serious about the collegiate model and the words *student-athlete* can't feel very good about what's happening in basketball with one-and-done student-athletes." At one point, Stern had worked for more sensible proposals. He once proposed an insurance plan that the NBA and the NCAA would pay into that would protect the top 50 or so college basketball players should one suffer a debilitating injury before entering the professional ranks. NCAA officials responded that insuring the top prospects would violate its rules of amateurism. "They said, 'Our rules require that you do that for all sports,'" Stern said. "We couldn't limit it to just basketball. I said, 'OK, I get it' . . . So the labyrinth of rules in the NCAA is off the charts, off the charts."

Stern settled into his chair. "I'm not sure how to react to Emmert's comments," he said. "I don't want to get into an epic confrontation." He took a moment. Stern reasoned that schools should not accept players who only planned to be on campus for a short time. The NCAA had a choice in establishing its own rules, just as the NBA did. "I think what really happens is those players ultimately get their credits in some online heaven," Stern said. "Online university in the sky, without having gone to classes, OK? So the hypocrisy lies with the schools, not with the league. I mean, Scott, those guys are in la-la land. No university president is going to say, 'All right, we're not going to have all these' . . . they call them one-and-done. It's very easy, don't have them. But then their alumni would [stop donating to the programs]. It's sort of like, to me, the professionals here are the purists. The amateurs are the hypocrites. The argument that—and just to go to the hardest part, because after thirty years I still can't articulate it exactly right—everybody gets a chance to set standards for employment. The *New York Times* says we want you to have experience as a journalist and maybe even a graduate degree in journalism."

The basis for an age minimum was simple, Stern said. The rule provided for a better product to enter the NBA, a player more mature physically and mentally, and for teams to make better-informed decisions on a player to whom they were obligated to offer a lavish contract. Stern had once said that the rule would tell communities that a kid would be more likely to become a scientist or a professor than an NBA player. In later years, he tried removing the societal implications of the change. "We're not in, and shouldn't be in, [the business of] telling people why what we're doing is good for them," Stern said. "I have never wanted to buy into that approach. So we're not going to [establish] rules so we don't have the next Lenny Cooke. I don't mean to be heartless about it because I'm not. I think it's horrible what happened to Lenny and I think they were let down by the system of sycophants and society professionalizing them. But that's not where my mind-set is on the way the NBA should interact. There's a difference between me, the person, and me, the CEO, on this. As a person, maybe you should have a set of rules that says you've got to do something to enable you to live. It isn't about school. It's about technical training. It's about skills for a job. It's about anything. But that's more for the high schools and the colleges. It's not for a professional sports league to spread its gospel and enact legislation."

Stern was present near the beginning of the migration of high school players into the NBA. He was practicing law, working as an outside counsel for the NBA at Proskauer Rose in 1975 when Bill Willoughby jumped straight to the NBA. Stern followed Willoughby's progress—or lack of it—closely once Willoughby entered the NBA. They grew up in neighboring New Jersey towns. "Willoughby was a— not a bust—a lesson," Stern said. "He made people think about it. And the college game had a certain allure for people who wanted to take advantage of using their skills to get an education. The bloom wasn't as quite off the college rose as it is now. Youngsters were more geared to focusing on continuing their careers in collegiate terms, and because the college game and the great reputations were made in college at that time." Kevin Garnett's declaration and success two decades later transformed that mind-set. Stern recalled reading about this extraordinary, rail-thin teenager, and that Garnett planned to take advantage of the rules available to him at the time. The thought of professional scouts milling around high school gyms, Stern said, always made him uncomfortable. "The word *unseemly* comes to mind," Stern said. When the Timberwolves selected Garnett fifth overall, they made a huge leap of faith to take a high school player that early in the draft. "What's good for the league is, on balance, to have nineteen-year-olds, rather than eighteen-year-olds," Stern said. "These are valuable picks and to use a pick on Korleone [Young] or Lenny Cooke or whatever is not a great thing. And we'll have the same players a year later, and there may be some advantage to them being more mature because having exercised their pick, it's more likely that we'll be able to judge their talent better, we'll be able to take a more mature player, we'll be able to make all kinds of interesting things. And, I don't know how fast Kevin Garnett was great, OK?" The flood of high schoolers entering the NBA started just a few years later. "It wasn't good from the league's perspective, from a business perspective," Stern said, adding that he did not really enjoy the influx of high school players from a personal perspective, either. "It wasn't good from a societal perspective, but I can never allow that to— I suppress that. The idea that we were not sure how good people were and people felt the pressure to draft such an athlete, because he was going to be great."

Stern has always argued that the age minimum was not based on financial motives. The collective bargaining agreement between the league and its players, Stern said, stated how the financial pie was to be divided up. Players were given a set percentage that did not change, no matter how it was divvied among them. "Billy Hunter was not constructive in this debate because he put out there, together with the union, that somehow this was designed to affect the cycle of how players were signed and keep them from becoming free agents a year earlier or something like that," he said. "The factual challenge underlying that assertion is that we're committed to paying fifty percent out. So all you're talking about is how it's distributed."

The conversation turned to Kwame Brown. "Poor Michael [Jordan]," Stern said. "That's the system we had. We had a lot of people who were going to be untried, we'll have to see how it works out. It wasn't an optimal business situation where we were going to expend these valuable picks and careers were going to be made or unmade on guesswork, really."

The same type of statements were made over and over again, like a mantra, by some of the most influential people in the NBA.

Said Phil Jackson, who coached a young Kobe Bryant: "You point to LeBron James, who came into this league and was there. He was comfortable. He was mature physically and relatively mature mentally. So there are exceptions to the rule and I think we make exceptions for that person or those particular people, not knowing there's another seventy-five percent, eighty percent of them that aren't going to be mature at the level or perform and they may get lost in the process."

Jerry Colangelo: "If the floodgates opened, there are going to be a lot more bad stories than good stories, because most kids are not ready emotionally. They may look like they have the physical talent to step in and do it, but they are not ready."

Rod Higgins, the general manager who drafted Kwame Brown with Michael Jordan: "For every success story, you probably could write a horror story."

They were wrong.

You cannot.

21.

Arn Tellem thought he had pulled it off again. A year earlier, in 1996, the agent had deftly orchestrated Kobe Bryant's path to Los Angeles. Bryant wanted to continue working out for teams, showcasing his talent and proving his NBA readiness in the days leading up to the draft. Tellem was one of the first to realize one of the quirks in the new rookie salary scale. Bryant's rookie salary would be determined by his draft position and there would not be much salary difference whether a team took him high or closer to the middle of the first round. Bryant's second contract would be much more lucrative when he could sign a rookie extension worth $70 million during his third season. Tellem recognized that the organization Bryant went to was of far more initial importance. When Tellem learned the full depth of the Lakers' interest in drafting Bryant, he declined subsequent workout offers from teams, gambling correctly that ill-prepared organizations would not draft Bryant without viewing him privately. To Tellem, the Lakers' organization manufactured stars in one of the game's biggest, most glamorous markets. He pictured Bryant trailing in the image of Magic Johnson. "This is one of the few rights we have," Tellem told Bryant. "We don't have to go to every workout." The maneuvering to land Bryant in Los Angeles culminated in Tellem running interference with John Nash and John Calipari, the Nets pair who would have changed the face of the NBA for much of a generation had they drafted Bryant after hosting him for three workouts. Tellem shared a relationship with both, but the future of his client trumped any collegial friendship. "It was extremely painful to go through that, but I did," Tellem said years later.

The following draft, Tellem believed that his new high school client, Tracy McGrady, would be drafted by the Chicago Bulls and paired with Michael Jordan. This too would require some outside-the-box thinking. Jerry Krause, Chicago's general manager, went so far as to sneak McGrady through a hospital's back doors in the middle of the night for a physical. Krause wanted questions answered about the durability of McGrady's back. But Jordan, of course, intervened and effectively killed the deal for McGrady that would have broken up his partnership with Scottie Pippen. "That's when it started to unravel," Tellem said. "I thought going into the morning of the draft, this was going to be the greatest thing. I'd have done it with Kobe in LA and now I'd have Tracy in Chicago."

The type of system manipulation that Tellem employed to maneuver Bryant to the Lakers and McGrady nearly to Chicago became impossible in subsequent years. There is little chance Bryant would have made it to the Lakers had he declared for the draft a few years later. By then, teams had to keep up-to-date on the best high school prospects or risk losing out on the next Bryant or Kevin Garnett. "Teams would take him, even if they weren't sure [about him], on hope and belief that you can't pass [him up]," Tellem said. "Then, with teams, there was enough doubt. Teams had the mind-set that they could take Todd Fuller over him. I don't see that happening in today's environment."

Among NBA agents, Tellem was one of the most powerful. He loved baseball while growing up along Philadelphia's Main Line and adored the Phillies. He filled most of his childhood by playing APBA Baseball, the mail-order board game, and poring over statistics. He came to the conclusion that his future would not involve a baseball playing career—or any sports playing career—and graduated in 1979 from the University of Michigan Law School. He was working at an LA firm, drowning in mundane work, when he one day thumbed through the pages of the *Los Angeles Daily Journal* and found a help-wanted ad for general counsel to the Clippers. The franchise was owned by Donald Sterling, the eccentric lawyer and real estate developer, known initially for his frugality and, in recent years, his racism. Tellem wanted his job application to stand out. He mailed his resume packed inside a deflated basketball. The Clippers hired Tellem, where he learned the inner workings of an NBA franchise through the prism of working in a dysfunctional front office. Sterling and the Clippers always seemed to be suing someone or being sued themselves. Tellem left the Clippers and began his own sports agency in 1989. He struggled initially, attending baseball's spring training to pitch clients. But his client list grew fast and coincided with the rising salaries of professional athletes, of which Tellem earned the standard 4 percent cut of each contract. A friendship with Sonny Vaccaro benefited both. They met while Vaccaro still worked with Nike to negotiate a shoe deal with Cheryl Miller, the great women's basketball player and the sister of Reggie Miller, another of Tellem's clients. Vaccaro felt he could trust Tellem. He was easygoing and they both loved to eat. Vaccaro advised players like Tracy McGrady and Jermaine O'Neal to sign Tellem to represent them. Meanwhile, Tellem's firm continued to expand rapidly. SFX Entertainment paid nearly $25 million for Tellem & Associates nearly a decade after Tellem started it with little more than his law degree, experience with the Clippers, and his avid interest in sports.

Tellem represented many of the players who jumped to the NBA from high school as they broke into the league. Some, many years after washing out of the NBA or not making it at all, regret the decision they made in not signing with Tellem when they originally declared. DeAngelo Collins was a mammoth talent who dominated his opposition through both skill and physicality. He went undrafted in 2002 after declaring for the NBA out of Inglewood High School. Teams shared concerns about his character and Collins believes an agent like

Tellem would have bolstered his image. "The only reason why I'm probably out of the NBA, I was supposed to sign with Arn Tellem," Collins said. "I didn't, I didn't do that." Instead, Collins signed with Immortal Sports & Entertainment, the same agency that initially represented Lenny Cooke during his failed NBA bid. "The only reason I was signed into that place was because of my other talent, as far as movies, music," Collins explained. "There were other talents that I had that I wanted to [pursue]. You only live once and I wanted to live. So that's what I was trying to do. And it didn't work out like that." Korleone Young shared similar misgivings. "I was gonna get with Arn, too," Young said. "Arn was honest. A lot of the real good agents were the most honest. But when you're from Wichita, I'll just keep it real. I hadn't really done a lot like this with white people, so that's part of the business. So I didn't trust them, long story short. How many of us do just trust them all the way?"

It is debatable whether Tellem was a skilled enough agent to resuscitate the careers of those who floundered for reasons beyond their choice of representation. But their belief in Tellem all these years later is a reflection of his sterling reputation. Allan Bristow, a former player and executive for the Charlotte Hornets, once allegedly became so incensed with Tellem during discussions over a new contract for Kendall Gill that he choked Tellem. Bristow, standing 6 feet 7 inches, denied choking Tellem, nearly a foot shorter, but said both had acted unprofessionally. "Bristow told the press that we'd had a 'heated, eye-to-eye discussion,'" Tellem later joked to *Sports Illustrated*. "That's true, but he lifted me a foot off the floor to conduct it." Bristow then asked if Tellem needed a ride to the airport. If so, Bristow could drive him. Players knew that Tellem would vehemently defend them in their darkest hour. He represented controversial players, like Latrell Sprewell, when he choked his coach, and Albert Belle, once baseball's bad boy. Tellem looked for the soft spots among his clientele—ways in which he could relate to them. Many of Tellem's clients developed an easy rapport with Tellem's three sons. Tracy McGrady would race back from workouts on many days to play Wiffle ball with Eric, Matty, and Mike in Tellem's backyard. The boys are grown now, but that doesn't mean Tellem's house is empty. Joel Embiid, a Cameroonian big man who spent a year playing at Kansas, signed Tellem to represent him in 2014. Embiid fractured a bone in his foot prior to the draft and spent the summer at the home of Tellem and his wife, Nancy, while recovering. He discovered how to order online food during his stay. Every 15 minutes or so, one of the Tellems would hear their bell ring late at night, signaling another deliveryman with another one of Embiid's orders—a drink from one restaurant, an appetizer from another, an entrée from another—until finally his meal was complete.

Despite the altercation with Bristow, Tellem tried avoiding confrontation. He preferred calling contract talks "discussions" instead of "negotiations," and tried to make any executive understand that he was acting in the team's best interest, as well as his client's. Tellem assumed the mantra of politician Daniel Patrick Moynihan, saying, "Everyone is entitled to his own opinion, but not to his own facts." In that way, he was still the boy who obsessively studied baseball statistics. He overprepared for each meeting with team executives, trying to figure out every possible outcome. "Their career length is higher compared with every other group of players," Tellem said of players who entered the NBA out of high school. "Put aside earnings, which are also off the chart, their [average] length of career is close to ten years. That's what bothers me. You're entitled to your opinion, but not your own facts. If you don't want high school players to go and you believe that's not the right thing, fine. You're entitled to your opinion, but you're not entitled to your own facts. The facts are the facts and let's talk about the facts."

Tellem and Bryant parted ways after Bryant developed into one of the game's best players. However, most of Tellem's relationships endured. Tellem enjoyed watching as Tracy McGrady and Jermaine O'Neal evolved from shy teenagers into stars and team leaders. O'Neal hardly looked up from his seat when he and Tellem met for the first time. Over the years, he became one of the game's more eloquent spokesmen. "I don't think anyone I've had came as far as him," Tellem said. "The other thing that he learned to do, which a lot of players can't do, is if he had an issue where something was bothering him, he could articulate it and tell you. That's huge. To have a client that can do that, it gives you the ability to forge a much better relationship." The players most deem as failures? Tellem still labels their careers as successes. Kwame Brown and Eddy Curry lasted longer in the NBA than most players. They drew lucrative salaries, even if their predicted stardom did not pan out. Brown was paid more than $60 million through 13 seasons. Curry made more than $70 million in 12 years, but still faced crippling financial problems. "With Tracy and Jermaine, in particular, what separated them from others who didn't succeed as long or as well, they're willing to listen," Tellem said. "They wanted to learn. The challenge with Kwame and [Eddy] Curry is it was much more difficult to reach them. They're very nice guys, really good people. I'm not blaming them. I'm not blaming us. It's not just high school players. It's anyone. There are some players where it's much more difficult to reach them." While Tellem guided several high school players into the NBA, one of the most well-known had branched off on his own. Aaron Goodwin had helped LeBron James secure more than $120 million in endorsements before he had played a single NBA game. Yet, James shocked the NBA when he severed ties with Goodwin in the summer of 2005. James joined Leon Rose, an agent with Creative Artists Agency, yet entrusted the bulk of his marketing future to his longtime friend Maverick Carter. In 2012, James turned to another friend, Rich Paul, to become his agent. "He used to listen to me and how I was going to get out of the inner city and make a difference, and I used to listen to him say how he was going to get out and make a difference," James told the *New York Times* about Paul. "Those conversations turned to how we are going to do it, and then to, why not do it together? I wanted him to be with me." News of both moves were initially met with skepticism and raised eyebrows across the league. Here was another example of a player having misplaced faith in those close to him. However, both Carter and Paul handled their newfound power and responsibility deftly, earning other clients across the league. Now, the moves are an example of how James has worked to comfortably steer his own future.

• • •

Tellem spoke at one of his favorite breakfast spots near his Brentwood offices. He wore a sports jacket. At 60 years old, Tellem still had boyish features that complemented his wavy, thinning hair. Tellem wanted to discuss the facts. "That group of [high school] players by far is the most successful, the most marketable, the most highly compensated, and the most decorated as far as achievement of any group of players in the last twenty years since Kevin Garnett went pro," Tellem said.

The evidence supported Tellem, who also had a vested interest in his clients realizing their earning potential. In 2004, before the introduction of the age minimum, Michael A. McCann published a paper called "Illegal Defense: The Irrational Economics of Banning High School Players from the NBA draft." McCann, then a Harvard Law School visiting scholar, studied the 29 high school players who had declared for the NBA draft and signed with agents from 1975 to 2003, finding that those players had stayed in the NBA much longer, while earning larger contracts and maximizing their earning potential, than their counterparts. "Simply put, for every Korleone Young, there are two or three Kevin Garnetts," McCann wrote. The NBA drafted 83 percent of the high school players who had declared, compared with only 46 percent of the players from 2001 to 2003 who had gone to college and then declared early for the NBA. McCann found that only three high school players who had signed with agents—Taj McDavid, Ellis Richardson, and Tony Key—had been unable to make a living playing basketball (although James Lang might be added to that list in the future for health reasons). McCann wrote that a player who bypassed college for the NBA was in line to earn as much as $100 million more in his career than if he had earned his degree. "In turn, since those players are often the most talented, they tend to develop at a uniquely accelerated rate, and thus their early arrival—and longer stay—ultimately benefits the NBA and its fans," McCann wrote. He predicted the future financial earnings of Tyson Chandler, who entered the NBA at 19 years old in 2001, and Shane Battier, a rookie the same year at the age of 23. McCann anticipated that in 2011, Chandler would be entering the prime years of his playing career and could sign a maximum contract he expected to be around $118 million over seven years. Battier, meanwhile, would be 32, on the downhill of his career's slope, and unable to sign a contract for nearly as much. In reality, that is close to what happened. Chandler signed a four-year, $58 million contract with the Knicks in 2011, while Battier joined the Miami Heat as a role player for three years and $9.4 million. In the summer of 2015, Chandler signed a four-year, $52 million pact to play for the Phoenix Suns. Meanwhile, Battier had retired from the NBA after the 2013–2014 season. To be fair, the trade-off is the difference in return teams garnered from the two early in their careers. Chandler experienced his growing pains in Chicago as a young player, while Battier entered the league as a capable two-way player.

Nearly all of the 17 players drafted after McCann's study in the two years the NBA continued allowing in high school players experienced sustainable professional careers after encountering initial growing pains. They ranged from those who progressed into franchise players, like Dwight Howard, to those who maximized earnings they would not have received had they gone to college and likely been exposed, like Robert Swift, to some who, while not becoming stars, made millions annually for years as journeymen, like Sebastian Telfair.

Tellem ordered an omelet made with egg whites and mushrooms, fruit, and whole-wheat toast. He had endured heart-bypass surgery nearly two decades earlier when his cholesterol levels climbed toward 400. He vowed to eat better—he was a sucker for bagels—only to continue a frenetic work pace. He completed a deal for Rex Hudler, a journeyman baseball player, just a few days after the heart surgery.

He returned to the facts. Today, the average NBA player will make about $25 million, while playing five years. It is impossible to state how long the average career length and salary will be among those who entered the NBA from high school. It is safe to assume that they will shatter the average. Many are still in the NBA a decade after the implementation of the age minimum, with several drawing maximum salaries. "Roughly twenty percent of the league is thirty or over," Tellem said. "So eighty percent of the league doesn't make it to age thirty. There's a lot who don't even make it to age twenty-five or twenty-six. So when you factor in injury and the desire of teams to have younger players, to lose that year in a career is incredibly detrimental. This is a young person's sport, much like tennis. This is not like baseball, where, once you make it, players can play well into their thirties. Here, there's fewer opportunities on everything from success to achievement to opportunity, and when you factor in just how the teams value players, how they put a premium on youth, to deny them that opportunity to go pro when they're ready is a huge miscarriage of justice for these players."

Tellem did not hide his frustration with Billy Hunter at the breakfast or before the ouster of the former executive director of the players union. Tellem had called for Hunter's removal earlier. Just before the 2013 All-Star Game, Tellem sent a lengthy letter to his basketball clients, heavily criticizing Hunter's tenure. *NBA players deserve better representation from the union they fund,* Tellem wrote in the letter. *I implore you and your fellow players to take control of your union and your future. It's time for Mr. Hunter to go.* To Tellem, Hunter broke the cardinal rule of entering negotiations: Know every option. "Rather than just blindly accepting their facts, their arguments, and then just playing defense, he never really understood or bothered or cared to understand [that] there are better alternatives than what they have to protect kids," Tellem said. For years, Tellem publicly disagreed with an age minimum and penned articles in newspapers that carried his opinions and the statistics. Tellem argued for a model most closely resembling that of Major League Baseball—to either allow players to become professionals out of high school or free them to leave college after two years (instead of baseball's three). He also preferred that the NBA develop a true minor league system. The NBA Development League has evolved greatly in recent years. More NBA teams are financially investing in the D-League, owning their own franchises and using them to groom players. But the NBA's roster for each team is maxed at 15 players. Teams usually expect their first-round selections to develop in the NBA. The vast majority of D-League players are not signed to the parent clubs due to these small numbers, although quite a few current NBA players have spent time in the minors. The top D-League players usually make only about $25,000, a mark that pales compared to what most are offered to play overseas. Tellem advocated teams being allowed to draft more players and submit them to the D-League for seasoning, maintaining their rights without their contracts counting against the team's cap. "But that goes toward protecting the individual," Tellem said. "If you care about protecting the individual, not punishing the individual, there are rules that could be modified, which is where I come from, and it's better for the teams. The teams want the best players. The teams that are building for the future want access to the best talent. It's in the league's interest to allow these players to come. It's clearly in the player's interest and there are ways that you protect those that this is not the right decision for. But you shouldn't punish future generations—the LeBrons, Kobes, Kevin Garnetts, Jermaine O'Neals, Tracy McGradys—and deny them the opportunity."

Tellem's phone buzzed. The caller ID revealed that the number belonged to Kendrick Perkins, another of Tellem's clients who leapt from high school and remained in the NBA. A few months later, Tellem would return to his roots of working for an NBA team by leaving his agency and becoming the vice chairman of Palace Sports & Entertainment, which owns the Detroit Pistons. "Part of me thought, 'I can't possibly accept,'" Tellem wrote in explaining his decision to *Sports Illustrated*. "I'm responsible for helping to guide the careers of scores of pro baseball and basketball players. But I grew pensive when I remembered something a friend once told me: that making a difference in a community gives you a deeper sense of purpose . . . I thought, 'I'm sixty-one. If not now, when?'"

But at the moment at breakfast, he was still one of the NBA's most powerful agents. The meal ended. Business had called.

22.

Rick Stansbury made the long, lonely drive from Starkville to Picayune a few times a month. He sometimes contemplated how fast life moved during the isolated stretches along Mississippi Highway 25. Basketball was his life. As a child, he worked on his family's rural Kentucky farm all day with his brothers. When the day ended, they lugged and moved hay, converting the barn into a dusty basketball court. They just hoped that an errant pass did not land the ball in cow manure. Stansbury worked his way up the coaching ranks when his playing career ended at Campbellsville University. He became an assistant at the school and later joined Mississippi State's coaching staff. In 1998, the Bulldogs named Stansbury head coach. He was 38 years old with job security and freshly married to his wife, Meo.

"I had just gotten married and was falling asleep, thinking about Jonathan Bender," Stansbury recalled.

Bender was the reason for those lengthy drives. In later years, once Stansbury had seen Kevin Durant's prodigious talents, he would compare a youthful Bender to the NBA's future MVP. Stansbury was an assistant at Mississippi State when he first saw Bender play in middle school. *This could be one of the best players to ever come out of the state,* Stansbury immediately surmised. Bender was quiet and modest, allowing his game to speak for him. He started playing ball as a youngster, following in the footsteps of his older brother, Donnell. He had been cut from his team in junior high only to grow another four inches that summer, sprouting to 6 feet 4 inches as an eighth grader. Bender had added another three or four inches to his frame by the time Stansbury took a serious interest in him. As a young assistant, Stansbury had been told at one of his first staff meetings at Mississippi State that the school could not land some of the top in-state recruits. Those prospects wanted a bigger spotlight elsewhere. Stansbury planned to change that, believing that Mississippi State was the perfect school for the top Mississippi high school basketball players. Stansbury became a masterful recruiter. He could relate to any kid, any family, anywhere because of his devotion to basketball. The better players began arriving at the school as a result of Stansbury's nudging. The Bulldogs appeared in 1996's Final Four—aided by the strong play of Dontae' Jones, who soon encountered a young Kobe Bryant in draft workouts. Stansbury thought Bender could continue the program's good fortune. They established a rapport, talking basketball while escaping on hours-long fishing trips. They maintained that rapport as other schools began noticing the silky-smooth big man with the skills of a guard. Bender committed to Mississippi State during Stansbury's first year as head coach. Stansbury considered the day as one of the greatest of his life. The frequent drives to Bender's hometown had paid off.

The school appeared on the brink of becoming a national powerhouse in an era before elite high school players routinely passed on college for the NBA. Once the exodus started, colleges lost out on players they had spent months or even years recruiting. The sidestepping impacted many high-stakes programs. Coaches could land lucrative jobs and teams could make deep tournament runs, providing a financial windfall for the university, off the strengths of one dynamic player alone. No university basketball program would be affected more by players skipping college than the Mississippi State Bulldogs and no coach would have more hard luck than Stansbury. "That was such a badge of honor before they changed the rule," said Phil Cunningham, an assistant coach under Stansbury at Mississippi State. "They all wanted to go and make money. No one said, 'Man, I want to go play for Alabama or LSU or Michigan State, rather than the NBA.' That's hogwash. Anyone who believes that is in a fantasy world."

Thoughts of making Bender the centerpiece of Stansbury's recruiting class began unraveling at the 1999 McDonald's All-American Game in Ames, Iowa. In a game with rosters full of future NBA players, Bender stood out. Stansbury watched from the stands. He cheered for Bender—until Bender started performing a little too well. Most of the crowd arrived in support of Nick Collison, a native of the state. Their allegiance changed once Bender released a barrage of outside shots. As the game wore on, fans clamored for Bender's teammates to pass him the ball. He felt as if he could not miss. The jitters started in his stomach once Bender realized he was closing in on the record 30 points that Michael Jordan had scored in the game in 1981. A free throw gave Bender 31 points. Anyone who breaks Jordan's record in anything basketball-related will garner attention. Unbeknownst to Stansbury, Bender had made joining the NBA out of high school a secret goal of his. He had watched Kobe Bryant and Tracy McGrady make the leap. He wanted to lift his family's spirits and finances. Bender's father, Donald, had died following a seizure six years earlier. The family lived in a brick home near railroad tracks where trains disrupted their sleep. To Bender, his performance at the McDonald's All-American Game simply cemented in his mind the notion that the jump was meant to be. He still had to persuade his mother. Willie Mae Bender recognized the value of an education. She worked nights at Walmart and attended classes at the University of Southern Mississippi during the day. At 44 years old, she earned her degree and graduated in the same class as her daughter, Valerie. Willie Mae Bender thought education provided a path out of poverty. Jonathan Bender convinced her that he would return for his education, that the NBA would provide the fastest route for a reprieve. She hesitated, but left the decision to her son.

Stansbury had heard the rumors and whispers that Bender would now skip college. He maintained hope. The conviction stayed with him when he checked into a New Orleans hotel to meet with his prize recruit. Bender and Thaddeus Foucher, his AAU coach, knocked on Stansbury's door. Stansbury knew that even if Bender declared, a chance remained that he could still honor his commitment to Mississippi State. Players could declare for the draft and work out for NBA teams, gaining a measurement of how they were valued by NBA teams. If they had not hired an agent, they could withdraw their names up to a week before the draft and retain their college eligibility.

But Bender had no plans of turning back.

He looked Stansbury in the eye. His voice did not waver. "I appreciate everything you've done, but I've decided to go pro," he told Stansbury.

Stansbury felt crushed. He tried, in vain, to convince Bender otherwise, but knew he did not have much to offer to counter the decision. Soon, Bender asked to leave the hotel room. He had never seen that look of disappointment in a man—a mix of anxiety, angst, and heartbreak. He needed a moment, but stayed firm in his conviction. "It was one of the most crushing blows I've ever had," Stansbury recalled. "For about two weeks, all I wanted to do was crawl into a hole. I put so much into that thing for five years. It was absolutely just a killer." It was hard, especially at the time, to admit it, but Stansbury knew he would have made the same choice if given the option. The Toronto Raptors drafted Bender fifth overall—the highest a high school player had been taken at that point—and dealt him to the Indiana Pacers. Bender's NBA career would be sidetracked by chronic knee injuries. He retired in 2006, unable to walk up stairs without experiencing jarring pain. A comeback attempt three years later with the Knicks ended briefly and quietly. But Bender was careful with his money. As a player, he read books and listened to advice. He became an entrepreneur and philanthropist, aiding several families displaced by Hurricane Katrina. "[Bender] made the next one not hurt quite as bad," Stansbury said with resignation in his voice. "By the time you got to Monta [Ellis], you just understood it. It was just part of it and I moved on."

The next one arrived in the form of a hometown product. Three years after losing Bender, Mississippi State poured its recruiting efforts into Travis Outlaw, a 6-foot-9-inch, 205-pound sky reacher. Outlaw grew up in Starkville under the colors of Mississippi State's maroon and white. His father, John, worked as an assistant chief in the police department. His mother, Markeeta, was a city clerk. Robert Kirby, another of Stansbury's assistant coaches, spent almost as much time at Outlaw's high school games as he did with Mississippi State's team. Outlaw finally disclosed his college choice at a morning press conference inside the Starkville High School library. He decided he would not go far and opted for Mississippi State. "I wanted to stay close to home," he said. "I'm kind of a momma's and daddy's boy. I also feel comfortable with the decision." Less than a year later, Outlaw announced another decision that made his pockets comfortable. He would be leaving home after all and joining the NBA when the Portland Trail Blazers drafted him in the first round.

The staff's final blow came from Monta Ellis. Ellis had experienced a dazzling career at Mississippi's Lanier High School. He was only around six feet tall, but the bigger the game, the better Ellis seemed to play. He punctuated one performance by scoring 72 points. Cunningham worked hard to recruit Ellis, landing his verbal commitment to Mississippi State in February 2004. "When we stopped worrying about Alabama, Texas, and North Carolina, we started seeing those NBA logos on those shirts at his games," Cunningham recalled. Cunningham still did not see much reason to worry. No guard of Ellis's diminutive size had successfully jumped to the NBA from high school. They, more than any other type of player, needed time in college to grow into their bodies. But Sebastian Telfair changed that. Telfair was a New York legend as a high school point guard who declared for the 2004 draft shortly after Ellis had made the decision to attend Mississippi State. Telfair stood just six feet tall. The best high school players had congregated in Colorado for a Team USA camp in 2004 as the draft looped on television. Portland took Telfair 13th overall. "When Sebastian got drafted, that kind of opened the door for smaller guards to think, *Hey, we may have the opportunity to do the same thing,*" said Lou Williams, a point guard from Georgia who went up against Monta Ellis in high school and also skipped college. "At least that's how I took it. So when he was drafted, and not only drafted—he was a lottery pick—that gave me a lot of confidence to feel like I could do the same thing. That was the main thing that went into my decision."

Ellis soon informed Cunningham that he would enter the NBA out of high school. Cunningham made one last-ditch effort. He scribbled the expected salary of each first-round pick—1 through 30—highlighting the salary differential between a player drafted early and one taken later. "Monta, think about this," Cunningham said. "If you come to Mississippi State for one year, you're going to be the best player in the [Southeastern Conference]. You'll be MVP of the SEC. You'll probably be first-team All-American. You think if you come here for one year, you can't be as good as Chris Paul and be a top pick in the draft next year and make this type of money as opposed to going in right now and [then] you're locked into this lower spot?"

Ellis flatly told Cunningham that he thought he was already a better player than Paul, a future All-Star. With that reply, Cunningham knew that another top high school player would never play at Mississippi State.

Rick Stansbury's recruiting mind-set did not change throughout the setbacks. "We went after the best players," Stansbury said. "Like any coach in the country will tell you, 'If I can get one for one year, I'll take him.'" But even the introduction of the age minimum did not help him during his run at Mississippi State. Stansbury believed he had finally lucked out when he landed Renardo Sidney, a talented big man. Sidney was one of those phenoms known from an early age. He was ranked among the top junior high players and his Mississippi middle school charged admission to watch him play. Some called him another Magic Johnson in the making. An NBA career seemed inevitable. But Sidney was born a little too late. The age rule was in place in 2009 by the time Sidney finished high school. By then, most colleges had backed away from recruiting Sidney, fearful that his association with shoe companies and agents would hurt his eligibility and put the university at risk for sanctions. Mississippi State remained one of the few schools who offered Sidney a scholarship. He accepted and enrolled, while the NCAA investigated his eligibility. The coaching staff believed Sidney would receive a short suspension and leave college after playing just one season. At several points during the season, Cunningham informed Sidney to be prepared to play. But the investigation dragged on. Sidney's weight ballooned. He practiced with the team, but devoured fast food when the squad went on road trips. The NCAA finally ruled Sidney ineligible for all of the 2009–2010 season and the first nine games the following year. Cunningham still thought Sidney would declare for the NBA. Instead, he stayed and showed only the occasional flashes of his past dominance on the AAU circuit. His tenure was mostly marked by disappointment. Most notably, Sidney fought with a teammate in the stands and drew another suspension. He went undrafted by the NBA in 2012 and played briefly in the NBA Development League.

After Sidney's final year at Mississippi State, an emotional Stansbury addressed reporters inside the campus's Bryan Athletic Building. He was now 52. The last season had been difficult on Stansbury. The team had once been ranked 15th best in the nation, but collapsed down the stretch. "We've had a couple of disappointing years by our standards, which we created," a red-eyed Stansbury said in announcing his retirement as the school's coach. "There's no one to blame but me for that. I'll take responsibility for that. And you've heard me say it—I want those expectations. We don't run from them."

Mississippi State experienced success during Stansbury's tenure. He guided the Bulldogs to a 293–166 record, but the team had last qualified for the NCAA tournament three years earlier. The team played in six tournaments, never advancing beyond the second round. One elite prospect for one year could have changed all that and much more. "It affected everyone's career so much because we had a great run," Cunningham said. "You look back on it and that was without Jonathan Bender, Travis Outlaw, and Monta Ellis. Throw all of those guys in there for just one year and think how that changes the talent of those teams they would have played on. Where is Rick Stansbury right now had those guys all gone to Mississippi State and he goes to the Sweet Sixteen a couple times, goes to a Final Four? Put one of those guys on our team and they make a run and all of a sudden you're an assistant coach on a Sweet Sixteen team. Now, you get a job, which never really happened for any of us assistant coaches at Mississippi State. It affected recruiting, too. You're always looking for the next thing to sell. We never could go out and sell that next guy that we've had a lottery pick, because those talents would get signed but never come."

. . .

If you want to take care of my family, you'll stay," John Calipari told DeMarcus Cousins in the spring of 2010. "If you want to take of your family, you'll go."

Calipari held similar conversations annually with his best players—usually those who had just completed fantastic freshmen campaigns under him at the University of Kentucky. Cousins had developed into one of the nation's top interior forces in 2009–2010. He was a massive talent with a bit of a mean streak. He possessed a bright future as a professional if he could harness his emotions. The university had been like a family to Cousins, with Calipari the father figure. Cousins shared his doubts about whether he should leave college after just one season for the riches of the NBA. Calipari presented his options in practical terms. "Once he put it in those words, it wasn't really a tough decision at all," said Cousins, taken fifth overall by the Sacramento Kings. Calipari dispensed his advice to his young players only after much deliberation. He advised an underclassman to declare for the NBA when his stock was at its highest. Even then, Calipari peppered the player with serious questions about his future. *What if you don't stay in the NBA? Are you ready to play somewhere foreign, where they do not speak English? Are you ready to watch us play on television in the NCAA tournament when you're somewhere by yourself in the middle of nowhere getting little playing time? What is your backup plan if you get injured?* Calipari's players came to realize that, first and foremost, he had their backs. He offered his insights straight, putting aside his own objectives. Calipari regarded himself as having gone from the business of basketball to the business of helping families. "It's not a secret," said Patrick Patterson, who declared for the NBA after his junior season at Kentucky. "It's not anything new. The NBA is about money. It's about profit. College basketball is all about family and basketball, togetherness. That changes completely when you get to the NBA."

Calipari had resuscitated his career after his short time with the New Jersey Nets, a stint most notable for him passing on the opportunity to draft Kobe Bryant. That decision could have changed everything. Instead, the Nets fired Calipari shortly into the 1998–1999 season with the team sporting a dismal record of 3–17. Calipari soon reappeared in the college ranks, where he seemed more comfortable as a molder of the game's future stars. In 2008, Calipari's Memphis Tigers advanced to the national championship game against the University of Kansas. That season's wins would later be vacated after the NCAA invalidated the SAT scores of the talented freshman Derrick Rose. The voiding marked the second time one of Calipari's teams had reached the Final Four, only to have the appearance rescinded. The NCAA again found that Calipari had no personal culpability in the breaking of its rules. To his detractors, Calipari always seemed a step ahead of reproach.

Soon, Calipari signed on to coach at Kentucky. He became a rock star of a coach, active on Twitter and friends to rappers like Jay-Z and Drake. He took advantage of the new age minimum in a way that Rick Stansbury and others could only imagine. The message was clear to the nation's top recruits. If you wanted to go to the NBA, Calipari could get you there the fastest. This was the new college basketball. Stars stayed only as long as it took for them to matriculate into the NBA, and Kentucky became the destination for one-and-done players.

NBA teams drafted 26 Kentucky players in Calipari's first six years at the university. Most left school after their freshmen seasons. Many became top NBA draft picks, and three—John Wall, Anthony Davis, and Karl-Anthony Towns—were picked first overall. Calipari labeled the 2010 draft as the greatest day in Kentucky basketball history when five Wildcats, including four freshmen, were drafted in the first round. Calipari's Wildcats started the 2014–2015 season with 38 straights wins, but had hopes of a perfect season derailed with a loss to the University of Wisconsin in the national semifinals. The NBA drafted six of the seven Kentucky players who declared for the draft after the season. The influx of talent became so heavy at Kentucky that it created logjams for playing time when a freshman had the chance to jump to the NBA but instead decided to return for another year of college. "We've got to make it evil," Calipari said. "Well, why is it not evil for [golfer] Jordan Spieth to leave after one year and do what he is doing? Why is that OK? Or a tennis star? Or Bill Gates? Or Steve Jobs? Is it because of who the kids are or where they're from? I don't understand the venom that was coming at us for helping prepare kids. I didn't understand it. I still don't today. If you're mad, do what we're doing. If you're not willing to do what we're doing, it's fine. Do what you do. But why would you be mad at kids? This is generational wealth. At times, generational poverty just ends with a family. It ends right there in that greenroom. For me, I just don't take it lightly. It's not hurt my career."

Kentucky was in the mix at the end of every college season—annually sporting a young, talented team. The process seemed disingenuous to some who sensed a loss in college basketball's purity. This seemed to be another way that Calipari had found to circumvent the system. His very process of often encouraging players to opt for the NBA after a short time on campus went against the fabric of the term *student-athlete*. "We're not here as a feeder system," Bob Bowlsby, then Stanford's athletic director, said to *USA Today*. "We're here to educate young people and that's what it ought to be about." But Calipari's detractors never had a true appreciation of his views, which came from the standpoint of a longtime college basketball insider. He helped families achieve their dreams. He argued that he worked within the confines of the system's rules—a system that he too disliked. He would not stop recruiting the country's best players, even if their college stays were brief. "Let me make this very clear: I want to coach players for four years," Calipari wrote in his book, *Players First: Coaching from the Inside Out*. "Very few of the young players are truly ready for the rigors of the NBA. All but a handful would benefit from more time playing college basketball, more class time and more time on a college campus." In his book, Calipari argued that the age minimum should be raised, so that a player cannot enter the NBA until two years after his high school class graduated. By that time, through summer classes, a player would be about a year from gaining his degree, instead of three years. Calipari wrote that it would be "stupid" for basketball to employ a baseball-like system, with players either declaring for the NBA out of high school or mandated to remain in college for at least three years. "I don't have another word for it," he wrote. "The NBA doesn't want high school kids and it doesn't have a whole minor-league system to develop them. The baseball rule would keep some kids in college basketball for three years who want to be in the NBA—without improving their situation in any way. Do we want a whole generation of kids, many of them urban kids, who don't strive for education? Are we encouraging them to go directly to the NBA out of high school?"

Calipari used the rules to his advantage. Most college coaches initially rejoiced after the implementation of the age minimum. The best players could no longer circumvent college. A coach who spent years recruiting a player would at least have the opportunity to coach him for a season. In 2006–2007, Texas coach Rick Barnes coached Kevin Durant for a season. At Ohio State, Thad Matta rode Greg Oden and Mike Conley Jr. into the NCAA championship game, then the pair declared for the NBA after their freshmen years. The age minimum helped restore college basketball's visibility. It confirmed the decision of CBS and Turner Sports to pour $10.8 billion into broadcasting the NCAA tournament as part of a 14-year deal inked in 2010—at least they would be able to broadcast the best players for a tournament before they declared for the NBA. That lucrative contract prompted a greater debate. The athletes who were televised did not share in the riches beyond their scholarships, due to the NCAA's archaic rules concerning amateurism. Players like O. J. Mayo were destined for the NBA from an early age. Mayo spent a short time in college at the University of Southern California before setting off for an NBA career. After his departure, it was found that Mayo had accepted benefits deemed illegal by the NCAA. He was already a professional by the time the NCAA penalized the university. But even coaches once wary of recruiting one-and-done players were forced to come around or risk being unable to compete. Mike Krzyzewski, the famed Duke coach, once refused to look at players he thought would quickly advance to the NBA. But in 2010–2011, Kyrie Irving played under him for just 11 games before becoming the NBA's top pick. Four years later, three Duke freshmen—Jahlil Okafor, Justise Winslow, and Tyus Jones—played pivotal roles in leading the school to a national championship before declaring for the NBA draft. Principle is one thing. Winning is another. In that vein, Krzyzewski was just like Washington's owner Abe Pollin, who at one point declined to scout high school players only to come around as the risks of possibly passing on the next superstar became too great.

The 2006 NBA draft featured only two players—Tyrus Thomas and Shawne Williams—who had declared for the NBA after their freshman season. The following draft's lottery featured six freshmen players, a number that remained relatively steady as high school players became disallowed to submit their names into the draft. The annual exodus of freshman became so noticeable that even President Barack Obama spoke about it. "I have to say that I don't begrudge young people if they've got an opportunity to look after their family to go ahead and get an NBA contract and then go back to school, hopefully, and get their degree if that's the right choice," Obama said while talking to ESPN's Andy Katz in 2014. "I'm more concerned with the young people who are not going to have the chance to go to the NBA, and are they getting treated well by these schools."

In 2013, Bill Self landed Andrew Wiggins at Kansas. Everyone expected Wiggins, the son of a former NBA player, to stay on campus just long enough to play his freshman season. Wiggins did just that before becoming the top pick in the 2014 draft. "I really don't know what the answer is," Self said. "I really don't. I find it very difficult to believe that a young kid coming from a poverty situation has a chance to provide in ways that they never dreamed about and the one holdup is, 'Well, he's not quite ready. He needs one more year in college.' That one year of college could potentially be detrimental. Even though, I think, in four out of five cases, it'd probably be very beneficial."

Self's comments echoed those of many college coaches. They remained split on how best to remedy the current structure. "The amount of distractions these guys have to deal with [is difficult], as people try to get to them or entice them or money is changing hands," said Billy Donovan, the former University of Florida coach before he decided to coach the NBA's Oklahoma City Thunder. "What ends up happening is the school pays the price. A kid or his family could be somewhat naive through all this stuff. It just creates a lot of uncertainty. My thing has always been, if a kid wants to go college and a kid wants to experience that, he should have the opportunity to go ahead and do that. If the kid wants to pursue a professional career, fine. But I also get the NBA's side, from an emotional standpoint, a maturity standpoint, and maybe a basketball standpoint. These guys aren't ready to contribute. If I was coaching in the NBA, I'd probably want more veteran guys. So I see both sides of it."

• • •

John Calipari was not the only who reinvented himself after the rule change. Sonny Vaccaro, the godfather of sports marketing who helped incentivize college basketball, returned to rail against the system he helped create. Vaccaro left the shoe business in 2007, shortly after the NBA raised its age minimum. He closed his camps and advocated paying college athletes, arguing against the belief that attending college

fit every single kid. From his personal history, he knew that some simply did not want to pursue a higher education. Now, the rules mandated they do so. He thought the system unfairly penalized the athletes
and he toured the country speaking out against the NCAA. He also
helped Ed O'Bannon, a former star at UCLA, and a group of plaintiffs
in their lawsuit against the NCAA for refusing to compensate players
for their names and likenesses. The irony of his position was not lost on
those who disliked Vaccaro, believing he spoke for or against the side
that most benefited him. "College is a trick under the system that's employed now," Vaccaro said. "I don't think college coaching has anything
to do with maturity if you're a super talent. I don't think by going to
college you actually get better. You put in time. There's nothing wrong
with going to college. But we've had the greatest success in the history
of basketball by kids who had never played college."

In time, Vaccaro found something of a loophole in the age minimum. The best high school players, he believed, could play professionally overseas for a season if they did not want to attend college. He
had the contacts and believed there would be an international market
for fans to see tomorrow's top NBA talent today. That way, the player
could be paid and devote his full attention to basketball, improving
his skills and boosting his draft stock. Vaccaro voiced those views on a
weekly radio show he appeared on called *Loose Cannons*. Soon after finishing one show, he received a telephone call from Brandon Jennings.

Vaccaro faintly remembered Jennings, who had played at a couple
of Vaccaro's sneaker camps. Once, Vaccaro recalled mentoring Jennings because he felt that the youngster was showing up his opposition
during a blowout win. But Vaccaro had not talked to Jennings in more
than a year before the phone call. Early in the conversation, Jennings
expressed his frustrations over trying to gain collegiate eligibility. In
high school, he had transferred from his school in southern California to Virginia's Oak Hill Academy. In Virginia, his game continued
to progress until he became ranked as one of the country's top point
guards. He planned to attend the University of Arizona. The Wildcats
had a rich history of steering talented point guards into the NBA. But

Jennings was now on his third attempt to gain minimum SAT scores, set by the NCAA. He did not achieve the needed scores his first time. His second attempt showed such a jump that the NCAA flagged it, instructing him to try a third time. A dismayed Jennings randomly came across Vaccaro's radio show. He asked Vaccaro if he really thought playing overseas was a viable option and whether he would be a candidate. "He was so damn strong-willed and that was his personality and still is," Vaccaro said. "To a fault sometimes, but that's who Brandon is."

Vaccaro wanted to see Jennings in person to judge whether or not he would be up to the challenge. Jennings told Vaccaro that he was in New York. Vaccaro planned to be there for that week's draft. He left a day early, meeting Jennings at an Italian restaurant.

"Do you know what you're doing?" Vaccaro asked. "They're going to beat you up."

Vaccaro believed that the first person who tried bypassing college basketball to play overseas would be held to an unfair standard. The player could be viewed as a pioneer or as an outcast. Some NBA teams, Vaccaro cautioned, would shy away from him for that reason alone. Jennings remained steadfast. He did not want to attend college. He wanted to become the best basketball player he could as quickly as possible. "It was one of those days in my life that I thought would never come true because I always advocated that and then he was the right kid at the right time because he was strong enough to do it," Vaccaro recalled.

They ended the dinner. Vaccaro left excited. Now, he had to get the ball rolling. He knew that after the draft, basketball's interest would shift to Las Vegas, where the NBA hosted its summer league. He only had a few days to make it all work. Vaccaro called teams, lining up representatives to watch Jennings work out in Las Vegas. Jennings impressed quickly by showing off his lightning-quick speed up and down the court. An Italian club, Lottomatica Roma, made an offer Vaccaro thought would be too good to pass on. In all, Jennings would make $1.2 million—which included a quickly arranged shoe contract with Under Armour, a burgeoning athletic apparel company.

"Brandon, this is a lot of money," Vaccaro told Jennings. "We can work out for the Israelis, the Russians, the Greeks. But shit, this is a lot. Let's go for it." Jennings agreed and signed the deal. "It wasn't the NBA," Jennings said. "But it was close enough." At the NBA offices, David Stern found the move interesting. How a player came to the NBA—from college or overseas—made little difference to him. "I was supportive," Stern said. "The NBA's rules were not a social program telling young men, predominantly African-American, that they had to get educated. In fact, it used to rile me because no one raised it about white tennis players, only raised it about young, black basketball players, which is a total fault line in the NBA's history. And so I was like totally torn because, goddamnit, this guy is allowed to do whatever he wants to do. He's earned it. He's a great talent. Apparently, he's going overseas. Great, why not?"

Jennings moved to Rome with his mother, Alice Knox, and his half-brother, Terrence Phillips. Together, as a family, they experienced the city. Knox learned how to navigate the area and drove Jennings to his two daily practices. A couple of other Americans also played on the team and Knox occasionally hosted them for dinner. But basketball was different. Playing time was sporadic. Sometimes Jennings played. Sometimes he did not. During games, Jennings's main objectives were to pass the ball and only shoot when completely open. For the most part—beyond a couple of hiccups when he complained to the American press—he listened and performed the tasks asked of him. Allan Ray was one of his teammates. Ray had played college ball at Villanova and the pair became friends. "During the whole year, Brandon never said anything or talked back to the coach," Ray said. "He just kept it cordial. He came to practice and worked hard every day. It was obvious how good he was. He would show glimpses in practice. I wish he would have played more. That experience alone prepared him mentally for life on and off the court. I really admire him for the way he handled himself in Rome. He was a true professional, even at a young age." Jennings averaged just 5.5 points and 2.3 assists in only 17 minutes per game. The meager numbers did not reflect his growth behind the scenes. Jennings grew as a basketball player through the tough, grinding practices. He grew as a man by experiencing life so far away from home. At times, he wanted to quit and leave it all behind. Instead, he persevered and entered the NBA draft once the season ended.

Vaccaro had not been as nervous for a draft since the Nets passed on Kobe Bryant back in 1996. His insides twisted in knots. He called around and surveyed his NBA contacts, trying to figure out where Jennings would be selected. He feared that Jennings would be punished by teams for initiating an alternate route into the NBA. Vaccaro sighed when the Milwaukee Bucks drafted Jennings with the 10th pick of the 2009 draft. He believed the teams that passed on Jennings would later regret the decision. That conviction gained traction early in the season. Jennings stunned professional basketball in just his seventh NBA game. He poured in 55 points against the Golden State Warriors, breaking Kareem Abdul-Jabbar's record for points scored by a rookie in a game.

Fresh off the success of Jennings, Vaccaro tried shepherding another prospect overseas the following year. It began the same way—with an unsolicited phone call. This time, Vaccaro received a call from the father of Jeremy Tyler, a young prospect in San Diego. Vaccaro had not heard much about Jeremy Tyler. Tyler's father, James, drove up to Santa Monica to fill Vaccaro in on the rest of the story. Jeremy Tyler was an early prodigy, having played varsity basketball as a sixth grader and advancing to dominate at San Diego High School. He had committed to playing at the University of Louisville, but his high school team encountered a myriad of issues. The San Diego Section of the California Interscholastic Federation had launched an investigation, finding that Tyler had become dissatisfied with the talent level of his teammates and threatened to change high schools if he was not surrounded by better players. (Tyler denied the allegations.) The talent started transferring into San Diego soon after, including two players from Washington and one from Oklahoma. By the time the investigation ended, two coaches—including the high school's head coach, Kenny Roy—had been fired and the federation had suspended three players. The family became disenchanted with the high school and trying to maintain college eligibility. Tyler was a high school junior with plans of becoming the first basketball player to skip his senior year of high school to play professionally overseas in hopes of entering the NBA in two years.

Tyler was a 6-foot-10-inch center. He had always been bigger and better than his opposition. For years, those around him had inflated his ego. "He's one of those guys that come along once in a lifetime. He's a [general manager's] dream and a marketer's dream. He could model or do movies. On the court, he does things you can't teach and has a fire that burns within him that you can't teach," Olden Polynice, an NBA veteran who was a volunteer coach at Tyler's school, told the *New York Times.*

Soon, coaches found they could not teach Tyler much of anything. Vaccaro again acted as a liaison, lining up representatives of teams from Israel, China, and Spain to watch Tyler work out. They settled on Maccabi Haifa, a club in Israel's top basketball division, and Tyler signed a contract for $140,000. The club believed Tyler would be a pioneer and offer a pipeline between them and other American teenagers who wanted to bypass college. Instead, Tyler acted his age. He had no support system around him. His brother, James Jr., initially hoped to move with him, but those plans fell through.

Tyler's teammates viewed him as soft. His coach, Avi Ashkenazi, found him uncoachable and lazy. *How could a player of Tyler's reputation arrive with so little basic knowledge of the game, like how to box out and rotate on defense?* Ashkenazi wondered. Tyler felt as if no one treated him with the respect he deserved. Frustrated after not playing in the first half of a game, Tyler ditched his uniform during halftime and spent the second half watching from the stands in his street clothes. Soon after, he quit without telling the team's management or his agent, Arn Tellem, and booked a flight back to the United States. Tyler lasted just 10 games in Israel. A daily newspaper in Tel Aviv described Tyler as averaging "two points, two rebounds and two temper tantrums a game."

Tyler still had the advantage of time. The following season, he played in Japan with the Tokyo Apache, under the auspices of Bob Hill. Hill had coached in the NBA in Indiana, San Antonio, and Seattle. He was a disciplinarian and would not accept laziness from his players. Hill's son, Casey, worked as an assistant coach for the team. Sometimes, he would play good cop to his father's bad cop in their dealings with Tyler. Once, Tyler messed up a play in training camp. Bob Hill yelled, making the team run the play over. This time, Tyler successfully finished it with a dunk.

"That's bullshit," Tyler said as he ran back up court, still upset over having to run the play again.

Bob Hill blew his whistle and stopped play. Spit fired from his mouth. "You haven't done anything in basketball yet," he said. "Why are you acting like this?" Tyler did not respond. Casey Hill recalled Tyler simply staring back with an expression on his face that reflected, *Oh, shit. Is this what it's supposed to be like? Is this it?*

Casey Hill tried to work with Tyler on harnessing his emotions. "He couldn't just play," Hill said. "The fact that he was playing against players who were strong and knew about him and wanted to beat him—he just wasn't used to that. He was just used to dunking on everybody in high school. And it had an effect on him. The way that those frustrations manifested themselves in him [was] not good. He would try to think of the meanest thing he could say to someone to piss them off. That's how mad he would be. It hurt relationships, and it gave him this bad reputation." To Hill, Tyler had simply skated by on his talents for years. No coach had ever held him accountable. "That persona allowed him to place the blame on everyone else but himself," Hill said. "The team in Israel—they never really disciplined him. He would just kind of go in there and have his emotional outbursts and they didn't know what to do with him, so they didn't play him. That was the worst thing. They didn't talk to him, [and] they didn't play him. It left him confused."

Tyler showed some of his promise in Japan. He averaged nearly 10 points and 7 rebounds before a catastrophic earthquake brought the season to a premature end. Tyler once expected to be one of the first players to shake David Stern's hand. Instead, on draft night of 2011, the Golden State Warriors paid $2 million to the Charlotte Bobcats in exchange for the 39th selection and the right to draft Tyler. The Warriors expected Tyler to be a project. Tyler did not view himself that way. He sounded like Ndudi Ebi during his downfall in saying a demotion to the NBA Development League "isn't in my membrane." The Warriors dealt Tyler to the Atlanta Hawks in a salary-slicing move in 2013. Atlanta waived him after just one game. Tyler has had trouble sticking in the NBA since. "The only thing I do think about is five years ago, I was the best player out of all these guys," Tyler said in the summer of 2013. "I'm a man of history repeating itself, so I just let it come to me and just keep playing hard and play poised and play with confidence and I'll be that guy that I always was."

Vaccaro once believed that a handful of the country's best players would annually choose playing professionally overseas instead of serving a season in college purgatory. That route never panned out, with Tyler's outcome serving as a cautionary tale for subsequent high school stars. Emmanuel Mudiay bypassed college to spend a year playing professionally in China before the Denver Nuggets picked him seventh overall in the 2015 draft. But the vast majority of talented teenagers elect to spend a year in college at institutions like the University of Kentucky instead of playing overseas. "My mistake was I didn't know Jeremy well enough," Vaccaro said. "I still think to this day, if he had started out right, he would have made it. But he doesn't like to play basketball. Unfortunately, that's not a solo thing. A lot of guys don't like playing the sport. They play it to make money."

23.

Kobe Bryant smiled after hitting his second free throw against Minnesota in December 2014. The beam was a rarity for someone who had preferred playing most of his 18 seasons through snarls and clenched teeth. With the shot, Bryant surpassed Michael Jordan's career point total. He now stood behind only Karl Malone (36,928 points) and Kareem Abdul-Jabbar (38,387) among the game's all-time leaders. The moment was not lost on Bryant. He would have been hard-pressed to pass Jordan had he attended college for two or three years. He had appreciated the chase and the journey—trying to match Jordan gave him a new obstacle to chase down as his career drew to a close. Jordan had been his idol. Bryant seldom disclosed this publicly, but he had carved his game in Jordan's image and spent nearly two decades in pursuit of a player many believe could never be replicated.

The Timberwolves, his opponent that night, stopped the game and hugs ensued. Bryant embraced his teammates on the court—none of whom had been a teammate when Bryant had last won a championship in 2010, when the Lakers outlasted the Boston Celtics in a hard-fought seven-game series. Glen Taylor, Minnesota's owner, walked onto the court and looped his right arm around Bryant's back. The two shared some brief words and Taylor, with his left hand, gifted Bryant the ball he had just used to pass Jordan's mark. It had been seven years since Taylor made the decision to trade away his own former high school star, Kevin Garnett. Minnesota had tired of treading water after several years, while maintaining one of the league's higher payrolls. Garnett preferred to stay in Minnesota. He was loyal to a fault. He had to be convinced to accept a trade to Boston and only relented when Taylor described the long rebuilding plan Minnesota had mapped out. In Boston, Garnett teamed with Paul Pierce and Ray Allen and in 2008 gained his elusive championship in a win over Bryant's Lakers. For their troubles, the Timberwolves received two first-round picks and five players for Garnett. Three of them happened to be players who bypassed college for the NBA—Al Jefferson, Gerald Green, and Sebastian Telfair.

Members of the Timberwolves congratulated Bryant as well. They included Shabazz Muhammad, a 22-year-old in his second season, drafted by Minnesota in the first round of 2013's draft. Muhammad was three years old when Bryant broke into the league. Had Muhammad been born earlier, he surely would have entered the NBA out of his Las Vegas high school. Instead, he spent an underwhelming season at UCLA and surprised no one by declaring for the NBA when his college season ended.

Next, Bryant raised his right arm to acknowledge the crowd and shared a long embrace with his coach, Byron Scott. Scott, in the last year of his playing career, was on the Lakers when Bryant entered the league. As a coach, Scott found it difficult to come up with the right amount of playing time for Bryant. In his mind, Bryant could still play like the teenager who took the league by storm. In reality, at 36 years old, his body could no longer handle the physicality that the game demanded. Bryant would rest the second games of back-to-backs and his minutes would be reduced soon after he broke Jordan's mark. The last years had been difficult on Bryant. His body no longer responded as his mind had grown accustomed to. Bryant fought off tears and stood with the help of crutches in April 2013, addressing reporters about an injury he had sustained. He had made a move that he had performed count-less times in his career late in a game against the Golden State Warriors and felt a pop. Bryant asked his defender, Harrison Barnes, if he had kicked him. Barnes said that he had not and Bryant feared the worst. He somehow went to the free-throw line and made two free throws before exiting the game. Tests revealed that Bryant had sustained a torn Achilles tendon. He trained hard to return to form early the following year—only to suffer a bone fracture in his left leg in a game against the Memphis Grizzlies. The following season, a torn rotator cuff prema-turely ended a third consecutive season. Bryant had entered the league nearly two decades earlier trying to make a name for himself. He never regretted his decision to skip college. He found that American players trailed in their development when compared to international players. In Europe, players like Tony Parker and Ricky Rubio played professionally as young teenagers. They devoted the bulk of their time to mastering their craft before entering the NBA as players prepared to contribute. "It seems like the system really isn't teaching players anything when you go to college," Bryant mused to reporters in 2014. "You go to college, you play, you showcase, and you come to the pros.

"We kind of got sold on that [college] dream a little bit," he con-tinued. "Fortunately, I didn't really listen to it. Neither did [Garnett]. Neither did LeBron. I think that worked pretty well for the three of us. I'm always a firm believer in us being able to make our own decisions, especially as it pertains to working and having a job."

Garnett's career came full circle a few weeks after Bryant broke Jordan's mark. In February 2015, Taylor and the Timberwolves traded for Garnett and returned him to the franchise. Garnett not only re-united with the organization, but also with Flip Saunders, who was again coaching the Timberwolves. In order to facilitate the trade, Garnett had to waive his no-trade clause with the Brooklyn Nets. In doing so, Minnesota received a different Garnett, one who was 38 years old instead of a teenager. They traded more for Garnett's leader-ship abilities to mentor a young team, rather than his on-court con-tributions. In the summer of 2015, Garnett signed a two-year deal to remain with the Timberwolves. If he fulfills the contract, Garnett will become the first player to play in the NBA in his teens, 20s, 30s, and 40s. The young players he was charged with mentoring included Andrew Wiggins and Karl-Anthony Towns. Both had spent just one year in college—Wiggins at the University of Kansas and Towns at the University of Kentucky—before becoming the first overall pick of subsequent drafts. They both would have almost certainly skipped college altogether had they belonged to another generation of NBA players. Instead, both were born at around the time Garnett first made his debut for the Timberwolves as a wide-eyed and superstitious teen. "Twelve days before I was born, it was his first game," Towns recited from memory. Garnett has said that one day he hopes to own the franchise. "It's perfect," Garnett told reporters at a news conference following the trade. "If you have a story, this is a fairy tale. This is a perfect ending to it. This is how you want to do it."

After half his life spent as an NBA player, Jermaine O'Neal retired from the league after the 2013–2014 season as a member of the Golden State Warriors. His brittle knees no longer allowed him to run up and down the court as he had as a spry youth. Toward the end of his career, he plopped an ice machine in the middle of his living room. He sat sullenly next to the machine for hours, with his long legs propped up, in search of relief from the constant pain.

His post-basketball career is already in motion. As a member of the Warriors, O'Neal wisely made contacts in Silicon Valley, meeting the movers and shakers of the region. He believes his future was achieved because of the tests he endured early in his career in Portland and Indiana in maturing from a teenager into a man. O'Neal agreed with Bryant's assessment. "We live in a country where [you] have the freedom to choose your occupation," he said. "You have the right to choose an occupation to take care of yourself and your family and build a way of living. I've been hearing people point out the [failures], but there are a lot of failures in corporate America with guys that went to four-year schools, graduate school, and failed at whatever they're doing. You got some of the brightest people in this world that did not attend college. So to me, it's something that's unfair. I think the biggest question is—and the focal point should be—what are the teams doing to do what Portland did, to understand what their investment is? You invest millions of dollars into these players. Why aren't you doing a better job at positioning these players to be successful? Rather than just drafting them and saying, 'Hey, I'm paying you, so you've got to get it.' There's no blueprint for the NBA. There's nothing like this. The only way you succeed in this is when you live it and understand what it is. That's why I'm against that. It's just not right."

Perhaps most striking about the age-minimum debate is how extreme the viewpoints can be of players who have lived the transition from high school into the NBA. Bryant and O'Neal are on one side of the argument and can make sense. Then again, Tracy McGrady can offer another rational stance and viewpoint. "You had Jordan and those guys still in the game," McGrady said of when he entered the NBA in 1997. "You had a lot of men. Now, it's a bunch of boys in the league." Back and knee pains dimmed McGrady's bright career. He played in China in 2012 as a fan favorite before returning to the NBA and finishing his career as a backup role player with the San Antonio Spurs. He later pursued a short stint chasing his first love— baseball—as a pitcher in an independent league. McGrady seldom felt that he had missed much by skipping college. Yet, he felt left out every time March rolled around. The rest of the players would boast about how far their teams would travel in the NCAA tournament. McGrady remained quiet. "College basketball is a place to mature, to prepare you for life after college," McGrady said. "You do a lot of maturing. You go through a maturation process from your freshman year to your sophomore year. It's amazing how much you can grow in that span in college. When these guys go one year and come to the league, that's still young. They're nineteen and twenty years old and a lot of them just aren't ready for it. I just think at the rate that they're going now, the talent is being watered down and college is being watered down. Imagine if you had to go to college for two or three years. Imagine the talent that would be in college basketball. Just go a couple years back.

If you look at that Kentucky team, all those guys Calipari put in the league—oh my gosh. College basketball would be awesome to watch."

The only thing all parties agree on is that no one is completely satisfied with the current rule—not the players it affects, not the NCAA, not the NBA. The debate will span the careers of Kobe Bryant and Kevin Garnett. The duo's generation largely defined the NBA for nearly two decades, leading its resurgence in the post-Jordan years and helping the game grow and gain financial stability. The reasons for allowing that type of player directly into the NBA are many. The potential earning career of an NBA player is short. Why should others be able to profit from their talent while they themselves cannot? The success stories outweigh those who did not make it and players are not really developing by spending a couple of semesters at college. Adam Silver replaced David Stern as the NBA's commissioner. Silver is well respected throughout the league, having been at Stern's side for decades, a Duke graduate who grew up in New York as a Knicks fan. He has made tacking another year onto the age minimum—boosting the minimum from 19 years of age to 20—one of his key objectives. His arguments mirror Stern's reasoning in originally implementing the age minimum. "I think that if the players had more of an opportunity to mature, both as people and in terms of their basketball skills, we would have a better league," Silver said. "We would have a better draft because there would be more of an opportunity for our teams to see them playing against top competition and I know firsthand that those years, at that point in a young man's life, make an enormous difference."

Like Stern, Silver said he was well aware of why players want to enter the NBA as young as possible. "We always shared the concern of this coded language of, 'These young men need college,'" Silver said. "You never hear that coming from us. There's a recognition always from the league [that] the college programs are far from perfect. They're not necessarily safe harbors. Plenty of bad things have happened on college campuses as well and there are benefits, true benefits, truly from a league standpoint and for our teams, to getting these players younger. The fact is, their ultimate goal is to be the best possible basketball players and they have a relatively short window in their lives to ply their trade. There is an argument that getting them to a professional level at a younger age will ultimately be beneficial for them and the league. Where I come out on the benefits of moving from nineteen to twenty, it's one of those issues where in my mind, on balance, I think it would be better." Silver will likely have the support of many of the league's owners when he argues his stance. "I can't speculate on what will happen in the future, but I'm a believer that the old straight out of [high school] and the current one-and-done [rule] creates a horrible culture of exploitation of teenage basketball players," Mark Cuban, the owner of the Dallas Mavericks, wrote in an email. "Too many are sold a dream of NBA riches. The longer a student-athlete stays in school, the better for the NBA. They have better skills, are more mature, have better life skills, and in some cases bring an established brand. I would love to see kids have to stay in school four years or play in the D-League, where we can focus on supporting their needs without worrying about wins and losses." The age minimum can only be altered through an amendment to the current collective bargaining agreement, which the sides agreed to in December 2011. The 10-year agreement contains opt-out clauses that can be employed by both sides after six years. Silver will find opposition from the players union in raising the age minimum. Michele A. Roberts replaced the deposed Billy Hunter as the union's head. In an interview with *Sports Illustrated,* she left no doubt on where she stood on the issue. "I'm adamantly opposed to [raising the age minimum]," she said. "I've been practicing law for thirty years. One of the beauties of being in that job is that I can practice until I lose my mind or die. That is not the case with athletes. You have a limited life to make money as a basketball player. Anything that limits those opportunities is distressing to me. I view [the age minimum] as just another device that serves to limit a player's ability to make a living."

And round and round they go, with the career and the future of the next phenom swaying in the balance.

They will certainly come around to replace this generation of NBA superstars. The careers of one of the NBA's greatest classes of players, those who entered a man's league directly from high school, are drawing to a close.

Time caught them all. They had entered the NBA as young teenagers with nothing but bright futures ahead of them. Gravity eventually pulled their games back to earth. It became harder and harder to free themselves up for open looks at the basket. Kevin Garnett still howls, but his bite—and shot—are not the same. Even LeBron James has spoken more often of late about his own athletic mortality.

They are forever linked with the few who took a big leap and fell short. Those are the names lost beyond serving as footnotes to a debate that has long passed them by. Time claimed them as well, although in a different manner. Their dreams of stardom, fame, and money have mostly faded. But their lives continue, those of onetime prodigies like Korleone Young, Lenny Cooke, and Tony Key.

24.

The waiter stood head and shoulders above everyone else at the chain restaurant deep inside the Bible Belt. The 6-foot-11-inch Tony Key had his hair in dreads and still looked as if he could bring backboards to a glorious death, as he had done in high school through the brute force of his dunks. His shift had started a couple hours earlier at Rafferty's in Bowling Green, Kentucky. It was a humid day in the summer of 2013, just a few months after LeBron James had captured a second consecutive championship with the Miami Heat. Key had watched the finals in passing. He once imagined himself playing in the NBA, making millions and crashing rims. Now, he had a few moments to spare before serving the next appetizer. Key had been at the job for about seven months, "which is actually surprising," said Otis Key, his older brother by eight years. "Me and my mom were thinking about it. This is the longest job that he's ever kept. But he gets unfocused, one thing leads to one bad decision and then another."

Otis Key tried talking to his younger brother when things started going awry. He argued until he felt the blood rushing to his head—the emotions boiling over. In nearby Russellville, Tony Key was a legend in 2000 when he guided his high school team to the state semifinals and shattered a backboard with a reverse alley-oop dunk in the process. College coaches frequented the high school to recruit Key. He had moldable potential, but few true basketball skills other than genetic gifts, his soft hands, and the ability to simply dunk on his shorter competition. Whenever his coach, Phillip Todd, tried to get Key to develop his game, to rebound and advance the ball, Key failed to listen. He regarded himself as just a big man and racing the ball up court was the work of a guard. He never allowed himself to know what it was like to push himself—to gain a second wind, to dig deeper and reach another level. Complacency settled in and the problems began.

Basketball coursed through the family. The sport had only become an option for Tony Key until he outgrew other ones. He had quit his middle school basketball team, preferring to play football and baseball. As Key made his run through the playoffs, Otis Key traveled the world as a member of the Harlem Globetrotters. Another brother, Thaddaeus Key, soon departed to play at Kentucky Wesleyan. Brenda Key, their mother, had to find work after splitting with her husband. The job kept her away most evenings. New people started popping up, Brenda Key noticed. Some tried to keep her away from her own son. The school informed Tony Key that he needed to make up half a credit in summer school in order to be eligible for his senior year. From afar, Otis Key pleaded with him over the phone. "Do the work," he said. "Tony, if you do this, you'll be able to accomplish anything you want to in life. If you don't, you'll fail at everything. Yes, you have a choice to do it or not, but it shows that you want to do something more. If you don't, you're just content with the status quo. You're content with just getting by."

Tony Key admitted his hardheadedness back then. He did not want to do the schoolwork. He did not want to listen to advice from his brother. His brother had forged his path. He wanted to make his own. "I know what I'm doing," Tony Key would constantly reply to the advice of his family. "I know what I'm doing."

He decided against putting the work in and having to either attend summer school or to repeat a grade. Instead, out of the blue and on the advice of a coach he had met over the summer, Key transferred first to a prep school and then to a high school all the way out in California, Compton Centennial. There, he measured himself against some of the top competition—players headed to the pros, like Tyson Chandler— and believed he was of the same caliber. In 14 games, he averaged team highs in points (23 per game) and rebounds (11). The federation that oversaw high schools in the area soon deemed Key ineligible. He said he had moved in with an aunt, although school officials never notified the federation to clear the transfer. That mattered little anyway. Key never had an aunt in California. He lived with the family of one of his teammates. Compton Centennial forfeited 11 of its victories.

College, if it had ever been an option, became even less of a viable one now. Tony Key estimated he attended about two classes in California. He spent his time hanging out and chain-smoking. An acquaintance introduced Key to Ron Delpit, an agent. Delpit had once been big in the game, a mover and shaker who had worked with Julius Erving. He was attempting a comeback and Tony Key said Delpit convinced him to sign with his agency and turn professional. "The way they explained it was, without them, I couldn't declare for the draft," Key recalled. "They said, 'You're gonna need an agent to declare for the draft, that's why you should sign with us, go ahead and get the ball rolling.'" Key left Los Angeles to work out in Las Vegas. For a kid from a small city in Kentucky, Los Angeles had been eye-opening. Las Vegas overloaded the senses. He partied more than he prepared for the draft. He bought a Cadillac. He had change in his pocket. He went on a shopping spree. He thought that it was something, just the beginning road to bigger, better, brighter things. He said he now realizes how little he had and how much more he could have worked.

Otis Key debated asking the Globetrotters if he could sit out that summer's tour, so he could take his younger brother in hand. He had played against professionals and knew his brother was still more boy than man. He was confident that he could get his brother focused and in shape, so that a team would at least take a flier on him. Once Tony Key got his foot in the door, he would see how hard he had to work and dedicate himself, Otis Key believed. He decided against it. He had a son and wanted to establish his own professional career. It is a decision he still thinks about today, wondering, *Maybe I should have made that sacrifice, and things would have turned out differently.*

At the 2001 draft, Tony Key knew the Nuggets had expressed interest in him. They bypassed him in the second round and instead took Ousmane Cisse, another high schooler whose NBA career never panned out. *Well, he didn't get drafted, but there are training camps*, Otis Key thought. *It's hard to pass up size and ability.* Instead, with major colleges no longer an option, Key ended up back in California at Los Angeles City College, a two-year school. He was kicked off the team and left for another small school, this one in Indiana. He asked for a second chance at Los Angeles City College and the coach relented. Tony Key seemed to finally be back on track when tragedy struck. His two sisters, Hanna and Jessica Key, were murdered in late 2002 by Hanna's boyfriend. The sisters had also both excelled in basketball at Russellville. The deaths devastated Tony Key. He was close to both, especially Hanna. "Don't tell me what you are going to do," she would tell him. "Show me."

"It seemed like for a while after that he was sort of lost," Brenda Key said. The family will forever grieve, she added. Brenda Key was still not sure if Tony Key had been able to face visiting their gravesites.

Key attended a small university in West Virginia before playing professionally in places like Mexico, Canada, and small domestic minor leagues. "He was determined to do it his way," Otis Key said. "He didn't want to come and ask for advice or seek out advice other than what people were telling him. When he was used and tossed to the side, it made him angry and led to more bad decisions."

LeBron James still stars in the NBA. Kobe Bryant and Kevin Garnett maintain, showing glimpses of their old selves through cemented legacies. Many others have secured their future while earning millions of dollars.

Meanwhile, Key returned to his high school nearly 15 years later, the same one in Russellville where he had once dazzled, and tried fast-tracking his way to stardom. Otis Key had left the Globetrotters to try out coaching. He headed the semiprofessional Bowling Green Hornets of the Central Basketball Association and added his younger brother to the roster. The league was mostly composed of former college players from the region. The players performed before a few hundred people for a couple of hundred dollars a game. On most nights, Otis Key could be seen alternately delivering praise and scolding Tony Key.

It could be his last chance, Otis Key said. Tony Key was 31 with two teenage daughters. He was still spry enough to make a living from the game—at least for a couple more years. All he needed was to be serious and someone, somewhere would give him a chance. Still, it remained difficult for Tony Key to accept the constant harangues from Otis.

"Tony, you're young enough where you legitimately have a shot left," Otis Key said. "You have two, possibly three, really good years left. If you take this seriously, you can turn this into something bigger. You have way more ability than I ever did. The only thing that I had was the wisdom to listen to people, to make good decisions, and then the discipline to put the work in. You're old enough now where you've made enough mistakes. You know which path is the right path and the steps you need to do. You've had enough experiences, good and bad, that you know if you put in the work, what's going to come."

Something continually held him back. Otis Key could never quite put his finger on the source. Tony Key would lose focus and hope. Both wondered if Tony Key wanted this for himself, if he loved the game or appreciated his gifts. It was hard finding the time to train, Tony Key said. He had a lot on his plate right now, "but it seems like if I could do that, life would be a whole lot easier now, but I don't know. I got a passion for it, but as far as eating, sleeping, and breathing basketball, I don't love it like that no more."

Real life beckoned. He returned to his shift. The dinner rush would start in force soon.

Maybe keeping the flickers of a dream alive was better than facing the reality of life without them at all.

AFTERWORD

2016

Mississippi State could finally rejoice. Rick Stansbury could exhale. He had landed the type of player who had eluded him for more than a decade, a blue-chip prospect with an NBA future, in Rodney Hood. Others like Jonathan Bender, Travis Outlaw, and Monta Ellis playfully flirted with the program only to launch themselves professionally into the NBA from high school. Hood followed their careers closely and had just entered Mississippi's Meridian High when the NBA changed its eligibility rules. "I geared my mind-set toward going to college for a couple of years and then going to the NBA," Hood recalled. He chose the Bulldogs, and as a rangy southpaw with an abundance of length for a guard, Hood performed capably in 2011–2012. The Southeastern Conference named Hood to its All-Freshman team. But Stansbury left the school following the season, and Hood followed suit. He had the NBA in his sights, but felt the need for further apprenticeship. Hood sat out the NCAA-mandated year for transferring before joining a powerhouse in Duke, playing a season in Durham before declaring for the NBA draft and being selected by the Utah Jazz.

By 2016, Hood had become numb to the rhythms of the NBA,

the predictable ebbs and flows that course throughout an alternately exhilarating and exhausting season. Hood had grown up like a million other kids in his generation, a shooter who wanted to be Kobe Bryant and mimicked him in the same manner Bryant once emulated Michael Jordan. Hood was about eight years old when Bryant fast-tracked his way to stardom, claiming championships while alienating teammates. But none of those other kids would face Bryant in his final NBA game.

Bryant had announced that he would retire following the season in late November 2015. The memory of vintage Bryant—quick-footed, high-flying—had mostly eroded. Aging and injuries had rendered him inefficient in recent years, his body no longer responding to the mind's commands. Many argued over the crippling millstone that Bryant's two-year, $48.5 million contract created for the dismal Lakers, openly wondering if Bryant, at 37 years of age, should give way to the team's younger core of players and allow them to develop on the court. But by disclosing his intentions in the winter, the rest of the season could serve as a protracted farewell.

The Lakers had been disqualified from the postseason for weeks by mid-April when Hood's Jazz arrived in Los Angeles. As Utah's team bus pulled into Staples Center, Hood noticed fans clad in purple and gold, number 8 and number 24 jerseys, already crowding the outside of the arena and celebrating Bryant's 20-year career with a block party. "Once we got in, it seemed that every star that you could name was in the building," Hood said. His Jazz had fought hard all season, through injuries and quality opponents, to knock on the door of playoff qualification. Instead, the Jazz learned shortly before the game that the Houston Rockets had toppled the Sacramento Kings that night to capture the Western Conference's final playoff berth. The Jazz had hoped that the combination of a win against the Lakers and a Houston loss would propel the team into the playoffs. "We had just found out that we weren't going to make the playoffs," Hood said. "It was a weird day."

Bryant sat on the bench in his warm-ups, watching teammates praise him from a video dedication on the JumboTron. More than nineteen thousand fans and nearly five hundred media members crowded inside the arena where Bryant had raised five title banners, and longtime Lakers public address announcer Lawrence Tanter introduced him for "the final time." Magic Johnson addressed the crowd, proclaiming Bryant the greatest Laker in the organization's history. "Kobe Bryant has never cheated the game," Johnson said. "He has never cheated us as fans. He's played through injuries. He's played hurt, and we have five championship banners to show for it." Another video tribute followed. Bryant sat wide-grinned as contemporaries congratulated him on his career. The tape included a message from Kevin Garnett. "I want to say congratulations on this night, man," Garnett said. "Lord knows, you earned it. I want to say thank you for these memories. As a friend and as a fan, man, I want to say salute and all the best to you, my dude." In a few months, shortly before the dawn of the 2016–2017 season, Garnett would announce his own retirement through a much quieter means. On Instagram, he released a short video of himself walking around a hallowed Target Center, the home of the Minnesota Timberwolves. "We gonna be aight, man," Garnett said in the video. "I don't expect this to be easy, but so far, so good. Stay tuned."

The Lakers and Jazz had played just a couple of weeks earlier, and Bryant had been chatty with Hood in that game. Bryant would exchange no pleasantries in the April meeting. "He just had a look in his eye," Hood said. "He was just all about business that day." Bryant missed his first shot of the game, a three-pointer heaved just 35 seconds after tipoff. He clanked his subsequent four attempts. A nervous energy emanated from the crowd. But midway through the first quarter, he blocked Trevor Booker's shot. Bryant received the ball on offense, pump-faked Utah's Gordon Hayward into the air, and converted his first bucket. The basket opened up from there. He finished the first quarter with 15 points. "It was basically like going against young Kobe," Hood said. "He was out on the island. You basically just felt helpless. He's just hitting knock-it-down shots, getting to the free-throw line, fadeaways, anything you could, really. It was just tough guarding him, especially everything surrounding it." Bryant nailed a fadeaway near the Jazz's bench in the second half. *There's just nothing we can do at this point,* Hood recalled thinking. Bryant turned in a case study on how a player of his stature could alternately draw praise and criticism, often in the same game. He totaled an electric, dizzying 60 points on the way to a victory, outscoring the Jazz by himself, 23–21, in the fourth quarter. He provided the final points of his career from the free-throw line with 14.8 seconds left in the game. He exited with 4.1 seconds left, serenaded by fans with chants of his name. Bryant took 50 shots, the most of his career, the most of any NBA player in three decades. "He got hot and he wasn't getting tired," Hood said. "He might have looked tired, but he was still shooting."

The matchup, beyond being Bryant's finale game, was inconsequential. That same April evening, at mostly the same time, the Golden State Warriors topped the Memphis Grizzlies and captured their seventy-third win of the regular season, eclipsing the 1995–1996 Chicago Bulls for the top regular-season record in NBA history. Somehow, Bryant made it all seem secondary, with Golden State's unfathomable mark almost serving as a matinee to his one-man virtuoso performance. "I feel like I didn't really realize it until a week later that the Warriors had broken the record," Hood said. "Everybody was still going crazy about Kobe." After the game, with a towel draped around his shoulders, Bryant took a microphone at midcourt. He talked about his journey of growing up a Laker fan and being traded as a teenager to the organization. "You can't write something better than this," he said. He thanked the fans, his wife and daughters. Bryant then, in an ode to his nickname, ended on, "What can I say? Mamba out." He smiled, dropping the microphone.

With that, the NBA became a little less dramatic, a little more predictable. Fans were left with one less icon to cheer, others with one less target to jeer. "Anyone who says they knew for sure the skinny seventeen-year-old we signed would play twenty years and be in the conversation when listing the all-time greats is probably blowing some smoke," said Del Harris, Bryant's first coach in Los Angeles. "On the other hand, it was easy to see that he had the potential for greatness and the work ethic to go with it. Soon, it became obvious he had the steely-minded determination and laser focus to accomplish great things. Still, a twenty-year career and to finish the final act with 60 points was an exclamation point on what was truly a most remarkable journey." Of the final game, Harris added: "I recorded that and kept it. It was magnificent. Yes, his teammates looked for him, but he made the shots, and made the shots and made the shots."

The sun set on the careers of Bryant and Garnett, trendsetters who paved the way for high school players to enter the modern NBA. Many others who followed in their path predated them into retirement. A few are still authoring their legacies. In June, with Bryant full-fledged into retirement and debuting a commercial for a new *Ghostbusters* movie, LeBron James made good on his promise to bring a championship to his home state in Ohio. His Cleveland Cavaliers overcame the historical, daunting odds and rallied from a 3–1 deficit to top the Warriors in the finals. The 31-year-old James earned unanimous Finals MVP honors after the dramatic Game 7 win. He averaged 29.7 points, 11.3 rebounds, and 8.9 assists in the series. Surprisingly, J. R. Smith became one of the team's most dependable players during its playoff run. Smith came into the league from high school in 2004, beset by numerous questions and concerns over his maturity for much of the next decade. The New York Knicks included him in a trade to Cleveland almost as an afterthought.

As James and Smith celebrated, a former Cavalier filed for bankruptcy. Darius Miles went against the advice of Alvin Gentry, his onetime coach with the Los Angeles Clippers. Miles acted in a movie the summer Gentry advised him to focus on his game and made cameos in a few more films. The Clippers traded Miles to Cleveland after two seasons. He became a journeyman until microfracture surgery ended his career at the age of 27. Gentry had once advised Miles he could make $85 million in basketball. His career did not meet expectations. Miles still managed to rake in nearly $62 million in a truncated career. In filing for bankruptcy in June, Miles cited a debt of $282,041 to the Internal Revenue Service, the *Belleville News-Democrat* reported.

He listed $460,385 in assets and $1.57 million in liabilities. He had squandered much of his fortune through fumbled real estate investments. In addition to his home, Miles, at the age of 34, owned twelve other properties, according to the newspaper. Bennie Lewis Sr., who coached Miles at East Saint Louis Senior High School, recalled that Miles did not take any college visits. "When you come from an area where you just haven't got that much money and you can go and get this right now, that was a plus for him to do that," Lewis Sr. said. "He did it, because he thought he had to do it, and I thought that he should've done it too."

The NBA provided a post–high school education for Miles, Bryant, and the rest. Life came fast for those teenagers. For most, money, fame, and attention arrived with it. Some lessons were never learned. Some were hard-learned throughout the years, as adolescence inevitably gave way to manhood.

In July, Bryant penned an open letter to his 17-year-old self for *The Players' Tribune*. In it, he wrote how he should handle his soon-to-come financial bounty. Bryant would experience a falling-out with members of his family, including his parents, as his career neared its end. Joe and Pamela Bryant had once moved to Los Angeles, shadowing a young Kobe entering professionalism. They were noticeably absent from his final game. "Your life is about to change, and things are about to come at you very fast," Bryant wrote. "But just let this sink in a bit when you lay down at night after another nine-hour training day. Trust me, setting things up right from the beginning will avoid a ton of tears and heartache, some of which remains to this day."

ACKNOWLEDGMENTS

This book only happened through the support, contributions, and guidance of many, many people.

The *Los Angeles Times* believed in me when it probably shouldn't have—when I was just 23 years old and it entrusted me with the beat of covering the Los Angeles Clippers. That was a dream job for a kid who grew up in the shadows of Los Angeles. It introduced me to the world of the NBA and got me on a track of wondering how these guys—some still teenagers—could possibly handle the pressures of living their lives on camera and being their families' patriarchs at such a young age. Thanks to Bill Dwyre, Randy Harvey, Efrain Hernandez Jr., Mike Hiserman, Barry Stavro, and Phil Willon.

Working at the *New York Times* helped me grow as a reporter and journalist and appreciate the deep talents it takes to crank out a newspaper of that quality on a daily basis. Thanks to Howard Beck, Greg Bishop, John Eligon, Terri Ann Glynn, Tom Jolly, Sandy Keenan, Patty La Duca, Bill Rhoden, Pete Thamel, Jay Schreiber, Jason Stallman, and Fern Turkowitz.

Bill Simmons has been nothing short of spectacular as a mentor and friend. Really, learning from him is like a basketball player being tutored by Michael Jordan. There is nobody I've met who works harder. More than anything, he taught me to make every article I turn in my best and hopefully this book meets that standard. The *Grantland* family he cobbled together has been amazing and many thanks go out to them and, in particular, Katie Baker, Bill Barnwell, Rafe Bartholomew, Jason Concepcion, Dan Fierman, Sean Fennessey, Kirk Goldsberry, Andy Greenwald, David Jacoby, Jonah Keri, Juliet Litman, Zach Lowe, Robert Mays, Chris Ryan, Monica Schroeder, Shea Serrano, Andrew Sharpe, and Robert King at ESPN.

The writers who cover the NBA are a special and talented group, and many of them were available for me to pick their brains for this project. Thanks to all, including Henry Abbott, David Aldridge, Sam Amick, Harvey Araton, J. A. Adande, Michael Becker, Chris Broussard, Jessica Camerato, Chris Hine, Benjamin Hochman, Justice B. Hill, Baxter Holmes, Lee Jenkins, Michael Lee, Holly MacKenzie, Jack McCallum, Dave McMenamin, Jason Reid, Ramona Shelburne, Marc Spears, Tzvi Twersky, Gary Washburn, and Adrian Wojnarowski. Jason Reid no longer covers the NBA, but is a wonderful journalist and the best mentor I could have asked for.

It took years to gather enough interviews to complete this book. I want to thank everyone interviewed who lent their unique experiences, thoughts, and knowledge. It would take a few pages to list everyone, but, in particular, I want to offer a special thanks to Mike Bass, John Black, Lenny Cooke, Tim Frank, Tracy McGrady, John Nash, Jermaine O'Neal, Joanna Shapiro, David Stern, Amanda Thorn George, and Sonny Vaccaro. All those interviews required a lot of transcription and Alex Shultz and Danny Chau helped out in a giant way with that job.

My agent, Daniel Greenberg, reached out to me before I even had a book idea in place. His faith went a long way toward making this happen. Thanks to him and Levine Greenberg Literary Agency. Nathan Roberson crisped up the book's pages as its editor. Thanks to him and Crown Publishing Group. And thanks to Adam Brinklow for fact-checking the manuscript.

My family supported me through this project and offered backing as only a family could. Thanks, Mom, Michelle, Danielle, Matthew, Whitney, Dan, Dannen, Nicole, Jamaal, and George and Angela Caldwell.

Finally, I am in awe of my wife, Tanya. She deftly handled giving birth to our first child, moving across the country, and having her husband traveling and working odd hours throughout the course of writing this book. She is the strongest person I know and, as a talented journalist in her own right, she was often my first line of defense in reading its pages. To our son, Jayden, this was all for you and just know: you are going to college—all four years.

Index

About the Author

JONATHAN ABRAMS is an award-winning journalist who covers the NBA for *Bleacher Report*. He was previously a staff writer at *Grantland*, the *Los Angeles Times*, and the *New York Times* and is a graduate of the University of Southern California.